UNHOLY GHOST

UNHOLY GHOST

Writers on Depression

EDITED BY

Nell Casey

WILLIAM MORROW
75 YEARS OF PUBLISHING
An Imprint of HarperCollins*Publishers*

Grateful acknowledgment is made to the following for permission to reprint previously published material:

From *The Savage God* by A. Alvarez. Reprinted by permission of Gillon Aitken Associates Ltd. © 1971 by A. Alvarez.

"Heaven and Nature" from *Tigers & Ice: Reflections on Nature and Life* by Edward Hoagland. Reprinted by permission of The Lyons Press. Copyright © 1999 by The Lyons Press.

"An Unwelcome Career" is, in part, from *Speaking to Sadness: Depression, Disconnection, and the Meanings of Illness* by David A. Karp. Reprinted by permission of Oxford University Press, Inc. Copyright © 1996 by Oxford University Press, Inc.

"Credo" and "Wood Thrush" from "Having it Out with Melancholy" by Jane Kenyon. Reprinted from *Otherwise: New and Selected Poems* with the permission of Graywolf Press, Saint Paul, Minnesota. Copyright © 1996 by the Estate of Jane Kenyon.

"On Living Behind Bars" from *Plaintext* by Nancy Mairs. Reprinted by permission of the University of Arizona Press. Copyright © 1986 by the Arizona Board of Regents.

"The Legacy" from *Family Therapy Networker* magazine by Martha Manning. Reprinted by permission of Martha Manning. Copyright © 1997 by Family Therapy Networker.

From *Walter Benjamin at the Dairy Queen* by Larry McMurtry. Reprinted by permission of Simon & Schuster, Inc. Copyright © 1999 by Larry McMurtry.

From *Darkness Visible* by William Styron. Reprinted by permission of Random House, Inc. Copyright © 1990 by William Styron.

HarperCollins books may be purchased for educational, business, or sales promotional use. For information please write: Special Markets Department, HarperCollins Publishers Inc., 10 East 53rd Street, New York, NY 10022.

FIRST EDITION

Designed by Richard Oriolo

Printed on acid-free paper

LIBRARY OF CONGRESS CATALOGING-IN-PUBLICATION DATA

Unholy ghost : writers on depression / edited by Nell Casey. — 1st ed.
    p.   cm.
    ISBN 0-688-17031-5
    1. Depression, Mental.   2. Writers—Mental health.   I. Casey, Nell, 1971–

RC537 .U546 2001
616.85'27—dc21   00-040098

01 02 03 04 05 QW 10 9 8 7 6 5 4 3 2

For Maud

Contents

~❧~

CREDO

Pharmaceutical wonders are at work
but I believe only in this moment
of well-being. Unholy ghost,
you are certain to come again.

Coarse, mean, you'll put your feet
on the coffee table, lean back,
and turn me into someone who can't
take the trouble to speak; someone
who can't sleep, or who does nothing
but sleep; can't read, or call
for an appointment for help.

There is nothing I can do
against your coming.
When I awake, I am still with thee.

WOOD THRUSH

High on Nardil and June light
I wake at four,
waiting greedily for the first
notes of the wood thrush. Easeful air
presses through the screen
with the wild, complex song
of the bird, and I am overcome

by ordinary contentment.
What hurt me so terribly
all my life until this moment?
How I love the small, swiftly
beating heart of the bird
singing in the great maples;
its bright, unequivocal eye.

—Jane Kenyon
from *Having it Out with Melancholy*

ACKNOWLEDGMENTS

I am so grateful to the following people for their advice and support: Laurie Abraham, Stacy Abramson, Mike Albo, Jane Barnes, Tessa Blake, Will Blythe, Alison Callahan, Clare Casey, John Casey, Julia Casey, Ros Casey, Shannon Worrell-Chapman, Elyse Cheney, Ernie Drucker, Jeri Drucker, Tim Duggan, Karen Durbin, Fiona Hallowell, David Isay, Caroline Kazlas, Janet McNew, Robbie Myers, Bob Perry, Lorraine Tobias, Joey Xanders.

To my generous editors, Taije Silverman and Robert Jones.

To Jesse Drucker for his humor and wisdom and love.

And, above all, to the writers whose exceptional essays make up this book.

EDITOR'S NOTE

There are three sets of companion pieces in *Unholy Ghost*. Russell Banks's and Chase Twichell's essays represent a call and response about depression; Rose Styron's piece about her husband's struggle with melancholy is placed alongside an excerpt from William Styron's *Darkness Visible;* and my own essay—about seeing my sister, Maud Casey, through her depression—is coupled with Maud's account of this period in our lives.

INTRODUCTION

～

*U*NHOLY GHOST, A READER ON melancholy, is a powerful collection of modern essays about an ancient topic. Here, writers who know, through experience, depression in one or more of its diverse guises, describe the sadness and dread that are at its core; they write about how it is to feel the draining out of vital forces; how it is to exist with, and live around, the sleeplessness, the restlessness, the inertia, and the hopelessness. They describe the lingering influences of melancholia on their notions of self and work, and they portray the damage that their despair brings to the lives of others.

Being writers, their struggle to define and describe depression is perhaps the most important process for the reader. Most rail at the desiccated language that is now the core of discussions of despair. William Styron, whose eloquent and graphic descriptions of suicidal depression are ones I frequently use in teaching medical students and psychiatric residents, has little use for the word "depression."

"For over seventy years," he writes, "the word has slithered innocuously through the language like a slug, leaving little trace of its intrinsic malevolence and preventing, by its very insipidity, a general awareness of the horrible intensity of the disease when out of control."

For Styron, the progression of his own illness was gradual and a nightmare: "The shadows of nightfall seemed more somber, my mornings were less buoyant, walks in the woods became less zestful." He was overtaken by anxiety, panic, and a "visceral queasiness"; he was haunted by "a fidgety restlessness" and "an immense and aching solitude."

Another essayist, Virginia Heffernan, describes the changes wrought both within and without: "Overnight, it seemed, I went from a twenty-eight-year-old optimist . . . to a person who is unreliable and preoccupied, a person other people find themselves trying to avoid.

"Depression," she continues, "brought to me a new rationing of resources: for every twenty-four hours I got about three, then two, then *one* hour worth of life reserves—personality, conversation, motion."

Thoughts of suicide are not uncommon in severe depression, nor have they been in these writers. Maud Casey, for one, notes that she "was forever staring at the tender blue veins along the inside of my wrists, fragile twigs trapped under ice." And A. Alvarez, whose *The Savage God* is a classic in the field of suicide studies, writes about the feelings leading up to his own nearly lethal suicide attempt: "My life felt so cluttered and obstructed that I could hardly breathe. I inhabited a closed, concentrated world, airless and without exits."

For many people, depression is an abrupt change in an otherwise full and happy life. It emerges suddenly and devastates by its very strangeness and pathology. For others, melancholy seems to have been the earliest of companions. Jane Kenyon, in *Having it Out with Melancholy*, writes:

> *When I was born, you waited*
> *behind a pile of linen in the nursery,*
> *and when we were alone, you lay down*
> *on top of me, pressing*
> *the bile of desolation into every pore,*
>
> *And from that day on*
> *everything under the sun and moon*
> *made me sad—*

Meri Nana-Ama Danquah, in reflecting back over her life, states that "there are times when I feel like I've known depression longer than I've known myself. It has been with me since the beginning, I think . . . My scales were never balanced."

As someone who has manic-depression and who has spent a good portion of my life thinking and writing about the beholdenness of certain kinds of creative work to the manic and melancholic temperaments, I have found the association one that is easy to romanticize, but also one that is too easy to dismiss. Several of the essays in this collection deal with the social and creative importance of pessimism and melancholy. Edward Hoagland, for example, writes that "People with sunny natures do seem to live longer than people who are nervous wrecks: yet mankind didn't evolve out of the animal kingdom by being unduly sunny-minded. Life was fearful and phantasmagoric, supernatural and preternatural, as well as encompassing the kind of clockwork regularity of our well-governed day . . . it was not just our optimism but our pessimistic premonitions, our dark moments as a species, our irrational, frightful speculations, our strange mutations upon the simple theme of love, and our sleepless, obsessive inventiveness—our dread as well as our faith—that made us human beings." In her essay "One Cheer for Melancholy," Susanna Kaysen concurs: "I think melancholy is useful. In its aspect of pensive reflection or contemplation, it's the source of many books (even those complaining about it) and paintings, much scientific insight, the resolution of many fights between couples and friends, and the process known as becoming mature."

For virtually all of the essayists, the melancholia, whatever adaptiveness it may or may not have held for them or their work, at some point became sufficiently paralyzing to force them to seek treatment. For some, psychotherapy or medication was an unalloyed godsend. For most, it was a more ambivalent thing. Some express their concerns about the effect of treatment on their creative process, fearing a loss of self, humanity, or motivation. Others fear the limitations of treatment: that it will not work well enough, or long enough, that it will strip them of an edge, or that they will have to endure untenable side effects. Lauren Slater eloquently raises the important concerns of a pregnant mother who needs psychiatric medications but fears their effect on her developing fetus. Martha Manning, while noting her dread of electroconvulsive therapy, concludes that it was, in fact, the tractor that pulled her out of the mud.

There are no easy answers and none of the writers tries to make issues less complex than they are. Experiences are as varied as the writers describing them. David Karp speaks for many when he writes, "Through the years my attitude toward drugs has remained steady, a mixture of hostility and dependence." Yet Jane Kenyon speaks for others in this excerpt from her extraordinary poem, "Back":

> *We try a new drug, a new combination*
> *of drugs, and suddenly*
> *I fall into my life again*

like a vole picked up by a storm
then dropped three valleys
and two mountains away from home.

I can find my way back.

This collection of essays is made even more forceful by including the descriptions of those who have lived with the depressed. Donald Hall and Russell Banks, in discussing their wives, Jane Kenyon and Chase Twichell, recount their initial attraction to the moodiness of their spouses. Banks, for example, writes, "I felt of her having more consciousness than I. Any aspect of her behavior that she explained as having been caused by depression, I took to be the result of her principled, clear-eyed, realistic view of the world that surrounded us." But over time it became apparent that depression was more than just a sensitivity to the world or an unduly responsive temperament. Kenyon tried to explain to Hall that "her despair had nothing to do with me. It was heartbreaking not to touch her, not to be able to give her comfort." Depression had moved from the attractive to the pathological.

Both Hall and Banks detail the effect of their mates' moods on their own. "When Jane went manic," Hall writes, "I fell into a deep depression. She soared up and I plunged down—a moody seesaw." Banks, too, speaks of the infectiousness of his wife's moods: "For the first time in my life, I was feeling, not sad and angry, not even melancholic or gloomy, but depressed . . . My response to all this was to blame Chase—to be angry at her, first, for not having allowed me to cure her of her depression, and then for infecting me with it."

Rose Styron writes, simply, of trying to contend with her husband's deepening depression. "Love," she states, "did not prepare me for 1985." His moods became "perceptibly blacker." He was "increasingly more irritated by noise," "demanded real solitude," and lashed out "unpredictably" at his family. Styron vividly describes the sense of desperation she and her children felt in the face of unremitting gloom.

The impact of Maud Casey's manic-depression on her family was similarly profound. She writes that her increasing dependence upon her mother was "a kind of *Invasion of the Body Snatchers* life-draining suck, the alien pod." Her mother's journal entries confirm this: "I feel Maud's misery and fear packed inside my senses. I wake in terror, always close to tears at dawn." Maud's sister, Nell (this collection's editor), recounts the frightening "absence" of her sister during her depression: "The remove of personality. The hidden, shadowy terror of devouring misery. The hollow lifelessness of her pupils, cartoonishly exaggerated into large, black pools from medication. The listless physicality."

No one who has experienced this "remove of personality," or the deadening and horror of deep depression, would minimize the suffering involved. For many, depression forced a lasting change in perspective, in friendships, and in an understanding of the self. Larry McMurtry, in describing the severe depression he went through after quadruple bypass surgery, concluded, "I had died for a few hours, been brought back to life, and now was attempting to live as someone similar to, but not identical with, my real self." And Chase Twichell speaks to the ultimate unknowability of self, mood, brain, and imagination: "But however the illusion of self is born, whether out of anger, ignorance, and greed, or trouble in the transmitters, it's that unstable mental projection that makes language, and in whose voice I'm doomed to speak. It's a phantom who swallows that scored pink oval each night, and a phantom who writes my poems."

For Lesley Dormen, the pain of depression allowed her to appreciate and fully participate in life: "I marvel at my ability to move in and out of ordinary feelings like sadness and disappointment and worry. I continue to be stunned by the purity of these feelings, by the beauty of their rightful proportions to actual life events. I'm hardly carefree—I still scan myself for depression as if checking for broken bones. But I consider my ability to participate at last in the everyday a gift. I don't know where depression comes from or where it goes. I do know that it was the crucible, the rite of passage, that allowed me to create my life."

Kay Redfield Jamison, Ph.D.
Professor of Psychiatry
The Johns Hopkins School of Medicine

A Delicious Placebo

~

Virginia Heffernan

THIS IS WHAT WOULD HAPPEN. In the middle of movie theaters, meetings, and restaurants, I would suddenly have to leave. Jamming my arms into my coat sleeves, I would face away from anyone who could see me, my wrists tightening. I felt asthmatic. If someone noticed that I was rushing, I'd evince artificial warmth designed to *get that person away*. "I need to quickly go outside, okay? Because the garage is closing. It's an early-closer. And I have to work," I'd garble, inventing words.

I developed a faith in motor memory. As I ducked out of the places I was supposed to be, I would stand up like an erect human woman, remembering the feeling of normal standing and pleasant hands. And then, over and over, I would say I was sick—sick with any documented ailment that came into my head, any ailment I could think of except "depression," which no one, no matter what the brochures with grainy girls' pictures and the word "reuptake" say, will ever believe is a real sickness.

I didn't think of it as a sickness either. I thought of it as work. Once I got outside, I would crawl into a taxi, sink down behind the divider, and start my classified work. I'd cry until I felt blood-poisoned with tears and keep crying. After a few minutes the driver would say, "Are you all right?" In careful adherence to my contract's confidentiality clause, I would always answer, "Yes!"

Adam broke up with me in January, at midnight, after two hours of stares and logic loops. Finally, he admitted he needed to get ahold of his feelings before he could see me again. I assumed the role of love executive and said, "Let's touch base later." But, at the door, a more proactive plea occurred to me. "You're denying exactly what's best about life!" I blurted, and that was my last coherent declaration for a long time.

At home in my apartment in Brooklyn, I scoured the cupboards for a sedative, hearing distant notes from a Wharton or Tolstoy medley. Was there an apothecary that still delivered brown-paper packages of laudanum to shrieking women? I drank wine from the bottle, took a double dose of cold medicine. In my hands, filings from the Sudafed package sparkled evilly. Then my mind began to blur. I panicked: if I drift off while I am so weakened, I will wake up demolished, my bones smashed. Frightened, I lay stiff but groggy on top of my bedcovers. Later, thinking I was awake, I dreamed of slicing, shape-shifting light.

That was the beginning. Overnight, it seemed, I'd gone from a twenty-eight-year-old optimist, the type advertisers and politicians take into account, who might find a career and start a family, to a person who is unreliable and preoccupied, a person other people find themselves trying to avoid.

In my first few weeks without Adam, I thought I could engineer a quick turnaround, working maniacally and seeing everyone I knew. When that failed to lift my mood, I submerged myself in the procedures of heartbreak, lolling around my room for weeks, reading the severe poetry of Louise Bogan and listening to overproduced songs by Fiona Apple. But then the lovesick vapors burned off and I discovered something stony, jagged, and permanent underneath.

Every day I felt sadder and stranger. If depression came into my life attached to heartbreak, as one virus piggybacks another, it soon asserted its independence, bringing conclusions to my mind that were captious, adamant, and dark. I began to see life as too long, too easy to botch, and, once botched, impossible to repair. I took stock of how other people had or hadn't ruined their lives; worse, I told them what I thought. "You married too early and should have moved to South America," I pronounced to a friend who lived contentedly with her husband in Colorado. Those flights of rhetoric put me in a bind: the beliefs and actions that grew out of being depressed justified depression, and renewed it.

After a month of vain displays of resiliency, I decided I was living in the aftermath of a huge mistake. The mistake appeared to be the begging but casually not begging letter that I sent Adam over Christmas. Then the mistake seemed to be my not having been receptive enough when, several months earlier, he appeared drunk at my door at two in the morning and caught me with a Clearasil face. But the probe went back further. I shouldn't have gone to graduate school, shouldn't have broken up with good guys, shouldn't have lied to my parents about how far along on my dissertation I was. That led me to more mistakes: lying generally, not being careful in my career, taking praise too seriously.

Truthfully, I thought, exercising my hot self-knowledge, the mistake must have been longer lasting, a perverted *pattern* of aspiring out of ordinary happiness and abrading life's delicate surface by thrashing out for—what?—some brilliance or beauty or fury or extravagance that I had rabidly decided I deserved, my confidence having been mysteriously canted up. After that, I would throw off the safety measures—friends, courtesy, family, money, work, health, sleep—and, on the brink of breaking out of the earth's atmosphere, suddenly come diving down, without security, and hit the ground flat on my chest, crunching ribs. Then: cold stunned sobriety, and the Icarus-like mortification at having overestimated myself and flaunted my dissatisfaction with normal life. Normal life now looked like paradise: I would have to apologize to it and plea-bargain with it and then seek atonement from it in order to get back in its good graces again.

This sine curve accounted—I decided—for screeds I wrote in college, assorted ideological frenzies, and numberless decisions I made to just *get in the car with these guys* or just, fuck it, *tell the faculty what I think*. I remembered scot-free forays into shoplifting and drunk driving and coke: *supposed to be bad for you*, I had told myself, *but for me they have no consequences*. Now here were my consequences. I clung to this realization, used it as a pivot to turn on my history and myself. Every day of my life seemed tainted by the Pattern—exorbitance followed by a crash and comeuppance. What once seemed a fresh life now appeared twisted and grim.

Along with the Pattern, treason was on my mind. I had betrayed something by getting depressed—whatever informal government supervises the tone of interactions in offices and social life, the one that frowns on euphoria but also mandates a measure of happiness. My punishments presented themselves: a laborious oblation, during which I would have to systematically shred my plans for a good life; house arrest, while I would wait it all out; or a lonely fugitive status, lived out on Amtrak and in the small tract houses of relatives. Or all three. Day to day, my gloominess resembled a Cold War–style job, more bureaucracy than adventure.

A hairdresser turned the bleached sections of my hair back to brown. Clerks at cheap, invisible stores—*Everything in Store Ten Dollars* stores—sold me natural fabric skirts and supportive, flexible shoes. I started to muffle my voice and keep my head down, eyes either on my watch or turned minimally to peer down the train tunnel from the subway platform. I couldn't disappear, but I kept my appearance discreet, my voice and movements small.

Down here, under the flickering, basement light of depression, my field of vision narrowed. I encountered yellowed labels inside shirts, limp one-dollar bills, and people with flat opinions about movies, spoken in the voice of a dial tone. The city was strewn with stained and frayed things, plastic coffee-cup lids and cracked, unspooled cassette tapes. As I brooded on how dingy everything seemed, I wondered if I had thrown myself into depression in order to avoid having a career. It seemed like a possibility, particularly since this theory implied that I was both melodramatic and lazy. Insights generally rang true to the degree that they were self-savaging.

How did I turn from a talkative, batgirl child into a stifled, abstracted monster? As I pressed through my history, in search of mistakes and patterns, I kept right on scaling down and crying for hours on end. I saw no reason to be supportive, to ask people about themselves, or to give some dolled-up rendition of what I was going to do with my days. In the beginning of February, I got into the habit of mumbling made-up lyrics to myself like *I'm in real trouble* and *Ain't no solace.* I mumbled them so often that the volume would accidentally slide up and up until I was singing out loud, in public. It made me feel a little better to talk to myself or sing or say *shhhh* like you would to a baby.

Through the long winter and into the spring, I managed to keep my job—no way out of it. I was trying to write my dissertation on finance and fiction, but mostly I was fact-checking the autobiography of a tycoon. Every day I had to call CEOs from my home and ask questions like, "Were you wearing a three-button suit at the merger meeting?" and "Was it 1986—I mean '85—that *Outrageous Fortune* went into production?" The phone sessions would last for hours. The gravelly voices of these men and the sporty voices of their assistants became a long, surreal radio show. One studio head confessed that his children bored him. A CFO worried that he had no friends because his whole company considered him "Dr. Downside" for pointing out financial risks. Their problems seemed like parables telegraphed from outer space. I began to think that melancholy was a dialect that only some people knew—or could even hear—and in my conversations, I sought these people out.

Sunday mornings I started to go to church, as I hadn't since childhood. I chose a cavernous Anglican church in Brooklyn Heights, and I went to the earliest service, often fighting tears through the prayers and hymns. One morning in early March, the deacon announced that the priest had AIDS. I scanned the small, largely female and Caribbean parishioners, many of them in winter hats; they took the news obediently. I wondered if all of us churchgoers were just exhausted by grief. For the dying priest and us, I thought, "God" always refused to become glorious, instead stubbornly remaining plain, a headache, a sorrowful knot of language. I was in a last-straw zone. On that day, I shipped way out, leaving the secular shores of sanity behind me.

Unless you are rich, and can convalesce in a sanatorium estate (where visitors come down a tiered, oceanside lawn to find you at your easel), you have to keep going when you're depressed. That means phone calls, appointments, errands, holidays, family, friends, and colleagues. For me, this is where things got tangled. Depression brought to me a new rationing of resources: for every twenty-four hours I got about three, then two, then *one* hour worth of life reserves—personality, conversation, motion. I had to be frugal while I was hustling through a day, because when I ran out of reserves, I lost control of what I said.

I would mention the Pattern, for instance, or treason. I'd spin out theories to movie agents on the phone or strangers on buses, whom I interrogated about their families and their faith. I couldn't stop myself. If anyone struck up a conversation with me, I drove it steeply deeper. I also talked this way to my friends, who told me that I sounded "abstract." Sometimes I thought they were right, and so I briskly invented an antidote, the Pillars—a rote series of activities designed to ground me like a middle-school curriculum: exercise, travel, religion, dates, art/music, job. Robotically, I went to the gym, to church, to the Met, to parties, to Seattle. I tried to confine my schedule exclusively to Pillars—checking them off like a tourist—to keep myself from meandering or morbid thinking. When I stuck with it, I congratulated myself on my own sad, neat world. *No one can call me abstract now,* I thought. But other times I thought, *To hell with people who think I'm abstract.*

Rejecting advice or wisdom made me feel solitary, bunkered, and furious. In those times, depression didn't stay pure; it got scorched with anger. That meant no more church and no more compassion. I paced briskly through the Pillar rituals, feeling hot flashes of mean-ness—glad to see people suffer, glad that someone got into a divorce mess, very glad that a man slept with an empty Mad Dog bottle hugged to his chest on my building's front steps. *Good, I hope he dies,* I thought, and it seemed like a new alliance—with death now, which I imagined as an I-beam, slamming through my chest.

Without knowing it exactly, I had felt this way before. Sitting on the steps of the concrete shower/bathroom unit at Camp Coniston when I was chubby and eight, watching badminton, casually pretending to be waiting on a friend, I looked down at my round body stretching out my pink ribbed blouse and overstitched fake denim jeans and thought, *I am such an idiot.* Dizzy with self-disgust, I spent a year clumsily dropping my three-ring notebook, dividers and worksheets spilling out, so many times that I added a prayer to my nightly ritual to prevent it. I called my new diary *Mental Pain.*

It came back: at sixteen, after my first breakup, outside a high-school dance, when the lacrosse captain Carl told me he had slept with someone on his summer abroad. I went down on the living-room sofa in tears that night and came up after what seemed like three hundred and sixty-five days, surrounded by tapes and self-help books, with my mother there, ready to talk me through my first shower. My mother was patient, too, when I sank again during my sophomore year in college and called her during the long weekends spent entirely in my room. She'd persuade me to go out, and I would, but only long enough to sign out more bleak German books from the library or to slump in seminars, where I paid grimly close attention to Shakespearean Evil and Faith and Doubt.

My star symptom was always tears, although this time—when I took a debased scholarly attitude, to the extent of reading *Listening to Prozac* and articles about blues in *Marie Claire*—I fixated on "loss of concentration" as a symptom I lacked. Did that disqualify me? Maybe that was a deciding factor, the absence of which meant that I had some unclassified and still-more-terrible brain fever. Whatever the significance, there was no mistaking my long attention span. The sight of ivy or a couple talking or a don't-cry-out-loud song could absorb me until I lost track of time.

I tried to milk whatever I encountered—Clinton's infidelity, an article about DNA, a violin—for meaning, a thickener that might make my life dense again. On Fridays, men at the mosque next door to my apartment knelt down and I watched from the window—the Tommy Hilfiger and Calvin Klein labels on the backs of their T-shirts—as they fell forward in supplication. *Allah*, I mused on the name, kiting my mind up and out over Saudi Arabia. I stared as they prayed and stared as they later took up their mats, and as the sun set, stared at the sidewalk where their mats had been.

The usual bland solutions droned through my mind: rest, therapy, time off. Starting small, I sought and found a counselor on the eighth floor of a building off Park Avenue. I liked going to her because it meant having another cry station, in a new Manhattan location. I would trudge up to her light blue office and cry and she would ask why and I'd talk about Adam or the Pillars. The Pillars had become my most exalted concept. I loved them; I loved the word "Pillars" and the idea of being ideological about them and not straying, and building a small devotional house out of them. They were, I told her, what I would systematically commit myself to, my good clean activities; I hoped that between now and the indefinite crisis I lately foresaw, they would keep me from sobbing on a park bench or shouting *caw, caw!* or worse.

Right away, she brought up medication. Firmly, I said no. Around April Fools' Day, my explanation for my dysphoria had developed a new twist. Despair was an astonishing break with the ordinary, I now reasoned, something that I had to feel to continue being human—something I should not dope myself up to avoid. I was in the middle of a regimented day of art history and Nautilus, feeling utterly evacuated, when it hit me. I didn't need a cure; I wasn't depressed at all. I had broken free, in fact, and was out from under some social tyranny. I was let loose into a liberty of desperate unhappiness, which was in fact glory. Maybe I was getting a true religion, after my lifetime of shallow faith; maybe these were revelations that would enlighten and stabilize me or even raise me up.

My mother had borne—even humored—each new idea, but this one about being spontaneously liberated frightened her. I could hear it in her voice when she called, when she suddenly resolved to fly to New York and move in with me. The Internet had armed her with some theories about mental health. Now she aimed to make my problems commonplace, telling me statistics and the story of Mike Wallace; she insisted that what I had was plain, run-of-the-mill depression. Sometimes it worked. I would hear her and calm down and then, in my next moment alone, I would jack back up again, and see my life as something enormous, great, and terrible.

My mother also encouraged me to get medication. I told her over and over not to worry. For brief periods, therefore, I stayed quiet, did not let her in on my scary ideas. I kind of thought that I'd either recover or die and both sounded very natural. But her worried voice did focus me, gave me a brief flash—like one frame in a twenty-four-per-second film—of what I looked like from the outside. For this fraction of a second, I saw that I shouldn't let myself drift too far, that someone was scared, that I shouldn't act too insane or think dying was okay.

Part of me was afraid my days were numbered, that sooner or later I would be revealed as a lost cause, ready for helmet and bib.

Another part was more afraid that I might get away with this forever!

In May, I returned to stoicism. Redoubled my commitment to the Pillars. No talking about myself. Make discipline my antidote. I am good now, I told myself, as I neatly scheduled more therapy. Good, well behaved, not depressed, a young worker, over her illusions, packed up and ready to be centered and independent and ask for what I want in a confident way, choose something over something else, get the job done, not a dreamer, not diffuse or overly poetic or abstract in her thinking, counts on her friends and family but not too much, not fake, not looking for the sublime, and most of all with no idea or hope that Adam will come back. ("He's not the source of it anyway," I parroted on command.) The phrases seized my memory like the pledge of allegiance.

But I wasn't better, and it was clear. I was still rushing out of places. The only word that fit me was sad. And the truth was—as a last-ditch effort—I was avidly seeking someone as sad as I was. That was my incentive for going out at all, striking up conversations, basically combing the population for tiny signs of mental illness to connect with and feel relieved by. When I found evidence of melancholy in an angry bodybuilder at a bar, or a friend who was sick of his job, I craved the details of their Mental Pain. ("I think I'm trying to split open my pectorals," the bodybuilder confessed.) This sense of shared grief, the citywide funeral, lifted me up.

On a cool, clear afternoon at the end of spring, I heard that a friend took St. John's wort, and I went with her and bought some. Day after day, for a week, I glugged down the big plastic pills. I didn't feel better, but the simple fact of buying pills and taking them made something happen: St. John's wort broke into my body, bore through the body/soul membrane, and cleared the way for medicine—the easy philosophical step to drugs that work. I listlessly realized I was bound for pills.

My mother wanted me to get away, and though neither of us had ever thought of spas before, the idea of a weekend at a spa was the closest we could come to Magic Mountain. Did I want to go? Yes. We booked three days at Canyon Ranch in Lenox, Massachusetts, where there are neither canyons nor ranches, a joke I made and which my mother gamely repeated seventy-five times in her effort to encourage me to find things funny.

The day I left New York I went to see an M.D. He asked me if I was a convict, if I'd ever been in the army, how I was sleeping, and a few other things. Then he wrote a prescription for an antidepressant—"It works *beautifully*," he said sexily—which I filled without taking any. Instead, I put the bottle in my bag and got on a train at Penn Station. As the train chugged into the Berkshires, I poured all forty pills out into my hand and stared into their small blue eyes. Was it possible that whatever was in them was all I lacked?

I could not find in myself a trace of love-of-life or even self-preservation. But a small readiness to be somewhere new—I found that. I envisioned a place that was not pining and not terrified, a view drained of the color saturation of bruised hearts. There were some things that I wasn't able to think about before that I was now able to say to myself. Childhood, okay. A new relationship, okay. The future, okay. I was not thrown down. But my attraction to this new thing was very light, seemed almost ready to blow away.

Canyon Ranch was a sprawling complex of StairMasters, pleasant music, and a talented, informed staff. In calligraphy, on a pastel, sponge-painted wall: DOUBT YOUR DOUBTS, NOT YOUR BELIEFS. Sentimentality didn't bother me. I was ready to be in that sloganeering AA frame of mind, break from the past, and cling to the phrases. Every time we trudged from the big beauty zone—with its extraction wing and reflexology terrace—into the fat-free dining room, I passed the slogan and ran through my doubts: religion, patriotism, and ideology couldn't deliver me, my life wouldn't get interesting again. I couldn't get my friends back, I'd never stop feeling sick, and I could never again be a solid, trustworthy citizen. I earnestly tried to doubt those doubts, and come up with new things to believe.

After our second grueling eight-hour day of workouts, my mother and I went to our room and peeled off our T-shirts. *Tootsie* was on Turner Classics. I really wanted something to happen then and there—anything that would signal an end to what my mother called my *bad phase*. While my mom took a bath, I called my voice mail. Adam had not called. He was gone: a fact, hard, like a free weight.

But as I sank into the perfectly white, thread-laden sheets, I contemplated something more surprising: my mother had spent a lot of money on this spa. And I wondered then if being depressed leads you inexorably to places where rich people go, and if depression, perhaps, was an epiphenomenon of prosperity. The concept held my interest. It also led to a new thought. I realized how grateful I was to my mother for letting me see the inside of this athletic and opulent palace, a thought which, in turn, led me to a deep and belated gratitude to my friends, who had talked to me and listened to me all through the winter and spring. I thought then that I had to thank them, rejoin them—not be the sick person anymore.

Out of gratitude I found a belief. I believed, finally, that time would pass—it just would—and before I knew it, days would accumulate, bank up like snow, whether I handled them well or not. That alone seemed kind of impressive.

I took the antidepressant the next day and almost immediately I began shelving the voluminous theories that had occupied my mind for six months. That was humbling. It seemed I had been working in isolation on dead-end research. My special, classified work had produced mostly obsolete and esoteric exercises. And the questions I had considered matters of life and death now struck me as a style of toy thinking (akin to "Does Truth exist?" and "How do we really know what the color 'blue' is?") to be put aside in adulthood. Even now it scares me to realize that my months of depression study came to so little; maybe I haven't realized it yet.

As I have gotten used to being steady, I have also longed for the old teetering, predepression exuberance. And I still haven't learned to like the therapy system—the "balance" and the take-control-of-your-life edict—anywhere near as much as the romance and logic of my treason and my Pillars, the whole weird internal theater. I know you're supposed to come to mistrust those symptoms, but I miss them. I'm like a former skier with a bad hamstring, wishing that I could have lived forever on a speedy and breathless high, and still having trouble facing that my substandard physiology won't allow it. So I have to live apart from the action, a few miles away, out in safer, suburban Therapyland. But I shouldn't complain! Or the depression sentries might shoot me their warning again: nice little life here; wouldn't want anything bad to happen to it.

Toys in the Attic

An Ars Poetica Under the Influence

Chase Twichell

A POEM IS A PORTRAIT of consciousness. It's a recording of the motions of a mind in time, a mind communicating to others the experience of its own consciousness. When I read or write a poem, I'm trying to open a window between my mind and the minds of others. Poetry is written for others. But it's also a study of the self, which is a private kind of work.

Already I've had to use the troublesome words "consciousness," "mind," and "self," which are approximate and overlapping in their definitions because the thing they describe is a slippery animal. Buddhism has a useful all-purpose name for what I am—a sentient being—but even this label doesn't account for the persistent evidence suggesting that I am a unique and identifiable individual, and can move as such through time. I want to explore this nexus of words—this atom of consciousness, mind, and self—by thinking about depression, from which I've suffered all my life, and its relation to poetry. For fifteen years I've lived with psychoactive drugs in my brain, among them Ambien, Celexa, Desyrel, Effexor, Elavil, Pamelor, Paxil, Serzone, Triavil, Valium, Wellbutrin, and Xanax, my Knights of the Round Table. I've studied the properties of each drug in the laboratories of my mind and body, and have made some unsettling but ultimately consoling discoveries concerning the nature of the self and its language. One is that the animal is slippery because it's mutable. It travels light, moving from drug to drug as if from country to country. The traveler learns that in all those foreign places the same language is spoken, precise and unadorned but also playful. It's the language I want for my poems because it's the language of my consciousness, my little piece of the flux, which happens to be something I fine-tune with psychopharmaceuticals.

In one of my earliest memories, I'm standing looking down into a storm drain, in which my younger sister is crouching. We're playing zoo, and she's the animal. I'm watching the elder sister, me, shove the heavy grate back over the opening. I'm slightly behind myself, like a shadow, a sensation I used to call "the eyes behind the eyes." In another memory, I'm about eight, reading in bed when my mother comes in to tell me that my dog, hit by a car the day before, has died at the vet's. I put my face in my hands, a self-conscious and exaggerated expression of sorrow. My first impulse is to act the part of a grieving child. I am a grieving child, of course, but the real grief is inaccessible to me at that moment. In its place is a calm, numb kind of consciousness, out of which I can fake the expected responses. I'm also playing my mother's words over and over in my head—she's said the dog's name, adding a *y* so that Centime (French poodle, French name) ends up *Centimey,* something my mother has never called her before. *Centimey died last night.* That *y* tells me a thousand things, among them that I am not completely inside myself the way I'm supposed to be.

The theme of third grade was Ancient Egypt. The teacher described how Howard Carter, excavating the Valley of the Kings for the first time, powered his steam engines by burning legions of "lesser" mummies. No doubt this lurid detail was meant to enliven the study of history, but the irony of the dead digging up the dead struck me as contrary to the natural order of things, and I told the child psychiatrist about it. Dr. C. was a slow-moving, gentle, elderly woman who gave me a series of Rorschach tests. I said that the butterfly, the obvious one they show you to get you started, was a dead angel, and that another, blatantly phallic, was a tree split by lightning. The doctor had asked me to secretly clink minds with her, but I saw through the trick. Outside myself as always, the watcher, the modifier, I lied to her in order to dramatize my pain, but also to keep her at a distance. I knew I wasn't normal—at school there was clear glass between me and the playground, me and my young fellow humans. I was the feral cat that slunk in and out of the garage at night, not the house pet asleep at the foot of the bed. I slept in my clothes and climbed down the drainpipe like a boy. But there was a joy that came with that loneliness. It was poetry, proof of a companion consciousness. As far back as I can remember, I recognized its language as my own.

What happens in depression, for reasons that are still unknown, is that the limbic-diencephalic system malfunctions. The biochemical chain reaction that results is extremely complicated, much of it still hypothetical. What is known is that certain neurotransmitters (especially serotonin and norepinephrine) do not work properly, causing a disruption in the flow of information between nerve cells. It's like a game of telephone; the message gets lost as it travels, eventually affecting cellular metabolism, hormone balance, and the circadian system, the clock that determines cycles of rest and activity. This translates into disturbances of mood, sleep, hunger, sex, memory formation, physical energy, hormone secretion (especially cortisol, the "fight or flight" chemical), and body temperature. As Dr. Demitri Papolos summarizes it, "Recent advances in the neurosciences are gradually revealing the central nervous system to look more and more like an interactive network of oscillating nuclei that exchange information across spatial and temporal boundaries that are modifiable by experience." Across spatial and temporal boundaries that are modifiable by experience—that's the part I'm trying to understand.

In my mid-thirties, which happens to be the average age of onset for clinical depression, I began shooting in the dark, as my doctor put it: searching through trial and error for a drug that would cure what ailed me with as few side effects as possible. Some of them make you dream, every night, the kind of dream you hate to wake from, rich and important feeling. Others keep you skittering along the surface of sleep as if a car alarm were going off somewhere in the neighborhood, but not on your street. Some make you black out if you stand up too fast, or glue your tongue to the roof of your mouth. One cures migraines, another exacerbates them. All of them affect the way in which the brain processes language. It's not something a person uninterested in words might notice, except for maybe a bit of tip-of-the-tongue syndrome, but to me it's obvious that my relation to language has been subtly affected. Before the long parade of drugs, words were like water—all I had to do was dip my mind and it would come up brimming with new excitements. I always thought of this ability as a "gift," a part of my being. Now the river of words flows around me as it always has, but I write as a translator trespassing outside the boundaries of my original language, fluent but no longer a native speaker. It's hard to explain. It feels like a new part of my brain has learned language, and the old part has atrophied. Maybe this sensation is just a physical metaphor for what the antidepressants do, I don't know, but I've come to see that this death of imaginary self (along with its language) is not necessarily a hindrance to my work, though it took me years to stop trying to call my "gift" back from its grave. Its loss functions exactly as form does in poetry: if the door's locked, try a window.

What if the Self is a fiction of the hypothalamus? Aside from the uncomfortable inference that I may be nothing but a poorly mixed cocktail of brain chemicals, this disturbing idea sounds like Zen, and also like science fiction. In the film *The Matrix,* a cyber-jockey called Neo (Keanu Reeves) is drafted by the underground to help bring about the downfall of the Matrix, a mutant computer program born of artificial intelligence, which has turned the human race into slaves. The "real world," based on urban America sometime early in the twenty-first century, is in fact computer-generated, a gilded cage for the population, which is unaware of the illusion that controls them. It's up to Neo and his new friends to reveal the truth, which, unhappily, turns out to be that the actual time is numerous centuries later than heretofore thought, and consists of a single surviving human city near the core of the earth, where there is still heat, and where the memory of freedom is kept alive by generations of escapees. I mention this particular science fiction because as a metaphor it expresses the essence of the Buddha's teaching: life is suffering. Full of craving, we try to cling to illusion, the flux. What we experience as our "self" is a mental projection, a changeable idea; to see the world as it is, we must forget the self. Forgetting the self means realizing its true nature, which is that the boundary between it and the world is imaginary. This is why Zen is said to be a study of the self.

Well, if the self is a fiction, then whose fiction is it? What consciousness determines how The Fiction should be feeling? What if The Fiction finds the magic wand of psychopharmacology among the toys in the attic? I can take a single daily pill that elevates my mood, improves my ability to concentrate, and redesigns the architecture of my sleep. Humankind has always tinkered with consciousness, of course, but recent advances in neurobiology have made it possible to do so with extraordinary specificity, especially considering that much of the current knowledge rests on vast hypotheticals. But however the illusion of self is born, whether out of anger, ignorance, and greed, or trouble in the neurotransmitters, it's that unstable mental projection that makes language, and in whose voice I'm doomed to speak. It's a phantom who swallows that scored pink oval each night, and a phantom who writes my poems.

Of all human languages, poetry is the most powerful and precise, even more so than mathematics, since poetry can account for math's logic but math cannot account for poetry's. This is a tanka by Saito Mokichi (1882–1953):

> *from where*
> *a red tomato*
> *lies rotting*
> *I am only*
> *a few steps away*

The demotion of the pronoun to the relative position puts the tomato in the position of the absolute. They have become "like the foot before and the foot behind in walking," as the eighth-century Chinese Master Shih-t'ou puts it in *The Identity of Relative and Absolute*. This is also the relation of the poet to the poem. The language of poetry is the means by which one human consciousness speaks most intimately, directly, and precisely to others. Yet it is also an empty mirror, if I tell the truth of what I see. To me, the pleasure of this poem lies in its disquieting perspective, which enacts the self dissolving.

It's hard to imagine what my relation to language might have been had I not been born with the genetic predisposition for depression. Studies of twins, both identical and fraternal, show that affective disorders are indeed hereditary. Depression (and manic-depression) tend to run in families—on both sides, in my case. In all likelihood I'll have to take psychoactive drugs for the rest of my life. I'll try the new ones as they come on the market. I'll inhabit subtly new selves, which will think in subtly new language. This no longer threatens my understanding of what it means to be a "self," or to write poems, though sometimes when I'm tired I long for a different kind of consciousness that might let me rest in the illusion of a unique personhood.

I used to think that everyone, especially poets, wanted to understand the true nature of the self, to know what it means to be conscious, and thus to think deeply about death. But most poems I read are about other things. This no longer surprises me, since the death of the self is not something the self likes to think too much about, fiction or not. Rereading Kerouac's *On the Road* the other day, I came across this passage in which Sal Paradise riffs on a dream he's had:

> Something, someone, some spirit was pursuing all of us across the desert of life and was bound to catch us before we reached heaven. Naturally, now that I look back on it, this is only death: death will overtake us before heaven. The one thing that we yearn for in our living days, that makes us sigh and groan and undergo sweet nauseas of all kinds, is the remembrance of some lost bliss that was probably experienced in the womb and can only be reproduced (though we hate to admit it) in death. But who wants to die? In the rush of events I kept thinking about this in the back of my mind; I told it to Dean and he instantly recognized it as the mere simple longing for pure death; and because we're all of us never in life again, he, rightly, would have nothing to do with it, and I agreed with him then.

I admire the way these sentences replicate the self's reflexive refusal of this knowledge, and the shrewdness of that last word, *then*, which admits the ultimate failure of the maneuver.

To me, consciousness is the supremely interesting thing, and poetry the ultimate art of self-annihilation. This is not a contradiction. Consciousness is the lens through which a self either sees the road to death, or does not, if the lens has cataracts, and the biggest, most opaque cataract of them all is the fiction of the self as a static uniqueness unassailable by time. I want to write in the language of the flux I know myself to be: physical and chemical; immortal and nonexistent. That's why, when language comes to me or I go to language, I always meet it somewhere outside of my self. From where a red tomato lies rotting I am only a few steps away.

Bodies in the Basement

An Ars Poetica with Attitude

Russell Banks

1.

WHENEVER I HAPPEN TO MEET and talk with people who are complete strangers to me but who know me, insofar as one can, only through my writings, they almost always say that they're surprised (and perhaps relieved) to find that I'm not depressed. And I'm not—neither clinically nor in affect. But I can understand why a stranger, having read my work, might expect me to be depressed, at least in affect—that is, withdrawn, down-at-the-mouth, enervated, possibly even surly and curt. In those novels and stories, after all, there are no happy endings; the characters endure lives led mostly in quiet desperation; and on the rare occasions when they do escape from their traps, they tend to do it in ways that only make things worse for themselves and for the people who love them. The comedy, when there is some, is likely to be on the dark side of pessimism and dread; and if at the end there is "redemption," it's only because we have seen that in this material world there is, gratuitously given, *something* rather than the merely *nothing* we properly deserve. Beyond that, everything the characters both do and don't do seems to derive its final meaning from the overriding fact that nobody gets out of here alive.

But even if I did express, through my personality and body, the affect that people seem to expect from a depressed person (withdrawn, down-at-the-mouth, enervated, etc.), it would only indicate that my view of the world has made me, not necessarily depressed, but sad and angry. And, indeed, it has. Thus (if only because the work has made him or her feel that way, too) the reader is right to expect to find me sad and angry (if only because the work has made him or her feel that way, too). Which is fine by me, if they feel that way, since I want the novels and stories to be true to my view of the world, and in my view the world is such that any other response to it than sadness and anger would be inappropriate.

Having said that, however, it should also be said that it's precisely the writing of those novels and stories, the act of making them up, that releases me in my day-to-day life and my personal dealings with other people *not* to feel sad and angry. So that, when I push myself away from my desk and rejoin the company of my dear wife, my family and friends, and even the company of strangers, I'm freed to overflow freshly with what feels like a natural sociability and *joie de vivre,* the way a comedian, finished with *his* act, is freed to walk off the stage and let his smile fade, to slump into his chair, look into his dressing-room mirror, and place his hands over his face and weep.

For this reason alone—that there exists a sharp distinction between my attitude and my consciousness—no person who is clinically depressed is likely to have written my novels and stories. Of course, no one other than I, depressed or not, could have written them anyhow; my point is simply that, given the nature of the work, I could not possibly be suffering from depression. Fiction, unlike poetry, is not so much a portrait of the author's consciousness as it is a dramatized expression of his attitude. I speak of the difference between fiction and poetry as one who has written fiction for nearly forty years and who began by writing poetry as well and has been married to a practicing poet for over a decade. Beyond that, from my experience of depression, which derives mainly from my continuing happy marriage to the poet just mentioned, a woman who happens to be clinically depressed, scrupulously self-analytical, and supremely articulate, I have come to believe that the consciousness of a depressed person rarely supports an attitude (or fiction) like mine. A depressed fiction writer with an attitude filled to the brim with sadness and anger nourished, not like mine by a hierarchy of value, but by her malfunctioning limbic-diencephalic systems, would probably be suicidal. Unable to separate her consciousness from such an attitude, unable to withdraw from it as the comedian withdraws from his comedy, she would likely be destroyed by it.

A fiction writer's attitude, generally referred to as an author's "vision," is what informs and gives meaning, especially moral meaning, to the plot, the form and structure of the narrative, the point of view, and the characters; it gives meaning even to the tiniest detail, to the sheen, if singled out, reflected off the dewy surface of a single oak leaf at dawn. Everything in a story or novel, by its nature and placement, by the very tone and inflection of the language in which it is borne, reveals, for better or worse, the writer's hierarchy of value. And as I've implied above, this characteristic of fiction is wonderfully liberating to the writer. Whether he's aware of it is irrelevant. The point is that he is able to distinguish functionally between his work and his personality, which is to say, between the manifestations of his attitude and those of his consciousness. (I might even say, between his body of work and his body.) For him, the two are under no compunction to be the same or even similar. Yet, for the poet, it seems, they

are. This, to me, is not just a crucial difference between the poet and
the fiction writer; it is also a crucial difference between a person who
is depressed and one who is not. And thus it represents a crucial difference between my wife and me.

2.

When I first came to know and love her, I had only a vague and, as it
turned out, wrongheaded idea of the true nature of depression. I
regarded it more or less the same way as do those readers who—
made sad and angry by my work, made "depressed" by it—expect to
find me withdrawn, down-at-the-mouth, enervated, etc. In other
words, despite what I knew about my bifurcated self, or selves, I
assumed that my wife's personality originated in her attitude, her
view of the world, and was therefore pretty much under her control.
I saw her personality, her consciousness, as a product of her will, and
if there was a downside, it was the price in easy sociability that,
unlike her sociable husband, she, who was clearly tougher than he
and more stringently self-sufficient, was willing to pay in order to
stay visibly consistent with her views. Which views I took to be characterized by sadness and anger—like mine. Other people might not
have understood her, but I did.

In fact, there was much about her "affect" (it was far more and
other than mere affect, of course, but I didn't realize it yet) that I had
not previously associated with depression, but should have, and found
seductive, interesting, and energizing. All right, sexy. She was a fast-
moving lady, someone who walked up the backs of other people's
heels on a crowded sidewalk, with quick, nervy (but not nervous) gestures and sudden shifts of expression, so that all my modes of attention were put on high alert. And to a fellow in middle age, especially
one grown a little jaded and inattentive, high alert can be pretty
exciting. Her insomnia suggested a sensibility more refined and
brightly lit than mine, and her history of migraines and fear of their

return lent drama to stress. Also, her careful hedges against stress, the elaborate ways in which she protected herself against it, simply meant to me that she lived a more agitated life than I, an unfortunate but redeeming consequence, I felt, of her having more *consciousness* than I. Any aspect of her behavior that she explained as having been caused by depression, I took to be the result of her principled, clear-eyed, realistic view of the world that surrounded us. And her account of having viewed herself since childhood as separated from her true self by a pane of glass, dissociated, yet always self-aware, as if trapped in an infinite regress—this struck me as a slightly heightened and metaphoric way of describing the detachment from one's self that all writers require and actually nourish: I merely thought that she was describing a familiar thing in a new way.

In those early months and well into the first few years of our life together, like all couples newly in love, we told each other the stories of our past marriages and love affairs and our complex, often painful relations with our parents, siblings, and, in my case, children. Like most such couples, we were better able to describe our lows than our highs, or perhaps felt freer to linger over unhappiness and dissatisfaction than their opposites, and emphasized traumatic disruption over easy, inevitable maturation, growth, and change. We described our difficult childhoods, our tormented adolescences, our past loves (in particular the ones we regretted and had suffered from), and our up-to-now neglected emotional, spiritual, and sexual needs: we told each other about the bodies buried in our basements. And in so doing, discovered that we were perfect for each other.

Time passed, and slowly, as in any marriage, a third person, who was neither of us, began to join us in our marriage, a person smiling beneficently between us, with an invisible arm draped across our shoulders. It was a person whose identity participated in both our separate identities and was, without our intending it or knowing how it happened, our mutual creation, containing both genders, both pasts, both personalities—someone utterly trusted in whom we each could see him- or herself *and* the other, but could see neither one nor the other alone. This third person, whose identity feels more real than one's own, makes a marriage transcendent, but also, when one or both the partners fail the marriage, makes divorce so difficult to endure, living on, as it must, for years after the marriage has been dissolved, keeping ex-husband and ex-wife from knowing who they are alone, what they like and dislike independently of the other, and what their own secret stories were and are. It's not unlike the invisible third person who appears in one's family when a parent or sibling or child is an addict or alcoholic and whose presence alters everyone's behavior and perceptions in tiny, incremental ways, until before long everyone in the family has changed to such a degree that no one, not even the addict, can know who he is anymore or who the others are without that third person present. It's how one becomes an "enabler." But in a marriage that's not organized around addiction or alcoholism, it's how one becomes a usefully sympathetic and understanding spouse.

In marriage we put our identities at risk, gambling that change will turn out to be improvement. I can't speak for my wife, but in my case, change has been improvement—at least insofar as I came over time to feel, not quite her pain, but her depression. And gradually came to realize that I'd had it all wrong.

3.

I began to suspect that I might have a few things wrong when I came to the surprising conclusion that, for the first time in my life, I was feeling, not sad and angry, not even melancholic or gloomy, but depressed. I was manifesting certain classic symptoms—small phobias, along with elaborately contrived avoidances, and the sort of distraction one associates with anxiety, especially the anxiety that arises from fear of losing control over every aspect of one's life. Also, minor sleep disorder and the anxiety that creates. I had never before asked myself, on waking in the morning, if I'd had a good or bad night's sleep, but now it was a regular morning interrogatory, a ruthless, irritated demand for an answer. And I was acquiring a new and noticeable (to me) detachment from myself, an alienation from the person who spoke and acted for me—an unwanted, counterproductive extension of the familiar and necessary detachment I'd long maintained from the man with my name who composed, with attitude, my novels and stories.

The phobias first, for they appeared first and were the tip-off. For years, certainly since her adolescence, my wife had suffered from what we half-jokingly called "urbophobia," fear of cities, especially New York City, an *urb* I rather loved, had visited all my life, and had resided in—from 1982 until 1988 (the year my wife and I set up housekeeping together in Princeton, New Jersey, where I was then teaching). Since my adolescence, I had responded to Gotham pretty much the way small-town American intellectuals have reacted since Whitman's time, romanticizing its history like Thomas Wolfe, glamorizing its funky bohemianism like Kerouac, and embracing its varieties of humanity like a social scientist on speed. Everything about the city excited me and nourished my mind; nothing repelled or scared me (although, naturally, I avoided danger with the same rational care that I took when crossing streets against the lights—I always looked both ways).

Until, having failed to displace my wife's phobia with my enthusiasm for the city, I began to see it with her eyes, instead of my own. The city hadn't changed; I had. Now it seemed physically and psychically threatening to me, noisy and invasive, chaotic and cruel; for the first time, I found myself judging my numerous friends who continued to love the city as I once had, viewing them as somehow more parochial than I and sentimental and self-deluded. None of this, of course, was my wife's doing, none of it was her desire—quite the opposite. She felt embarrassed by her fear of the city, handicapped by it, and the last thing she wanted was to share that fear with me. Yet there it was: in looking out for her, I had begun to look out *with* her. Failing to protect her from a thing she feared, I had come to fear it myself.

It was the same with all but a few of her other symptoms of depression. Although I had never suffered from migraines, I now worried that perhaps I would, or should. And although I had never slipped into the slough of near-suicidal despond that she sometimes endured, I began to magnify my own occasional dips and slips into morbidity and to rely less on humor to get me back on track and more on anxiety and agitated will, which, predictably, got focused on issues of control: the more I felt able to control matters both large and small, the less likely the fall into despondency. It was a mildly effective solution, but the end result was a raised level of ongoing anxiety and the constant care and feeding of a fast-growing control freak.

My reaction to all this was to blame my wife—to be angry at her, first, for not having allowed me to cure her of her depression, and then for infecting me with it. Crude, I know, but not uncommon, I fear (especially among custodial males with the bodies of failed fathers buried beneath their basement floors). Happily, it didn't take long for me to see that my wife was not responsible for my condition; I was. Physician, I told myself, cure thyself, and saw then that this self-inflicted "infection" was in fact a homeopathic cure, in which like cures like and by means of which I was allowed to see the extreme and defining difference between my minor case of depression, contracted by my having confused empathy with sympathy, and my wife's major case, which went, not with her choice of spouse or diet or job or residence, but with her brain chemistry. It went with her body. And bodies don't have attitudes; they have consciousness.

In the intervening years, much has changed, and all for the better, partly because of my growing comprehension of the nature and etiology of my wife's condition, but mostly because of the rapid development and deployment of antidepressants. In the meantime, I have learned a great moral lesson and have tried to apply it to as many aspects of my life with my wife and others as possible. I have

learned to feel *for* my wife and to avoid feeling *with* her. To sympa-
thize and not empathize. It now seems clear to me that it is arrogant
for me to claim to feel another person's pain—unless I'm willing to
become that person. A fiction writer can do that with his characters,
and perhaps, if he wishes to write fiction that will matter to
strangers, he must do that. But a husband cannot become his own
wife. Not if he wants to go on loving her in sickness and in health;
not if he wants her to love him back.

One Cheer for Melancholy

~

Susanna Kaysen

SADNESS OR GLOOM, SAYS THE dictionary, from the Greek "black bile." Definition two is, Pensive reflection or contemplation. Keats wrote an ode to it; Robert Burton wrote an anatomy of it; Freud wrote a major essay about it. Before somebody rechristened it depression, it was common, and commonly accepted as part of life.

That's all over now—the commonly accepted part, anyhow. Commonly complained about is more like it, to judge from the flood of memoirs and preventive manuals. I'm guilty of contributing to that flood. Consider this a sandbag.

I think melancholy is useful. In its aspect of pensive reflection or contemplation, it's the source of many books (even those complaining about it) and paintings, much scientific insight, the resolution of many fights between couples and friends, and the process known as becoming mature.

Here are the characteristic feelings: It's all wrong. I did it wrong. I'm no good at this. This idea stinks. That paragraph doesn't mean anything. These data don't add up to squat. We always end up yelling about the same two things. I can't ever seem to bring anything I start to completion.

Next step: Why bother?

Some people stop there. Some people get stuck there for months or years. Some people move to, But suppose I did it this way? Half the time, "this way" leads back to, It's all wrong. Even when it doesn't, It's all wrong might turn up at any moment.

Those feelings are unpleasant, but they spur change. What would we be without self-doubt and despair?

More energetic, more productive, and happier, say the depressophobes. In my continuing argument with them (which occurs only in my melancholic mind) I object that though we would probably be more energetic, we wouldn't necessarily be more productive. There's no certainty that our products would be better because there were more of them, anyhow. I'm not even convinced that we'd be happier.

A couple of my friends are chronic optimists. They are often disappointed because things didn't work out as well as they have expected. I have never had such a feeling because I'm a pessimist. I get my disappointment over with beforehand. If things don't work out, I'm smug because I predicted it. If they do, I'm pleasantly surprised. Any psychiatrist can tell you this is a standard defense mechanism against disappointment and loss. But so is optimism—and optimism is a lousy defense mechanism because more than half the time it leaves you feeling bad.

My main objection to optimism is that it's incorrect. Things are somewhat more likely to turn out badly. Taking the long view, things are definitely going to turn out badly, since we all die at the end. I once read about a study of "depressives" and "normal people" predicting outcomes in real-life situations. The depressives' predictions were more often right. The pessimistic outlook is actually the realistic one.

If the price of being happier is an occluded worldview, I don't want to pay it. I'd rather see things clearly. Seeing things clearly, for me, is a sort of happiness, even if what I see is banal or sad. Does one of my friends turn on me every time I get depressed? Does another get pleasure from putting me down? Do the idiotic events of history continue to repeat themselves, with tragic consequences? Yes, yes, and yes—but at least I know what I'm up against.

I also know that I am supposed to say that there are serious drawbacks to the melancholic temperament. Deep depression is debilitating. As doctors and drug manufacturers like to remind us, depression can be fatal. Public health officials talk about all the time "wasted" by being depressed. And yet, it's not an uncommon activity, wasting time in this way. If the depressive and manic-depressive constitutions are such a liability, why are they rather prevalent in the human population?

One answer may be balance. I've learned this from my optimistic friends. I rely on them and their cheerful attitudes. Together, we make a complete picture. My doom and gloom may be more often right, but they aren't the whole story. My optimistic friends are more likely to take a risk than I am. They don't think it's risky, since they think things will work out well. They can prod me to try something I'd talk myself out of on my own. On the other hand, I've pulled them back from the brink of a few big messes, which they'd convinced themselves were going to be fabulous.

Extrapolate this to the general population and you have an American Constitution situation in which nobody gets too carried away. Checks and balances: not a bad arrangement.

Let's suppose this is true, that there is a species benefit to having a majority of can-do types mixed with a significant minority of worriers and brooders. Most people would rather be part of the optimist group than the pessimist group, at least in modern America, where optimism is highly valued and irony, pessimism, and sadness are seen as "negative thinking."

Americans are saddled with the idea that we can and should be happy. It's as if we've misread the Declaration of Independence and think it guarantees us the right not to pursue happiness but to achieve it. We have a low pain threshold for sadness, which inevitably means we complain a lot about it—especially when decades of prosperity have given the middle classes more time to ruminate on whether we feel good or bad.

The consensus seems to be that we feel bad. On talk shows and in support groups, in memoirs and collections of essays, we reveal that we've been abused, thwarted and disappointed, and are now depressed. Misery has come out of the closet. Now it's like a hyperactive jack-in-the-box that won't go back in.

It's telling that I wrote the word "hyperactive" there. Things that used to be adjectives are now diseases. Kids who were wriggly and irritable fifteen years ago have Attention Deficit Disorder nowadays. I won't even bother with the Love/Gambling/Credit Addiction stuff. The general climate is a pathologizing one, and it's not hard to see why. Extraordinary leaps in medicine have raised extraordinary expectations for the cure (or at least mitigation) of ailments that have plagued people for millennia. Combine those expectations with our equally unreasonable expectations for happiness, and you get a lot of people clamoring to label themselves diseased in the hope that they can be cured. This faith in science is ill-advised. Despite Prozac and her daughters, there's no cure for sadness.

I can hear the objections. Sadness isn't depression! Depression kills! Depression, in its severity and duration, is different from what Freud called common misery. That's true, but I'm not convinced most people can tell the difference these days. People are often attracted by the idea that they have something really bad.

Here's an anecdote. When my book was having its moment of success, I was part of a group of "experts" on a TV talk show about (what else?) Prozac, though I'd explained to several people connected with the show that I'd never taken it and knew nothing about it. The discussion was heated. I got into a wrangle with a woman in the studio audience whose dog had died. "I couldn't function," she said. "I *had* to take Prozac." When I pointed out that grief was a normal, healthy response to the death of her dog, she became furious. "You've never been really depressed," she told me. I didn't want to get into a competition about who'd been more depressed, so I repeated my idea that some things in life were truly sad and worth feeling depressed about. She just wasn't having any. "You don't understand clinical depression," she said. I gave up.

The important word was "clinical." She'd latched onto that, though I wasn't sure why. Maybe naming her feelings and labeling them a disease relieved the guilt and shame that often accompany depression. Maybe it helped her stop punishing herself for a failure of will.

The Failure of Will theory is equally popular with people who are not depressed. Get out and take your mind off yourself, they say. You're too self-absorbed. This is just about the stupidest thing you can say to a depressed person, and it is said every day to depressed people all over this country. And if it isn't that, it's, Shut up and take your Prozac.

These attitudes are contradictory. Conquer Your Depression and Everything Can Be Fixed by the Miracle of Science presuppose opposite explanations for the problem. One blames character, the other neurotransmitters. They are often thrown at the sufferer in sequence: Get out and do something, and if that doesn't work, take pills. Sometimes they're used simultaneously: You won't take those pills because you don't WANT to do anything about your depression, i.e., Failure of Will.

The one thing these attitudes share is the idea that sadness is bad and must be eliminated.

I don't think it's so bad. I think depression and despair are reasonable reactions to the nature of life. Life has its ups and downs. It is unreliable and conditional and provisional. It can be, as we used to say in my youth, a real bummer. Failure, disease, death: standard life events. Is it any surprise if some of the time, some of us feel like hell?

The worst thing about depression—the thing that makes people phobic about it—is that it's a foretaste of death. It's a trip to the country of nothingness. Reality loses its substance and becomes ghostly, transparent, unbelievable. This perception of what's outside infects the perception of the self, which explains why depressed people feel they aren't "there."

This tells us something important about what it means to *be* "there." It means believing the evidence of our senses, believing in heat and cold and hunger and smoothness and sexual desire. What philosophers the melancholics are, positing a world in which the tree doesn't make a noise even when it falls right in front of your face!

When I'm feeling good, I sometimes think of feeling depressed, the sliminess of it, when what I see has a shimmer of not-thereness and what I feel has a slippery way of falling off after a minute, so that I can't sustain the sensation of being alive. But it's far away at that moment—as far as vivacity is when I'm depressed.

I know they are both real.

The melancholic temperament is equipped to perceive and, more important, to tolerate the fundamental ambiguities of life. The transient nature of happiness, beauty, success, and health may come as a shock to the upbeat person but it's old hat to the depressive. And, I think depressive people have more fun. Human nature being what it is, we enjoy more whatever is hard to get and in short supply. Happiness is certainly both, and nobody knows that better than someone who spends half the time sunk in gloom.

"Ay, in the very temple of Delight / Veil'd Melancholy has her sovran shrine," said Keats. He was right: everything passes, everything can become its opposite at a moment's notice. Read it and weep—or laugh, if you're a melancholic sort.

HEAVEN
AND NATURE

∿

Edward Hoagland

A FRIEND OF MINE, A peaceable soul who has been riding the New York subways for thirty years, finds himself stepping back from the tracks once in a while and closing his eyes as the train rolls in. This, he says, is not only to suppress an urge to throw himself in front of it but because every couple of weeks an impulse rises in him to push a stranger onto the tracks, any stranger, thus ending his own life, too. He blames this partly on apartment living, "pigeonholes without being able to fly."

It is profoundly startling not to trust oneself after decades of doing so. I don't dare keep ammunition in my country house for a small rifle I bought secondhand two decades ago. The gun had sat in a cupboard in the back room with the original box of .22 bullets under the muzzle all that time, seldom fired except at a few apples hanging in a tree every fall to remind me of my army training near the era of the Korean War, when I'd been considered quite a marksman. When I bought the gun I didn't trust either my professional competence as a writer or my competence as a father as much as I came to, but certainly believed I could keep myself alive. I bought it for protection, and the idea that someday I might be afraid of shooting myself with the gun would have seemed inconceivable—laughable.

One's fifties can be giddy years, as anybody fifty knows. Chest pains, back pains, cancer scares, menopausal or prostate complications are not the least of it, and the fidelities of a lifetime, both personal and professional, may be called into question. Was it a mistake to have stuck so long with one's marriage, and to have stayed with a lackluster, well-paying job? (Or *not* to have stayed and stuck?) People cannot only lose faith in their talents and dreams or values; some simply tire of them. Grow tired, too, of the smell of fried-chicken grease, once such a delight, and the cold glutinosity of ice cream, the boredom of beer, the stop-go of travel, the hiccups of laughter, and of two rush hours a day, then the languor of weekends, of athletes as well as accountants, and even the frantic birdsong of spring: red-eyed vireos that have been clocked singing twenty-two thousand times in a day. Life is a matter of cultivating the six senses, and an equilibrium with nature and what I think of as its subdivision, human nature—trusting no one completely but almost everyone at least a little. But this is easier said than done.

More than thirty thousand Americans took their own lives last year, men mostly, with the highest rate among those older than sixty-five. When I asked a friend why three times as many men kill themselves as members of her own sex, she replied with sudden anger, "I'm not going to go into the self-indulgence of men."

They won't bend to failure, she said, and want to make themselves memorable. Suicide is an exasperating act as often as it is pitiable. "Committing" suicide is in bad odor in our culture even among those who don't believe that to cash in your chips ahead of time and hand back to God his gifts to you is a blasphemous sin. We the living, in any case, are likely to feel accused by this person who "voted with his feet." It appears to cast a subversive judgment upon the social polity as a whole that what was supposed to work in life—religion, family, friendship, commerce, and industry—did not, and furthermore it frightens the horses in the street, as Shaw's friend Mrs. Patrick Campbell once defined wrongful behavior.

Many suicides inflict outrageous trauma, burning permanent injuries on the minds of their children, though they may have joked beforehand only of "taking a dive." And sometimes the gesture has a peevish or cowardly aspect, or seems to have been senselessly short-sighted as far as an outside observer can tell. There are desperate suicides and crafty suicides, people who do it to cause others trouble and people who do it to save others trouble, deranged exhibitionists who yell from a building ledge, and closemouthed, secretive souls who swim out into the ocean's anonymity. Suicide may in fact be an attempt to escape death, shortcut the dreadful deteriorating processes, abort one's natural trajectory, elude "the ruffian on the stairs," in A. E. Housman's phrase for a cruelly painful, anarchic death—make it neat and not messy. The deed can be grandiose or self-abnegating, vindictive or drably mousy, rationally plotted or plainly insane. People sidle toward death, intent upon outwitting their own bodies' defenses, or they may dramatize the chance to make one last, unambiguous, irrevocable decision, like a captain scuttling his ship—death before dishonor—leaping toward oblivion through a curtain of pain, like a frog going down the throat of a snake. One man I knew hosted a quietly affectionate evening with several unknowing friends on the night before he swallowed too many pills. Another waved an apologetic good-bye to a bystander on a bridge. Seldom shy ordinarily, and rarely considerate, he turned shy and apologetic in the last moment of life. Never physically inclined, he made a great vault toward the ice on the Mississippi.

In the army, we wore dog tags with a notch at one end by which these numbered pieces of metal could be jammed between our teeth, if we lay dead and nameless on a battlefield, for later sorting. As "servicemen" our job would be to kill people who were pointed out to us as enemies, or make "the supreme sacrifice" for a higher good than enjoying the rest of our lives. Life was very much a possession, in other words—not only God's, but the soldier's own to dispose of. Working in an army hospital, I frequently did handle dead bodies, but this never made me feel I would refuse to kill another man whose uniform was pointed out to me as being inimical, or value my life more tremulously and vigilantly. The notion of dying for my country never appealed to me as much as dying freelance for my ideas (in the unlikely event that I *could* do that), but I was ready. People were taught during the 1940s and 1950s that one should be ready to die for one's beliefs. Heroes were revered because they had deliberately chosen to give up their lives. Life would not be worth living under the tyranny of an invader, and Nathan Hale apparently hadn't paused to wonder whether God might not have other uses for him besides being hung. Nor did the pilot Colin Kelly hesitate before plunging his plane into a Japanese battleship, becoming America's first well-publicized hero in World War II.

I've sometimes wondered why people who know that they are terminally ill, or who are headed for suicide, so very seldom have paused to take a bad guy along with them. It's lawless to consider an act of assassination, yet hardly more so, really, than suicide is regarded in some quarters (or death itself, in others). Government bureaucracies, including our own, in their majesty and as the executors of laws, regularly weigh whether or not to murder a foreign antagonist. Of course the answer is that most individuals are fortunately more timid as well as humbler in their judgment than government officialdom. But, beyond that, when dying or suicidal, they no longer care enough to devote their final energies to doing good works of any kind—Hitler himself in their gun sights they would have passed up. Some suicides become so crushed and despairing that they can't recognize the consequences of anything they do, and it's not primarily vindictiveness that wreaks such havoc upon their survivors but their derangement from ordinary life.

Courting the idea is different from the real impulse. "When he begged for help, we took him and locked him up," another friend of mine says, speaking of her husband. "Not till then. Wishing to be out of the situation you are in—feeling helpless and unable to cope—is not the same as wishing to be dead. If I actually wished to be dead, even my children's welfare would have no meaning."

You might think the ready option of divorce available would have cut suicide rates, offering an escape to battered wives, lovelorn husbands, and other people in despair. But it doesn't work that way. When the number of choices people have increases, an entire range of possibilities opens up. Suicide among teenagers has almost quadrupled since 1950, although the standard of comfort that their families enjoy is up. Black Americans, less affluent than white Americans, have had less of a rise in suicides, and the rate among them remains about half of that for whites.

Still, if a fiftyish fellow with fine teeth and a foolproof pension plan, a cottage at the beach, and the Fourth of July weekend coming up kills himself, it seems truculent. We would look at him in bafflement if he told us he no longer likes the Sturm und Drang of banging fireworks.

Then stay at your hideaway! we'd argue with him.

"Big mouths eat little mouths. Nature isn't 'timeless.' Whole lives are squeezed into three months or three days."

What about your marriage?

"She's become more mannish than me. I loved women. I don't believe in marriage between men."

Remarry, then!

"I've gone impotent, and besides, when I see somebody young and pretty I guess I feel like dandling her on my knee."

Marriage is friendship. You can find someone your own age.

"I'm tired of it."

But how about your company? A widows-and-orphans stock that's on the cutting edge of the silicon frontier? That's interesting.

"I know what wins. It's less and less appetizing."

You're not scared of death anymore?

"It interests me less than it did."

What are you so sick of? The rest of us keep going.

"I'm tired of weathermen and sportscasters on the screen. Of being patient and also of impatience. I'm tired of the president, whoever the president happens to be, and sleeping badly, with forty-eight half-hours in the day—of breaking two eggs every morning and putting sugar on something. I'm tired of the drone of my own voice, but also of us jabbering like parrots at each other—of all our stumpy ways of doing everything."

You're bored with yourself?

"That's an understatement. I'm maybe the least interesting person I know."

But to kill yourself?

"You know, it's a tradition, too," he remarks quietly, not making so bold as to suggest that the tradition is an honorable one, though his tone of voice might be imagined to imply this. "I guess I've always been a latent maverick."

Except in circumstances which are themselves a matter of life and death, I'm reluctant to agree with the idea that suicide is not the result of mental illness. No matter how reasonably the person appears to have examined his options, it goes against the grain of nature for him to destroy himself. But any illness that threatens his life then changes a person. Suicidal thinking, if serious, can be a kind of death scare, comparable to suffering a heart attack or undergoing a cancer operation. One survives such a phase both warier and chastened. When—ten years ago—I emerged from a bad dip into suicidal speculation, I felt utterly exhausted and yet quite fearless of ordinary dangers, vastly afraid of myself but much less scared of extraneous eventualities. The fact of death may not be tragic; many people die with a bit of a smile that captures their mouths at the last instant, and most people who are revived after a deadly accident are reluctant to be brought to life, resisting resuscitation, and carrying back confusing, beamish, or ecstatic memories. Yet the same impetuosity that made him throw himself out of the window might have enabled the person to love life all the more, if he'd been calibrated somewhat differently at the time of the emergency. Death's edge is so abrupt and near that many people who expect a short and momentary dive may be astounded to find that it is bottomless, and change their minds and start to scream when they are halfway down.

Although my fright at my mind's anarchy superseded my fear of death in the conventional guise of automobile or airplane crashes, heart seizures, and so on, nightmares are more primitive and in my dreams I continued to be scared of a death not sought after—dying from driving too fast and losing control of the car, breaking through thin ice while skating and drowning in the cold, or falling off a cliff. When I am tense and sleeping raggedly, my worst nightmare isn't drawn from anxious prep-school memories or my stint in the army or the bad spells of my marriages or any other of adulthood's vicissitudes. Nothing else from the past half century has the staying power in my mind of the elevated-train rides that my father and I used to take down Third Avenue to the Battery in New York City on Sunday afternoons when I was three or four or five, so I could see the fish at the aquarium. We were probably pretty good companions in those years, but the wooden platforms forty feet up shook terribly as trains from both directions pulled in and out. To me they seemed worse than rickety—ready to topple. And the roar was fearful, and the railings left large gaps for a child to fall through, after the steep climb up the slat-sided, windy, shaking stairway from street level. It's a rare dream, but several times a year I still find myself on such a perch, without his company or anybody else's, on a boyish mission, when the elevated platform begins to rattle desperately, seesaw, heel over, and finally come apart, disintegrate, while I cling to struts and trusses.

My father, as he lay dying at home of bowel cancer, used to enjoy watching Tarzan reruns on the children's hour of television. Like a strong green vine, they swung him far away from his deathbed to a world of skinny-dipping and friendly animals and scenic beauty linked to the lost realities of his adolescence in Kansas City. Earlier, when he had still been able to walk without much pain, he'd paced the house for several hours at night, contemplating suicide, I expect, along with other anguishing thoughts, regrets, remembrances, and yearnings, while the rest of us slept. But he decided to lie down and die the slower way. I don't know how much of that decision was because he didn't want to be a "quitter," as he sometimes put it, and how much was due to his believing that life belongs to God (which I'm not even sure he did). He was not a churchgoer after his thirties. He had belonged to J. P. Morgan's church, Saint George's, on Stuyvesant Square in Manhattan—Morgan was a hero of his. But when things went a little wrong for him at the Wall Street law firm he worked for, and he changed jobs and moved out to the suburbs, he became a skeptic on religious matters, and gradually, in the absence of faith of that previous kind, adhered to a determined allegiance to the social order. Wendell Willkie or Dwight D. Eisenhower, instead of J. P. Morgan, became the sort of hero he admired, and suicide would have seemed an act of insurrection against the laws and conventions of the internationalist-Republican society that he believed in.

I was never particularly afraid that I might plan a suicide, swallowing a bunch of pills and keeping them down—only of what I think of as Anna Karenina's kind of death. This most plausible self-killing in all literature is frightening because it was unwilled, regretted at midpoint, and came as a complete surprise to Anna herself. After rushing impulsively, in great misery, to the railway station to catch a train, she ended up underneath another one, dismayed, astonished, and trying to climb out from under the wheels, even as they crushed her. Many people who briefly verge on suicide undergo a mental somersault for a terrifying interval during which they're upside down, their perspective topsy-turvy, skidding, churning; and this is why I got rid of the bullets for my .22.

Nobody expects to trust his body overmuch after the age of fifty. Incipient cataracts or arthritis, outlandish snores, tooth grinding, ankles that threaten to turn are part of the game. But not to trust one's *mind*? That's a surprise. The single attribute that older people were sure to have (we thought as boys) was a stodgy dependability, a steady temperance or caution. Adults might be vain, unimaginative, pompous, and callous, but they did have their affairs tightly in hand. It was not till my thirties that I began to know friends who were in their fifties on equal terms, and I remember being amused, piqued, irritated, and slightly bewildered to learn that some of them still felt as marginal or rebellious or in a quandary about what to do with themselves for the next dozen years as my contemporaries were likely to. That close to retirement, some of them harbored a deep-seated contempt for the organizations they had been working for, being ready to walk away from almost everybody they had known, and the efforts and expertise of whole decades, with very little sentiment. Nor did twenty years of marriage necessarily mean more than two or three—they might be just as ready to walk away from that also, and didn't really register it as twenty or thirty years at all. Rather, life could be about to begin all over again. "Bummish" was how one man described himself, with a raffish smile—"Lucky to have a roof over my head"—though he'd just put a child through Yale. He was quitting his job and claimed with exasperation that his wife still cried for her mother in her sleep, as if they'd never been married.

The great English traveler Richard Burton quoted an Arab proverb that speaks for many middle-aged men of the old-fashioned variety: "Conceal thy Tenets, thy Treasure, and thy Traveling." These are serious matters, in other words. People didn't conceal their tenets in order to betray them, but to fight for them more opportunely. And except for kings and princelings, concealing whatever treasure one had went almost without saying. As for travel, a man's travels were also a matter of gravity. Travel was knowledge, ambiguity, dalliances or misalliances, divided loyalty, forbidden thinking; and besides, someday he might need to make a run for it and go to ground someplace where he had made some secret friends. Friends of mine whose husbands or wives have died have been quite startled afterward to discover caches of money or traveler's checks concealed around the house, or a bundle of cash in a safe-deposit box.

Burton, like any other desert adage-spinner and most individuals over fifty, would have agreed to an addition so obvious that it wasn't included to begin with: "Conceal thy Illnesses." I can remember how urgently my father worried that word would get out, after a preliminary operation for his cancer. He didn't want to be written off, counted out of the running at the corporation he worked for and in other enclaves of competition. Men often compete with one another until the day they die; comradeship consists of rubbing shoulders jocularly with a competitor. As breadwinners, they must be considered fit and sound by friend as well as foe, and so there's lots of truth to the most common answer I heard when asking why three times as many men as women kill themselves: "They don't know how to ask for help." Men greet each other with a sock on the arm, women with a hug, and the hug wears better in the long run.

I'm not entirely like that; and I discovered when I confided something of my perturbation to a woman friend she was likely to keep telephoning me or mailing cheery postcards, whereas a man would usually listen with concern, communicate his sympathy, and maybe intimate that he had pondered the same drastic course of action himself a few years back and would end up respecting my decision either way. Open-mindedness seems an important attribute to a good many men, who pride themselves on being objective, hearing all sides of an issue, on knowing that truth and honesty do not always coincide with social dicta, and who may even cherish a subterranean outlaw streak that, like being ready to violently defend one's family, reputation, and country, is by tradition male.

Men, being so much freer than women in society, used to feel they had less of a stake in the maintenance of certain churchly conventions and enjoyed speaking irreverently about various social truisms, including the principle that people ought to die on schedule, not cutting in ahead of their assigned place in line. But contemporary women, after their triumphant irreverence during the 1960s and 1970s, cannot be generalized about so easily. They turn as skeptical and saturnine as any man. In fact, women attempt suicide more frequently, but favor pills or other passive methods, whereas two-thirds of the men who kill themselves have used a gun. In 1996, 87 percent of suicides by means of firearms were done by men. An overdose of medication hasn't the same finality. It may be reversible, if the person is discovered quickly, or be subject to benign miscalculation to start with. Even if it works, it can be fudged by a kindly doctor in the record keeping. Like an enigmatic drowning or a single-car accident that baffles the suspicions of the insurance company, a suicide by drugs can be a way to avoid making a loud statement, and merely illustrate the final modesty of a person who didn't wish to ask for too much of the world's attention.

Unconsummated attempts at suicide can strike the rest of us as self-pitying and self-aggrandizing, however, or like plaintive plea bargaining. "Childish," we say, though actually the suicide of children is ghastly beyond any stunt of self-mutilation an adult may indulge in because of the helplessness that echoes through the act. It would be hard to define chaos better than as a world where children decide that they don't want to live.

Love is the solution to all dilemmas, we sometimes hear. And in those moments when the spirit bathes itself in beneficence and manages to transcend the static of personalities rubbing fur off each other, indeed it is. Without love nothing matters, Paul told the Corinthians, a mystery which, if true, has no ready Darwinian explanation. Love without a significant sexual component and for people who are unrelated to us serves little practical purpose. It doesn't help us feed our families, win struggles, thrive and prosper. It distracts us from the ordinary business of sizing people up and making a living, and is not even conducive to intellectual observation, because instead of seeing them, we see right through them to the bewildered child and dreaming adolescent who inhabited their bodies earlier, the now-tired idealist who fell in and out of love, got hired and quit, hired and fired, bought cars and wore them out, liked black-eyed Susans, blueberry muffins, and roosters crowing—liked roosters crowing better than skyscrapers but now likes skyscrapers better than roosters crowing. As swift as thought, we select the details that we need to see in order to be able to love them.

Yet at other times we'll dispense with these same poignancies and choose only their grunginess to look at, their pinched mouths and shifty eyes, their thirst for gin at noon and indifference to their kids, their greed for the best tidbit on the buffet table and penchant for poking their penises up the excretory end of other human beings. I tend to gaze quite closely at the faces of priests I meet on the street to see if a lifetime of love has marked them noticeably. Real serenity or asceticism I no longer expect, and I take for granted the beefy calm that frequently goes with Catholic celibacy, but I am watching for the marks of love and often see mere resignation or tenacity.

Many men are romantics—likely to plunge, go for broke, take action in a spirit of exigency rather than waiting for the problem to resolve itself. Then, on the contrary, still as romantics, they may drift into a despairing passivity, stare at the TV all day long, and binge with a bottle. Women too may turn frenetic for a while and then throw up their hands. But though they may not seem as grandiosely fanciful and romantic at the outset, they are more often believers—at least I think they tend to believe in God or in humanity, the future, and so on. We have above us the inviting eternity of "the heavens," if we choose to look at it, lying on our backs in the summer grass under starlight, some of which had left its source before mankind became man. But because we live in our heads more than in nature nowadays, even the summer sky is a minefield for people whose memories are mined. With the sky no longer humbling, the sunshine only a sort of convenience, and no godhead located anywhere outside our own heads, every problem may seem insolubly interlocked. When the telephone has become impossible to answer at home, sometimes it finally becomes impossible to stride down the gangplank of a cruise ship in Mombasa, too, although no telephones will ring for you there.

But if escapist travel is ruled out in certain emergencies, surely you can *pray*? Pray, yes; but to whom? That requires a bit of preparation. Rarely do people obtain much relief from praying if they haven't stood in line awhile to get a visa. It's an appealing idea that you can just *go*, and in a previous era perhaps you could have, like on an old-fashioned shooting safari. But it's not so simple now. What do you believe in? Whom are you praying to? What are you praying for? There's no crèche on the courthouse lawn; you're not supposed to adhere exactly even to what your parents had believed. Like psychotherapy, praying takes time, even if you know which direction to face when you kneel.

Love is powerfully helpful when the roof falls in—loving other people with a high and hopeful heart and as a kind of prayer. Yet that feat too requires new and sudden insights or long practice. The beatitude of loving strangers as well as friends—loving them on sight with a leap of empathy and intuition—is a form of inspiration, edging, of course, in some cases toward madness, as other states of beatitude can do. But there's no question that a genuine love for the living will stymie suicidal depressions which are not chemical in origin. Love is an elixir, changing the life of the lover like no other. And many of us have experienced this—a temporary lightening of our leery, prickly disapproval of much of the rest of the world when at a wedding or a funeral of shared emotion, or when we have fallen in love.

Yet the zest for life of those unusual men and women who make a great zealous success of living is due more often in good part to the craftiness and pertinacity with which they manage to overlook the misery of others. You can watch them watch life beat the stuffing out of the faces of their friends and acquaintances, although they themselves seem to outwit the dense delays of social custom, the tedious tick-tock of bureaucratic obfuscation, accepting loss and age and change and disappointment without suffering punctures in their stomach lining. Breathlessness or strange dull pains from their nether organs don't nonplus them. They fret and doubt in moderation, and love a lobster roast, squeeze lemon juice on living clams on the half shell to prove that the clams are alive, laugh as robins tussle a worm out of the ground or a kitten flees a dog. Like the problem drinkers, pork eaters, and chain-smokers who nevertheless finish out their allotted years, succumbing to a stroke at a nice round biblical age while the best vitamin-eating vegetarian has long since died, their faces become veritable walnuts of fine character, with the same smile lines as the rarer individual whose grin has been affectionate all of his life.

We spend our lives getting to know ourselves, yet wonders never cease. During my adolescent years my states of mind, though undulant, seemed seamless; even when I was unhappy no cracks or fissures made me wonder if I was a danger to myself. My confidence was such that I treaded the slippery lips of waterfalls, fought forest fires, drove ancient cars cross-country night and day, and scratched the necks of menagerie leopards in the course of various adventures which enhanced the joy of being alive. The chemistry of the mind, because unfathomable, is more frightening than mere chanciness. In the city, I live on the waterfront and occasionally will notice an agitated-looking figure picking his way along the pilings and stringpieces of the timbered piers nearby, staring at the sliding whorls on the surface of the Hudson, as if teetering over an abyss. Our building, standing across the street, seems imposing from the water and over the years has acted as a magnet for a number of suicides—people who have dreaded the clammy chill, the onerous smothering essential to their first plan. One woman climbed out, after jumping in, and took the elevator to the roof (my neighbors remember how wringing wet she was) and leapt off, banging window ledges on the way down, and hit with the whap of a sack of potatoes, as others have.

Yet what is more remarkable than that a tiny minority of souls reach a point where they entrust their bodies to the force of gravity is that so few of the rest of us will splurge an hour of a summer day gazing at the trees and sky. How many summers do we *have*? One sees prosperous families in the city who keep plants in their apartment windows that have grown so high they block the sunlight and appear to be doing the living for the tenants who are bolted inside. But beauty is nobody's sure salvation: not the beauty of a swimming hole if you get a cramp, and not the beauty of a woman if she doesn't care for you. The swimming hole looks inviting under the blue sky, with its amber bottom, green sedges sticking up in the shallows, and curls of gentle current over a waterlogged birch tree two feet beneath the surface, near the brook that feeds it. Come back at dusk, however, and the pond turns black—as dark as death—or on the contrary, a restful dark, a dark to savor. Take it as you will.

People with sunny natures do seem to live longer than people who are nervous wrecks; yet mankind didn't evolve out of the animal kingdom by being unduly sunny-minded. Life was fearful and phantasmagoric, supernatural and preternatural, as well as encompassing the kind of clockwork regularity of our well-governed day. It had numerous superstitious (from the Latin, "standing over") elements, such as we are likely to catch a whiff of only when we're peering at a dead body. And it was not just our optimism but our pessimistic premonitions, our dark moments as a species, our irrational, frightful speculations, our strange mutations upon the simple theme of love, and our sleepless, obsessive inventiveness—our dread as well as our faith—that made us human beings. Staking one's life on the more general good came to include risking suicide also. Brilliant, fecund people sometimes kill themselves.

Joy to the world.... Let heaven and nature sing.... Repeat the sounding joy.... The famous Christmas carol invokes not only glee but unity: heaven with nature, not always a Christian combination.

It's a rapturous hymn, and no one should refuse to surrender to such a pitch of revelation when it comes. But the flip side of rapture can be a riptide of panic, of hysterical gloom. Our faces are not molded as if joy were a preponderant experience. (Nor is a caribou's or a thrush's.) Our faces in repose look stoic or battered, and people of the sunniest temperament sometimes die utterly unstrung, doubting everything they have ever believed in or have done.

Let heaven and nature sing! the hymn proclaims. But *is* there such harmony? Are God and Mother Nature really the same? Are they even compatible? And will we risk burning our wings if we mount high enough to try to see? I've noticed that woods soil in Italy smells the same as woods soil in New England, when you pick up a handful of it and enjoy its aroma. But is God there the same? It can be precarious to wonder.

I don't rule out suicide as being unthinkable for people who have tried to live full lives; and don't regard it as negating the work and faith and satisfaction and fun and even ecstasy they may have known before. In killing himself a person acknowledges his failures during a time span when perhaps heaven and earth had caught him like a pair of scissors—but doesn't repudiate his life span. Man is different from animals in that he speculates, a high-risk activity.

POODLE BED

～

Darcey Steinke

LIKE MOST LITTLE KIDS I had a blankie. I can still remember its yellow silk top and shredded wool weave and that awful day when I lost it in JCPenney's toy department. Maybe it's because of this early separation from my familiar that I have always been inordinately attached to my bedspreads. I can remember each of my childhood quilts; the thin one with pink rosebuds; and the green wool blanket with the fat black stripe. It wasn't until high school though that I dragged a blue gingham quilt into my closet and curled up within. My brother coined the term "poodle bed" when he caught me lying in a fetal position on top of my tennis shoes.

In its heyday the poodle bed consisted of a comforter thrown onto

a dark closet floor or the space underneath a table or a closed-in corner between, say, the refrigerator and the wall. When I was sad— and
I was desperately sad throughout my teens and twenties—I'd lie in
the dark poodle bed crying, then staring at the wall before finally
falling asleep. I employed the poodle bed in a variety of tiny apartments. Haunted by the vagaries of my twenties—financial insecurity
and unsteady relationships—I often suffered from crying jags and anxious insomnia. I wasn't yet familiar with my own volatile temperament, and sadness often overwhelmed me like an ice-encased sapling.

The culmination of this period came when I was twenty-four-
years old and living with my boyfriend in an apartment on San Francisco's Bush Street. My parents had split up the year before and my
embittered mother served my father papers while he was visiting me.
She accused him in the documents of numerous infidelities as well as
being a psychopath. I also quit my Stegner Fellowship at Stanford
that year. The head of my writing program was a high-strung former
Jesuit. His false gestures were flamboyant, and once when I met with
him he went on so long I almost missed my train back to the city.
Later, my vision went out in the middle of the train ride and I was
suddenly so nauseated I threw up. It was the first migraine of a series
that would last all year. Then there was my editor, Jacqueline
Kennedy Onassis. I can still hear her distinct lilting voice on the
phone of my graduate-school hovel. *Do you know the French word*
fleur, *Darcey?* I did not. *That's a shame really because your novel
needs more of that.* I was uncertain about the quality of my prose, and
Jackie's largesse, while encouraging and perceptive, often disoriented
me. Once she accused me playfully of being overly nervous *like those
lovely little terriers at foxhunts* and she insisted I do as Truman
Capote had done and use pink pages for my rewrites.

The Bush Street poodle bed consisted of a ratty blue comforter,
stained with ink dots and blotches of spilled coffee. Lying in its folds
in the closet, I could see the water-stained wall, by the line of light
underneath the door, dust gathering on the wood runner. Once, I
noticed with a wave of disgust that the material I was wrapped in

smelled like leftovers and that I'd just spent the last twenty hours lying in my messy dog's bed.

A month later, when I left my boyfriend, I got my own place. I moved to a studio apartment in the Mission, nailed fabric up over the windows, pushed a futon into the alcove, and bought a bookshelf and table from a thrift shop. My new lover was a fellow student at Stanford. He was short, with red hair, and I was, in my fucked-up way, extremely fond of him. Our relationship was one of those weird in-between affairs, detached and otherworldly from the start. He knew I was sad and unsteady, and was always thinking of ways to cheer me up. When I was sick he would go down to the Lucky Lady candle shop, a voodoo-Catholic place, and ask the lady to mix a special mint potion that he would then sprinkle over the hot skin of my back. He sang me old Elvis Costello songs before I went to sleep at night and read to me from *The New Yorker* while I took long hot baths.

A few days before I was to leave San Francisco and take a Grey-hound back east to Virginia to live, my old boyfriend came over to my apartment and tried to exact a promise that at some future point we would again live together. I reassured him, though I knew for certain that this would never be. There was danger in this self-conscious duality. My old boyfriend talked about reuniting in Charlottesville, where we had met, or getting an apartment in New York City. *Sure sure, don't worry that will happen,* I told him. Each time I spoke I felt like the floor underneath me was giving way and that I would finally fall into the abyss. Ultimately I didn't believe I deserved a life of my own—that is, a life of my own construction, directed by my own desires rather than someone else's. My bohemian-chick period had been a failure; I couldn't handle free love. And those other values sub-scribed to by my mother—marriage, a nice house, and a baby—seemed downright idiotic. All this was simmering, sad but okay until I watched my old boyfriend gloomily descend the stairs. Hearing footfalls below, I glanced at the clock and realized my red-haired boyfriend was coming up. I couldn't breathe as I saw my current boyfriend's startled green eyes, mouth hanging open like a baby. He said "hi" and jerked his hand up jauntily. He always became as stylized as a cartoon character when things got weird. My old boyfriend paused slightly as if he'd forgotten where he was, but then moved on down the stairwell, never acknowledging the greeting and quickly passing out of sight. At first I was relieved no fight had ensued, but then I felt this nonevent left my life without any congruent reality, that I myself was no more substantial than a girl made up of dust. I felt doomed, as if I would always divide my affections and never find a happy regular life. The raw nub of my soul bobbed up to the surface, ugly and ungainly, and I was suddenly pierced with panicky malaise.

I sent the red-haired boyfriend away that night, folded my futon in half, wedged it into a corner, wrapped the blue comforter around me, and sobbed. The identity I'd cobbled together was coming apart like tissue paper in water. I felt as if I had to hold on to the edges of the futon. My body began to feel as dull and dead as the bookshelf or the hardwood floor. At three in the morning I called my mother, who got so upset over my sobbing that she called my little brother, who was also living in the area. He dutifully came over in the middle of the night and slept on the floor beside my poodle bed.

In the morning he helped me pack up my stuff and drag the furniture to the street corner. In the late afternoon we took the bus up to Bernal Heights to his girlfriend's apartment. My mother bought me an emergency plane ticket home even though I already had a bus ticket to Virginia; she understood I couldn't handle the droning three-day ride. My brother ordered Chinese food and we ate silently while I cried. He was afraid to touch me, and when I clung to his neck, he patted my back, his palm flat and awkward. I knew my brother loved me but his gesture embarrassed me. His girlfriend was more comfortable with my endless crying. She made me a kind of poodle bed on their couch with a woven Mexican blanket and a tapestry pillow stuffed into a white case. They slept on the other side of French doors and the form of their bodies under the blanket, spooned together, made me feel like a disembodied spirit. They were vital people with an apartment and a singular, loving relationship. I had killed myself and was only a ghost now come back to lurk around and mooch off their young lives.

When a strip of light appeared at the horizon, I got up to shower. I remember the spray of water, the way the first light fell into the liquid strains and made it look metallic, and how the water seemed to scald my body. I glanced out the little bathroom window. The scene was like a miniature medieval painting, with slanted roofs spread over a pinkish mountain, and again I had the painful sensation that I was dead, or worse, had never been born. Time zigzagged sideways. I didn't exist, so I could take no pleasure in the material world. In fact, I held a grudge against everything that contained mass, from the bar of soap in the dish to the navy shower curtain with the overly cheerful yellow and red dashes of color.

My brother rode with me on the airport shuttle bus. I remember the faces of the people coming out of their homes, and how each time a new person with an anxious expression stepped inside and sat down on the vinyl seats, I felt sadder. Everything seemed to increase my misery, the changes in the morning light, the blue mailboxes on the occasional street corner, the fact that a whole year of my life had been wasted. I felt like I'd been found incompetent and fired from my own life. My brother put me on the plane but there was no one to sit with me on my layover in Pittsburgh. I became lonely and started to call people from the writing workshop at Stanford. I was intent on speaking to a girl named Betsy. Her father was the mayor of Cincinnati and there was something about her baggy jeans and long friendly face that had always comforted me. When the answering machine clicked on I heard her father's smooth political baritone and started to sob.

My mother picked me up at the airport in Virginia and we drove to our worn suburban ranch house. The empty rooms were filled with boxes. My mother was breaking down the place. It upset me to see the box with my father's old shoes and another one with family photos. My face ached from crying and I had an unbearable headache, so I collapsed on the twin futon my mother had set up for me among the chaos in my brother's old room. As soon as I heard her go down into the basement to load the washing machine, I pushed aside my brother's boxes of baseball cards and curled up with a blanket inside his closet.

The next day I had an emergency session with a blind shrink. As I came into the consultation room, Dr. John, who was blond, with narrow shoulders and an aristocratic nose, rose up to shake my hand and asked me to take a seat on the chair across from him. He said, "You're so thin." Did he know this from the handshake? The feel of my narrow fingers and skinny wrist? I told him my story—my parents' breakup, another relationship failed, my fear of not being able to finish my book—all the while staring at his eyes. One was a regular blue eye covered with a milky film. The other was shocking. A moon eye; greenish yellow and slightly protruding, it glowed a little, and I felt it peering into my soul. As I talked Dr. John sat in his wing-back chair with his long fingers folded together in his lap. I have had many shrinks since then but none so like an oracle. He asked me practical questions. Was I eating? Was I able to sleep? I told him about the poodle bed but he was more interested in the fact that I had actually slept a few hours the night before. He assured me this was a sign I was getting better and that rather then dwell on this episode I should go along with time and try to get well. Eventually, I was able to comply. With this advice and with my mother's great silent support, I started to eat and sleep and remember a few of the things I liked about myself. After a month I was stable enough to go live on the island I'd waitressed at throughout college and live off the money I'd gotten from selling my first book.

I was often sad there, often up too early trying to find a morning news program on my transistor radio, often taking afternoon naps that lasted all night. I didn't have a closet in the tiny bed-and-breakfast room, so I sometimes lay under my twin bed or wiggled into the space between my desk and the wall. Day by day, I began to feel better. The world of objects muscled up. I found momentary pleasure in simple things like a tangerine or a calico seashell. I was able to reclaim my place in the world, and while I was still trepidant, still uncertain who, after my collapse, I really was, these flashes of personal homecoming were a great relief.

Lately, the poodle bed urge has splintered. I am often equally sad, but somehow the stability of writing regularly and motherhood have mitigated the low-lows. My treacherous transition from childhood to adulthood is complete and I no longer have the compulsion to pull my blankie under the table. Though sometimes I do lie perpendicular to the wall with my cheek resting against my arm. And for a while I used to sleep with the silky lining of my winter coat pressed to my cheek. That coat is long gone to the Salvation Army, but I still have a swatch of its lining in my underwear drawer. Life is hard. People dis-appoint one another. I don't always understand myself. I like knowing it's there just in case.

FROM *WALTER BENJAMIN*
AT THE DAIRY QUEEN
~~~

Larry McMurtry

THE FOLLOWING REFLECTIONS WERE AN *attempt to explain—to myself and my friends—the nature of a severe depression I fell into following quadruple bypass surgery, which I had in the winter of 1991. The conclusion I reached then: that I had died for a few hours, been brought back to life, and now was attempting to live as someone similar to, but not identical with, my real self, is still how I feel.*

For heart patients, and many others, the spookiest, most Wellsian, most noncommonsensical weapon in the modern operative arsenal is the heart-lung machine. In my own efforts to understand the after-effects of bypass surgery, now that I've lived with them for eight years, the heart-lung machine figures powerfully and ominously. Of course the bypass operation, as it has been practiced now for more than thirty years, would not be possible without this machine. The heart-lung machine may not really be able to keep *you* there, but it does keep your body viable, breathing for it and circulating its blood.

But the *you* that involved thought and personality, where did *that* go during the five hours or so when the heart-lung machine was taking care of your basic biological functions? Your brain is not dead, but it has been neutralized, keeping only its own secret register of what is going on.

The fact that two major involuntary functions, blood circulation and breathing, have been assigned to a machine takes you about as far from common sense as one can go. While the operation is happening you are neither really alive nor truly dead.

Then there are the aftereffects of this noncommonsensical experience—life after such surgery will feel, for many, only somewhat like life. It may also feel somewhat like death—personality death, at least.

In my case the most startling evidence of the profound effects of bypass surgery was that, about two months after the operation, I ceased to be able to read. (The surgery itself was performed at Johns Hopkins, flawlessly.) My recovery had, up to the sixty-day mark, involved no pain and little discomfort. I went to Tucson to get my strength back and was soon hiking in the desert and feeling fine. I had taken with me, to read during my recovery, the little twelve-volume Chatto and Windus edition of Proust, and also the five-volume Hogarth Press edition of Virginia Woolf's diaries: the White Nile and the Blue Nile of language, that is. I read all eighteen volumes with great pleasure, at the rate of about fifty pages a day.

When I came to the end of these two great riverine discharges of words and observations I felt as if my recovery was probably complete, so I went back to my normal life, which involved running bookshops, traveling, lecturing, writing fiction, writing movie scripts, and so forth. But within a few days of leaving Arizona, I realized that my recovery wasn't working. The content of my life, which has been rich, began to drain rapidly away. I had been leading a typical type-A East Coast life, reading three newspapers a day, reading many magazines, and in general, trying to stay informed. But more or less overnight, staying informed ceased to matter to me. Though I subscribed to *The New York Times* in three cities I put it aside one day and didn't read another issue for seven months. From being a living person with a distinct personality I began to feel more or less like an outline of that person—and then even the outline began to fade, erased by what had happened inside. I felt as if I was vanishing—or more accurately, *had* vanished. Thanks to the popularity of *Lonesome Dove* (the miniseries, not the book), I had, about this time, acquired a number of impostors, most of them just middle-aged bullshitters hoping to get a little attention by pretending to be me. During this period I began to feel that I, too, was one of my impostors, doomed to impersonate a person I now no longer was. I became, to myself, more and more like a ghost, or a shadow. What I more and more felt, as the trauma deepened, was that while my body survived, the self that I had once been had lost its life.

At about the time that I ceased to read I began to experience strange night terrors, waking each morning precisely at 3:15 A.M. and staying awake, tense and frightened, until I saw the sunrise, after which, slowly, I would relax and go back to sleep.

The trauma imposed many restrictions. I ceased to travel, except to see my grandson. I was taken in by a friend and her daughter and scarcely left their house for two and a half years. Fiction still came, but it came rapidly and impersonally; my pages were like faxes I received each day from my former self. Many days, after typing my pages, I merely sat on a couch and stared at the mountains, doing nothing at all.

The thing, more than any other, that convinced me I had in some sense died was that I couldn't read. I went to my bookshops but could not connect with the books. Books, magazines, newspapers, review copies, book catalogues arrived, only to be tossed aside. Reading was the stablest of all pleasures, and now it was gone.

The fact was that even then I *could* read professionally: I read seven scholarly books on the Nez Perce, in order to write a film script. But read for pleasure, no. I had floated down the Nile and out to sea.

Now, looking back from a distance of eight years, I realize that even in the first months after the operation, when I thought I was feeling fine, what I was really feeling was relief that I was alive and not in pain. After all, I had had my breastbone sawn in two, my heart put in coolant. I wasn't quite myself, but I hadn't started grieving either, for the self or the personality that had been lost during the process. The violently intrusive nature of that operation—of any operation, really—was bound to dislocate one for a bit, I thought. Car metaphors seemed to apply. I had had some serious engine work done and then been jump-started back into drivability. If there was a little sputtering at first, well, that was only to be expected.

In the fourth month matters worsened—the sense of grief for the lost self was profound. I didn't feel like my old self at all, and had no idea where the old self had gone. But I did know that it, he, me was gone, and that I missed him. I soon came to feel that my self had been left behind, across a border or a canyon. Where exactly was I? The only real sign of the old self was that I could still connect with my grandson, Curtis McMurtry. Otherwise, I felt spectral—the personality that had been mine for fifty-five years was simply no longer there—or if there, it was fragmented, it was dust particles swirling around, only occasionally and briefly cohering. I mourned its loss but soon concluded that gone is gone—I was never really going to recover that sense of wholeness, of the integrity of the self.

That being the case, I began to put a kind of alternate self together, and the alternate self soon acquired a few domestic skills, on the order of loading the dishwasher or taking out the trash. But I still couldn't read. I was at the time owner of perhaps two hundred thousand books and yet I couldn't read.

The problem, I eventually realized, was that reading is a form of looking outward, beyond the self, and that, for a long time, I couldn't do—the protest from inside was too powerful. My inability to externalize seemed to be organ based, as if the organs to which violence had been done were protesting so much that I couldn't attend to anything else. I soon ceased to suppose that I would ever reassemble the whole of my former self, but I could collect enough chunks and pieces to get me by—as I have.

Such surgery, so noncommonsensical, so contradictory to the normal rules of survival, is truly Faustian. You get to live, perhaps as long as you want to, only not as yourself—never as yourself.

Sometime in the third year I slowly regained the power to read. I bought Diana Trilling's *The Beginning of the Journey* and slowly read it through with pleasure. In the fourth year I recovered my interest in the rare-book trade, something that has been a fascination for most of my life. My memory for bibliographical minutiae returned. Once again I could open a copy of *The Sun Also Rises* and turn automatically to page 181, where in the first issue, "stopped" is spelled "stoppped." I began to recall the provenance of books sold long ago, where I found them, where they went when they left my hands. I was cheered to find that a few of my book scout's skills were coming back.

Even now, reading is an uneven experience—though I began to read again several years ago, I am only now regaining my velocity— the ability to read several books more or less at the same time, at a fast clip. If many looked-forward-to books fail to engage me I suspect it may be because the operation left me with a less generous level of attention to bestow.

I think of the heart surgery now mostly in metaphors of editing. I am nervous about letting an editor edit my manuscripts—even editors who have known me for years—and yet I let the surgeon, a man

I had met for only ten minutes, edit my body on the basis of information from machines. This is not to blame the surgeon, who did a fine job. I merely call attention to the oddity of letting the body be abruptly edited by one who has no knowledge of the self of which the body is but one expression. All the machines can tell the surgeon or cardiologist, after all, is about the defects and flaws of a given body; the machines can't read strengths, particularly not psychic strengths. Longevity is bound to be a chancy thing, a matter of gains and losses, but surely personality and spirit are factors in longevity, too. Before the operation, despite my physical flaws, I was whole—something had compensated for the blocked arteries, perhaps for some while and at least long enough for me to finish *The Evening Star*. From the machines' point of view I had been living wrong for a long time, eating what I wanted, exercising only when the mood struck me. Dietary caution is probably the last thing one should look for in an artistically active person. Did Dostoyevsky watch his weight? The artists I have known best never give up anything—sex, rich food, Baby Ruths, Dr Pepper, opium. In choosing the operation I did the correct, the intelligent thing, but it wasn't the passionate thing and I did it without conviction. I came out of it with a sense that we are now, indeed, in Wellsian time, able to leave our basic functions, for quite long stretches, to machines. The question is how long we can hand over these functions without, at the same time, relinquishing our personalities, and our spirits, too. The personality might slowly elide until it is no longer recognizable or regainable as itself; it may cease to be the personality that goes with a particular self.

Throughout the whole experience I felt no pain at all in my body, where the intrusion occurred, but a long and complex pain in my spirit. Bypass surgery as I experienced it raises questions that are both haunting and unanswerable. Would I have died, sometime in the last eight years, if I hadn't had the surgery? Would I have lifted one too many pile of books, eaten one too many cheeseburgers, and dropped dead; or would the survival skills my body had obviously already acquired as it dealt with the arterial blockage have been enough to keep me going? I will never know, but I consider it a toss-up.

Most vivid to me still are the two and a half years in which I couldn't read. I would hold a book in my hand but be unable to read it, as if, having lost sight of myself, literature, too, had become invisible, or at least distant and indistinct. In vanishing, my self took literature with it—and when the fragments of my personality began to cohere again, literature came back with it.

I've related my experience of heart surgery for what help the record might give to those who have this surgery and find that they no longer feel quite themselves. Of course, it needn't be only heart surgery that produces this feeling. Almost any surgery will do it to some degree. The anesthesia itself produces detachment—if it didn't, it wouldn't work. The most passionate natures are sometimes humbled by surgery—quelled by it. Life itself involves a continual leaving behind—of stages, of parts of self. What major surgery produces is a certain quality of loss, a loss with its own nuances, its own character. Proust, had he experienced it, would no doubt have been able to exhaust it as a thing to be described.

The fact that Proust and Virginia Woolf were the last writers I read before losing reading has given them a Delphic weight in my life. I am always flipping through them now, trying to find paragraphs that I remember reading just before reading faded. Sometimes I will seek a passage in Proust that is actually in Virginia Woolf, and vice versa. The two have merged in my memory.

I once heard a famous Washington hostess say of Max Lerner: "Good God . . . I'd rather fuck him than read him!"—an aperçu I've long pondered. She wasn't saying she *wanted* to fuck Max Lerner, merely that, compared to reading him, it would be the less distasteful alternative.

I recall the remark whenever I notice that in the main I'd rather read biographies of writers than read their works. Proust and Virginia Woolf are two exceptions, perhaps because their works are not only rivers of language, they're rivers of gossip, too. My time with these two masterpieces I owe to the heart surgery because, without it, I might never have been open to them so profoundly. This is a bonus that goes far toward overshadowing the trauma. The trauma has faded, but the grandeur of those books, the White Nile of Proust, the Blue Nile of Virginia Woolf, will be with me all my life.

Noontime

❦

Lauren Slater

SEPTEMBER 21, 1998

I HAVE WAITED ALL NIGHT. Twice I've wanted to get up but don't, instead letting the hormones leach into my bladder, which by now is brimming with the liquid of, if I am lucky, a newly gravid woman; she is me—married, white, comfortably off, and, of course, going gray.

The sky outside is not going gray, but turning many tender and sentimental shades of pink. I can see clouds from the bed where I lie with Benjamin, who is also awake and waiting with me. We say not a word. We watch the digital numbers flip on the clock—5:40, 5:41. I will take the test at six. Our anxiety is palpable, laughable, as though we are waiting for death, not life.

"I'm going to take the test now," I say to Benjamin. "All right," he says. My anxiety is just, well, over-the-top. My fingers are freezing. The floor is freezing. In the bathroom I line up the kits in preparation for the big event. Notice, if you will, the plural. Not kit. Kits. I am married, white, comfortably off, dosed on Prozac, a perfectionist with some fine accomplishments on the one hand, some bloated angst on the other. I work, so I have money to spend. And these kits are expensive, these store-bought crystal balls with lovely names like Clear Blue, with its suggestion of sky and indigo, or Immediate Response, with its appeal to the instantaneous, or Fact, which I have also bought, and then Fact Plus, just too tempting to pass by, with its bold, postmodern hint of results, consequences, stories swimming in a realm beyond what we can measure.

I pee into a plastic cup. My urine feels thick, full of sediment and gold. My period is late. I must be pregnant. I know I'm pregnant. At thirty-five, I have so little time left in which to be pregnant! Before I put the dropper in, I lift the cup to my nose. I do something strange. I taste the urine. It used to be that doctors diagnosed diabetes by tasting the output of their patients—a sugary flavor said yes. Could it be that pregnancy is also a flavor; I taste talcum, cornstarch, bitter, flesh. I taste yes.

Still, I do the tests, all five of them. Drip drop drop. I watch the white windows where the answer will appear, and sure enough, after only a few moments, blue lines, purple dots, plus signs and red crosses emerge like hocus-pocus from the blandest of backgrounds. I am pregnant, the crosses say so, carmine crosses, florid, hysterical, they glow like icons in a lavish church where, at midday, tired housewives come to pray.

"I'm pregnant," I say to Benjamin. I show him all five tests, and he studies them, and then—no, we do not kiss or weep or spend some sweet moment conjuring up the limbs of our future little one—and then we shake hands. We give each other a firm, hearty handshake and I collapse back onto the bed, exhausted. "I am never," I say, "having sex again." Benjamin nods sympathetically.

"Me either," he says.

I rest my hand on his chest. "That was awful," I say.

"Awful," he repeats.

"Six months of trying," I say. "It was a triathalon."

"We won," he says.

Winning. This is a tale about winning, not losing. This is a tale of health, not illness, fertility, not infertility, for there is absolutely nothing wrong with either Benjamin or myself in the reproductive department. My piping is clear and open, my ovaries stuffed with human caviar, my uterus pear-shaped and warm. Benjamin has over sixty million little swimmers in every spurt—he would want me to mention this, as it's a point of pride with him. No, we are perfectly fertile, there is nothing unexplained or damaged, and six months ago we set out to conceive, mostly at Benjamin's urging. I was not sure I wanted children. I had had several abortions in my teens. I had had several psychiatric hospitalizations in my twenties, and although I considered myself recovered, I could not claim it so with any confidence. Now "recovered," I was a psychologist, a writer, I had a close group of friends, my life at last lacked for nothing, and a child, well, like so many women of my generation, there were simply no empty spots for a child to fill.

But Benjamin had always wanted one of those munchkins, those sweet little terrors in bibs, and what was I to say? No? How do you deny the man you love, the marriage you've made, a presence such as youth? And, truth be told, I was only partially opposed. All around me I saw women my age mourning their barren wombs, toting vials of Fertinex in their lunch packs, secret shots in staff bathrooms, and their desire, the keening, intense desire, had an effect on me. There is no need, even greed, quite like that created by the infertility industry, an industry which brings a grown woman, "barren" or not, way down into her womb. All around me I saw wombs, I heard wombs, I read full-page advertisements in major papers picturing dark drops of eggs burgeoning into babies—*come now*, the ads said. *Let's have a kid,* Benjamin said, and I thought maybe we should, maybe I could warm to the idea, it had been years since I'd suffered a serious psychiatric crisis, just maybe I'd at long last become normal enough to take on this, the most normal and terrifying of roles. Understand, I had no passion or longing or—the term I hate most of all—baby lust. I had no lust, just the inchoate sense, rooted partially in alarm, that it might be time to pursue a new project, this one with lungs and hair. I said okay.

SEPTEMBER 27

I take Prozac. In fact, I come close to holding the world's record for the longest time spent on the drug—ten years. I was at a party a little while ago, one of those Cambridge parties where everyone's a writer and in some sort of therapy, and a man named Jay, a friend of a friend of a friend, came up to me. "So I hear you've been having some trouble with your medication," he said.

In Cambridge, understand, everyone knows everyone else's psychotropic drug of choice. It gets around, just like news about who's won the NEA.

"Yeah," I said. "Ten years on Prozac, maybe I should switch."

"Eleven years," he said, putting his hand to his chest, smiling with mock pride.

"Well, I'm on Klonopin, too," I said. "For my anxiety."

"Klonopin here, too," he said. "Plus Wellbutrin."

"Okay, you win," I said, and we smiled sadly at each other.

Because it's no joke, this medication issue. There are some funny parts, but the bottom line is, it's no joke. When Benjamin and I decided to get pregnant I visited four perinatal specialists to find out what the risks to the fetus would be if I stayed on my medication regime. The doctors, given the seriousness of my struggles with depression and anxiety, said "stay on." They used words like "risk benefit analysis" and "statistical significance," and those words made no difference to me. They said it would be more dangerous for me to go off my medication than for the fetus to be on it, but even as they announced this, I saw a look of alarm in their eyes. I decided to listen to their words, not their looks. On my own, however, I did research, and this is what I found. In rare instances, Prozac-exposed embryos have:

- fused fingers and toes. *Mermaids they are. Split their tails and every step will be a sword.*
- an extra flap of skin beneath the eyelid. *Doubly drowsy, will they sleep their way through life?*
- extreme jitteriness. *They wiggle and wiggle and get no rest.*
- spontaneous abortions. *Made precocious by Prozac, they tumble from the uterus, lungless and bloody.*

I have started to bleed. Five days of it now, a steady brown staining, the baby dead or alive, I don't know. I think about it being dead. If it is dead, then my body has turned into a tomb, housing this little pharaoh.

I wish not to be a tomb.

I wish to be a woman.

If I stop the Prozac, then will I feel more like a woman, like a mother? If I stop the Prozac, and cleanse myself with vinegar, and pee out green in toxic steams, then will I feel like a good mother? I don't feel good downing these pills every day, no matter what some specialists say. It would be so easy to go from four pills to three, three to two, then one, then zero, then maybe the staining would cease.

Here's the problem. Zero. "0." I can see it's shape in the air, the Munch mouth, how my life looked before the medication. I have been told I need these pills to survive, same as a diabetic needs his insulin, how ridiculously simplistic, but I'll tell you it's true. These pills, more than any egg or sperm, have brought me to the point in my life where pregnancy is possible. They threaten the embryo at the same time that they have ushered it from nothingness.

And what was my life like before the pills? This is a question people always ask, a question I detest. Because I am an author of autobiography, I have had to answer this question on television and radio and in newsprint, and whatever I say sounds like a bad soap opera. I recount the five hospitalizations, the slow suck of depressions, the slashes on the arms, and none of that captures the experience. How can I explain it? Zero. 0. Say it. Feel the sharp buzzing edge of the *z* in your mouth; picture the hole and you falling through. "What is depression like?" interviewers ask, and you answer obediently, laying out all the horrifying things you did to yourself, to your skin, when what you really wish they'd ask is, "Where did it hurt?" and you would say, "In my throat, at the backs of my eyes, deep down in my gut, in every tooth."

And yet, even with all that, I think I'll stop the Prozac. I'm running to the bathroom every ten minutes, peering down to see if the stains have ceased. I've rubbed myself raw. I want to be pregnant. I go to the medicine cabinet, tap four pills, my usual dosage, into my palm. I won't take them. *Where does it hurt? They ask. You answer. In my throat. In my fingers. Twisting up my tongue.*

In the end I compromise, take half my usual dose—two pills— and go upstairs to my study.

SEPTEMBER 30

Four Prozac to two, two to one, I think I want to keep the baby . . . safe.

Who's safe?

OCTOBER 5

By the time I get to the clinic I am a wreck. I'm still bleeding.

"Slater," the technician calls.

In the ultrasound room I take off my pants, climb onto the table. The condom-covered probe is as big as a dildo, slick with gel, it goes inside me. Click click click.

"There it is," the technician says, and I turn toward the screen, toward a tiny orb of light, it is not a heart but a star living galaxies away, so distant and minute that the light, as it reaches us, must be millions of years old.

"That's the heart?" I say. "That speck?"

"Uh-huh," she says.

"It doesn't look like a heart," I say. "It looks very faint. Like it might go out any minute."

"Oh no," she says. "This is one strong heartbeat. One hundred and ten beats per minute. This is a healthy, healthy little thing. One of the best I've seen."

I smile then. I positively beam. I feel like a parent whose kid got double 800s on his SATs. How could I have thought any less? I am healthy. I am bright. Ben is brighter. We are chromosomally complete, of the genetically robust race. I suddenly love my DNA.

"You sure?" I say. "Really one of the best?"

"Oh," the technician says, and I listen hard to see if she's humoring me, if she says this to everyone, "just superior. Look at it! So steady. A winner."

A winner! "Oh, thank you," I say, "thank you thank you," and a flood of such intense joy rushes through me that I reach out to hug her.

She must be used to this, naked women deranged by anxiety, impaled on a probe, hugging her, for she very calmly hugs me back, pats me on the back, and says, "Why don't you get dressed?" Then she presses a button and before she leaves hands me a printed picture of the life within my life.

OCTOBER 7

Four to two. Two to one to zero. 0. In the place of Prozac, prenatals, big as the Mellaril pills they used to feed me in the hospital. Extra folic acid, tiny white disks, let the spinal column fuse. Let the brain bloom. Let the tongue form. Let whatever she says be sane.

OCTOBER 20

Sunday. A perfect New England autumn Sunday and Benjamin and I go out to breakfast. I've felt no nausea, which disappoints, even frightens me. Are my hormones high enough? Despite the heartbeat, might the pregnancy still go south? How odd that in pregnancy, the presence of illness confirms health.

As for me, I feel fantastic goddamn it. The day is fantastic, a snap in the air, mums and pumpkins piled high in people's gardens. I have stopped trying to trick myself into nausea. It does no good. Today I order three blueberry pancakes with warmed syrup, a mound of whipped butter melting down the steaming stack, and I taste each blueberry as though it is brand-new, bursting like ink in my mouth, but fresh, but sweet.

It is the kind of day when you really must be outside. I take the dogs to the woods, where we will hike. "Be careful," Benjamin says to me, for the woods near where we live are almost always beautiful and occasionally vicious—a man murdered, found in the stream, a pair of lovers who never returned. It doesn't scare me. The lovers were two men. The murdered man was gay. This is the stomping ground for Boston's homosexuals, the place where they love and rage, ruin and touch. I am irrelevant here.

And on a Sunday like today, all the other irrelevants have come out to play. The field leading into the trails is packed with happy heterosexuals flying kites, carrying kids on their shoulders. The dogs and I trot past this parade and enter the thicket of trees.

I smell water. The summer has been a wet one, and all the bogs are brimming. The streams are gurgling, and giving off a silvery vapor. My nose feels absolutely alive, like it's separate from my face, its own little humming unit, it takes in odors and breaks them down into all their component parts, the silvery water which is fish skin, mercury, silt, and damp stone; the red-gold leaf I press to my nostrils, pepper and bark, the earth, which is everything, rottenness, ruin, glowing tulips, all rising up to meet me.

I enter the woods. I walk the path. I touch my nose as the dogs canter off, their own dark snouts twitching with stimulation. Up ahead, the trees thicken and close, blocking out the sun. I lift my face to the sky and scent the sun; it is surprisingly strong, like gas and lemon, I go down.

A gale of nausea sweeps over me, and I am utterly surprised by its swiftness, its strength, my stomach seizing up, breakfast burning at the back of my throat, I retch and retch; *okay*, I think, *enough*, I think, for it is starting to hurt, and then, just like that, it's over.

I straighten up, a little shaky, wipe my mouth with the back of my hand. "Musashi," I call, "Lila." My voice wavers, all broken and fantastically fragile—I am pregnant!—and before me stands a man, smiling.

"You okay?" he asks. He is wearing the tiniest pair of shorts I've ever seen; and no shirt at all. He has the requisite earring in one ear, a little gold dollop, and his hair is straight seventies, feathered and soft.

"Fine," I say, smiling at him. "I'm, I'm pregnant," I say proudly, gesturing vaguely toward the mess I've made on the ground, as though it contains the contents of the pregnancy, not my most recent meal, and he, he must think so, too, for he looks.

"Pregnant," he says to my vomit, and then he nods. "Yup."

I can't wait to get home and tell Ben. The excitement is just now beginning to build. I've puked. I've puked! I have arrived. I am just so pleased, so tickled, so pink, so silly. This man, my witness, is suddenly so special to me. It does not matter that he wears no shirt in October, that his shorts ride up between his crotch, contouring a bulge too big to be believed; it does not matter that he has a scar on his stomach, oddly caesarean, a pink welt at the bikini line. The excitement is suddenly racing through me, making me tremble, and my nose feels very alive.

"I'm eight weeks pregnant," I say. "It's really a hassle."

"Oh, I know, I know," he says. "I'm pregnant, too."

"You, too?" I say, beginning to laugh. I could laugh and laugh— something is wrong but it's too much fun—the ease of my laughter, lubricated and high, I am slippery, I am slipping, two weeks now without my medication.

"It's not funny," he says, touching his scar.

"Oh, I know," I say, and I switch into seriousness, we are dead serious here, there is nothing funny. Someone, somewhere, suffers.

"You don't believe me," the man says, and he looks sad.

"No," I say. "Of course I don't. Only women get pregnant."

He shakes his head. He looks genuinely mournful, harmless. I want to help him. Crazy people rarely scare me, they are my bread and butter after all, and in their skin I sense myself. Myself, slipping, thrilled, I want to help the whole world.

"Touch my stomach," he says, "and you'll see."

"Okay," I say, and I do, I touch his stomach, hard as slate, and he moves my hand down, down—I start to get scared now, sensible now, I thought he was gay—so why is he moving my hand down, and down, and then he stops at his scar, just above the belt line.

And sure enough I feel it, deep in this man's belly, a tiny flutter, very fast, or is that just his pulse, I jerk away, back away. "Musashi," I call, "Lila," I call. I am sound again, sane again, the dogs come bounding back and we are running; running out of the woods and into the light, which feels too bright, solid chunks of light, a clashing sound, coyotes. Howl.

OCTOBER 31

I cannot sleep. It's been three days and I cannot sleep. I attribute this to my nose, which has the sensitivity of a canine's snout, billions of nerve endings soaking in the jumbled nights—there, six blocks away, a skunk has crossed the street, a woman brews a cup of coffee, the tang of aftershave, the urine of a cat.

I lie here, scenting. I sweat, although its autumn. My lungs feel full of holes, and I gasp and flop, gill-less and oxygen-starved.

I know these symptoms. I do not have emphysema, or a bad heart. I am slipping—without my medication I always slip. I must go back on. "I just couldn't put my child at risk like that," I recall a friend of mine saying when, in the middle of her anxiety-ridden pregnancy, she was offered Paxil. "I would always look at my child and wonder what I had done to him."

I look at my child. I can see it perfectly. No not him. No not her. It. It. There are no genitals yet. I want to scream this to the street. There are no genitals. There are no hands. It has no brain; it can feel no pain. I feel the pain. And pain exists in the present tense only. It has no past, it has no future, just a never-ending now—NOW— where is relief?

I get up, go to the medicine cabinet. I can hear the doctor's words. I know all the rationalizations. Stress, after all, may be worse for the fetus than the pills used to combat it. You cannot take care of a child unless you take care of yourself. I know all this. It barely informs my motives. I gulp down two pills like an addict, looking for relief. NOW.

In the bathroom it is dark, our medicine cabinet stocked with good things, vitamins, sunscreens, hot compresses, what we use to nurture. My hands. They are not the hands of a nurturer. Of a mother. I have two hands, and with them I vote, first, for myself.

And so the pills go down. I flip on the light, look at my face in the mirror. Exhausted. Blue bags beneath the eyes. After the baby comes, this is what my face will look like for months, or even years. I try to imagine it, late nights, a bottle hissing on the burner, you can kiss your sleep good-bye. You can kiss your life good-bye. This is crazy. I am crazy. I have made a big mistake.

NOVEMBER 5

My moods are all over the place. The books say to expect that, especially in the first trimester when your hormones are wild, but this is much more than I bargained for. Benjamin and I pulled into a gas station the other day and the sight of a woman in a yellow head scarf just made me weep. "What is it, what is it?" Benjamin asked, and I couldn't answer, I was crying hard. My tears felt thick and hot; they stank of HCG, progesterone, estrogen, my body emitting these sex steroids like a skunk, her pungent smell.

And Benjamin, poor Benjamin, he looked genuinely alarmed. He dashed into the gas station's food mart, came out with a box of Kleenex, blotted my eyes, my nose. I am the baby here. I need good care.

"What is it?" he said again, and I watched the saffron woman walk away, all gilded with light.

"My mother," I said. "I think I miss her."

"Look," said Benjamin, opening his fist. "I bought this for you in the food mart."

And there, nestled in his palm, was the tiniest pumpkin I'd ever seen. I started to sob anew.

"It's just a pumpkin," Benjamin said. "What could be so bad about a pumpkin?"

"I'm supposed to think it's cute," I said. "Right? Any normal woman would think, 'Oh what a cute little pumpkin,' but I don't think it's cute."

"Neither do I," said Benjamin, nodding seriously, taking the pumpkin and turning it slowly. "No, this is not a cute pumpkin."

"You don't think so?" I said.

"No," he said.

"If you don't think the pumpkin's cute," I said, "then what would you call it?"

"What would you call it?" he said.

"Interesting," I said.

"Genetically engineered," he said.

"Is it edible?" I said. "My main impulse is to eat it."

"Let's eat it," he said.

And so we did. We went home and ate the pumpkin—it was, after all, he reminded me, just a pumpkin, Lauren—the orange skin, seeds popping in the pan.

NOVEMBER 10

Somewhere in here daylight savings has come. Nights now are early, fast plunges into frosty darkness, the trees nude and spiked.

Harper's called today while I was at work. They'd commissioned an autobiographical piece from me, which I'd written and submitted according to the proposal.

"I'll be honest with you," the editor said. "The women liked it, the men didn't. The women liked your extended use of first person and the men, well, the men wanted more theory, less subjectivity, something broader . . ."

"But our contract stated—" I said

"Could you put a lot more theory in it," the editor said, "make it less memoirish," and I knew what she meant, make it less womanish, less lubricated, altogether drier, I got mad.

"No," I said.

"No?" she said.

"I won't rewrite it," I said.

"You know memoir's getting stale," she said.

"If I were Joseph Epstein or Phillip Lopate, we wouldn't be having this conversation," I said. "A man writes a personal essay and gets compared to Montaigne. A woman writes a personal essay and gets compared to——"

Who? I couldn't think who. Hysterical we women were. Sensationalists, myopic, childishly self-referential, my anger went away. It just went away. I hated women. They stank. They swelled. They wept at the sight of passing yellow. The woman's world was saffron, brimming red, crisis orange, like a goddamn Gymboree. Inside her, the child tumbles and scrawls, illegible, illiterate. I hated her.

"If you won't rewrite it," the editor said, "then——"

"I'll take my kill fee," I said. My voice was soft, without strength.

I'm home, back in my study, a single light burning on my desk. It is only four P.M., but the darkness is almost absolute. Rain darts down outside, and tomorrow, I know, the puddles will be webbed with ice, silver and crackly, the yard hard as concrete. "Kill fee kill fee," I keep thinking. I say the word over and over to myself. It has such a sound, such a slash. I wish I were a man. I wish I were a woman with the mind of a man. Kill fee. Kill she. Kill her. Men, in general, are more successful at pulling off a suicide. Women botch it, leave the bathtub bloody. Maybe women don't really want out of the world, just out of their gender, released to a place dry and white.

I do not want this child. Sitting here, in the hard darkness, rain scratching at the windows, I suddenly know. I do not want this child. I've spent years and years pulling myself together, pulling myself up, getting my advanced degrees, working seventy-hour shifts, modeling myself after the fathers of the world; how can I, then, become a mother?

And yet I am. Becoming a mother. At this very moment fetal stem cells form her heart. A grief unlike any I have ever known pulses over me. I want my old, austere life back, my quiet world of words and books and late-night movies. I cry and cry. I cannot believe

I can cry so hard, that such sounds can come out of my mouth, that the air could be so difficult, so scraping going down.

And then, at some point, the rain stops. Clouds scoot across the sky, leaving behind a washed black backdrop for billions of jittery stars. I stop crying. I open my study window and smell the air, the after-rain November air, soaked pavement, decomposing bark, the log pile where the raccoons nest. As a child, I had a pet raccoon. I had mice and rabbits, a horse named Tanya, so even today the smell of manure floats me back to the barn where leather harnesses hung.

And I remember Tanya foaling, contractions rippling down her flanks, two wet beads of colostrum forming on her milkbag, hot and hard, she lay down. I was twelve, with not yet even a period. Still, I knew Tanya's body was mine. I knew the smell of hay, the lazy munching, the deep red vulva parting for his head, all marbleized and wet, with two tiny ears tamped down and a muzzle to find the milk. Later on, days later, when the foal was old enough to nicker and cavort, I found him in a field and offered him my finger. I remember the strength of the suck, it sent contractions through me, I was the mother, and I thought, *yes*.

Now I touch my own stomach. My eyes sting from so much salt. *Yes,* I think, recalling Tanya.

No, I think, looking at my clean walls, my daybed with its narrow shape, starched white sheets, *for only me*.

Yes, I think.

No, I think.

In between those two proclamations I stand, held very still by the centrifugal force, spinning and spinning so fast no one can see how sick my motion makes me.

NOVEMBER 13

Because I am a psychologist, I know all the signs. Disturbed sleep. Disturbed appetite. Neurovegetative symptoms. Psychomotor retardation. It is difficult to move; my limbs say no. I stand at the stop of the stairs, holding with one hand to the newel post, looking down the slant and considering. I spend a long time weighing the pros and cons of staying put, or descending. The decision feels tricky and enormous.

All the signs above are symptoms of depression. They are also, however, symptoms of pregnancy, so maybe I'm not depressed. Maybe I'm just pregnant. Maybe to be pregnant is to be depressed. Then would the converse also be true, that to be depressed is to be pregnant? Of course not! Why can an equation work one way but not the other? Why does two plus two always equal four, but four is not always the same as two plus two? Why, if penicillin cures a cold, is the cold not caused by a lack of penicillin? My brain swims in my head, the questions are overwhelming, my heart flaps.

I make a decision. I get to the bottom of the stairs. Musashi comes over and licks my knee. He keeps licking and licking my knee in one specific spot and at last I see why; I have a skinned knee, with blood and all, I don't know how this happened. Perhaps I fell down the stairs, although I highly doubt it. In any case, the hows do not matter, only the whys. Why Musashi licks my knee is because there's blood on it, I have an answer. I have an answer! His tongue looks pretty, a flickering red, but I know it's crawling with bacteria, that I should push him away from the cut, but I don't. I cannot find it in myself to care.

What I find in myself is a fatigue that flees during the night so I am wide-awake and blinking, and descends during the day, without warning, each nap a small delectable death. I nap at all the wrong times, in staff meetings, on the phone with a social worker, please God not with a patient, of course I am with a patient, she being me, napping and then jerked away, my heart's rhythm all wrong. "What's wrong?" Benjamin says each evening when he comes home from work. I say, "It's back, depression's a real mental illness you know," and he nods. He doesn't know. He brings me food, all of it very unappealing, especially the texture of toast. He brings me sliced tomatoes and I am nauseated by the way they look, like fresh peeled scabs on a white platter.

I have never had schizophrenia, voices, pink elephants or burning buildings, but I have for a long time considered myself a person with a psychiatric handicap, formidable if banal. My prior episodes have always been banal, without delusions or deities. This time around, however, feels different. I say to Ben, "This one's different," and he doesn't know what to say, so he says "Okay." The difference is this: Inside me now is a coiled thing going from parasite to personhood, and as it does it emits horrid toxins. I am awash in stinking hormones. The little embryo ejaculates human chorionic gonadotropin. All day long the embryo sits in my stomach and jerks off in spurts; sex steroids. These are my thoughts. The depression is deadness—go ahead and lick my knee—but also a hyperawareness, a needle on the floor, shining like the highest wheedling note of a violin; a person's face all funny, in separate pieces, the isolated mouth moving, the blink of an eye excruciating, the silky crash of lashes. What a weird hallucinatory world. I can only cry.

The sun is an assault. I am, by the way, on the street, taking a walk or running an errand. Because I am mentally ill, I've decided it's essential that I get an abortion. Can a mentally ill woman be a good mother? It's such a sane question; I'd like to take a poll. A woman walks by me pushing her carriage, one of those ridiculous double-wheeled canopied gizmos, equipped with mesh storage pockets in every possible place. "Are you mentally ill?" I say, and she says, "Yes, but only at certain times," and I say, "What times?" and she says, "Noontimes, and then I am fine," and just like that she fizzles away. She never existed, fooey on you. I made her up, a little narrative trick, a bit of projective identification, it doesn't matter. Noontimes, she says. Sometimes, I say. Sometimes I have it, and I take medicine for it, and I have been hospitalized years of my life, and then other times, remission, I'm fine. Should a woman like that become a mother? How will she mother at noontime? Will the child languish? And what if, this time, noontime never goes away, my greatest fear. What if one day an episode comes and never leaves, around the clock, tick-tock, trapped.

I go home. I pull out the Yellow Pages and look for abortion clinics. I can just hear my friends. I know what my sister would say. "But, Lauren, you always recover. Your fear that you won't is just part of the illness." True and not true. Point and counterpoint. The kings clash. I have so far always recovered. But I am in the field, so I know. Each episode takes its toll on the brain, erodes it that much more; bouncing back gets harder, and harder still.

Benjamin comes home. Key in the lock. Door opens. "What is it?" he asks.

"I want an abortion," I say. "Look at me. I am not fit to be a mother. Once a mental patient, always a mental patient. Look at me."

So he does. Benjamin looks at me. He has never seen me break down, because for our entire five-year relationship I've been maintained on medication.

"You shouldn't have gone off the drugs," he finally says.

"Well, I'm back on them," I say. "Full dosage. And they're not working."

"You're not as bad as you think," Benjamin says. "You have strengths you don't even know about. I see things in you that you can't."

"How can you say that?" I practically scream. "This is serious." I walk over to the couch, sit down. "Listen, Benjamin," I say. "I have an illness. I warned you about it before we got married. I got pregnant because I thought the illness was under control, but it's not, it never will be, it might go away but it will always be back, each time probably worse, and I could never mother a child with this handicap."

"So don't," he says.

"Abortion?" I say.

"No," he says. "So don't mother. Who says just because you have the child, you have to mother it? I'll raise the child myself."

His response takes the wind right out of my agitated sails. "You will?" I say.

"I will," he says.

"What role will I play?" I ask.

"Incubator," he says.

"But after that?" I say.

He shrugs. "I want a child, and if you can't take it on, I will. I'll hire help."

"But I'll have to be something," I say. "How about if I'm the father and you're the mother? We'll switch."

Benjamin stands still, considering this. "No," he says. "I've always wanted to be a father. I've never wanted to be a mother."

"Well, maybe I've always wanted to be a father, too," I say.

Benjamin smiles. I smile, for I see how silly this is, and yet, at the same time, how utterly sober, how sociologically complex, a Goffman drama.

"You can be the aunt," Benjamin says.

"Aunt," I say, trying out the word. I've always liked that word. It reminds me of ant, ants, my favorite insects.

"I could be the aunt," I say, excitement now mounting, for I can see my way out of this dilemma, and it's on the segmented black back of an ant, we can have our cake and eat it, too, us ants.

"Well, will we have sex anymore?" I say. "The father's not supposed to sleep with the aunt."

"We'll have sex," he says.

"So we're not breaking up," I say.

"No," he says. "We're not breaking up."

I spend the rest of the evening awash in relief, which feels like it's own kind of chemical pumping through me, at first soothing, and then staccato. My pace picks up, I have found a way out. I am very excited. I wash all the floors, sponge down the baseboards, consider the architecture of my home. It's a single-family, but with a little bit of work, a wall or two, some soundproofing, we could turn the third floor into a separate apartment, where the aunt would live amid books and metaphors, occasionally descending to dine with Dad, to rock the baby, everything hazy and scented, katydids thronging in the grass.

I fall asleep with blueprints on my mind, but by the time I wake up, at four in the morning, I know the fantasy's over. I just forgot about my body for a little while, but now my body's back, and it sends its undeniable signals, breasts aching at their roots, my uterus aflutter. You can never be *just incubator*. I've spent years of my life learning to think linearly, statistically, logically, learning to separate and segment, but motherhood will not cooperate. It will not be just biological. The child is yours not because you bore it in your womb, but because every physical symptom gave rise to an image—it is moving now, the heart beats now—the child is yours because you have imagined it, a girl maybe, with dark eyes and a bright bow of a mouth, or a boy with shoepolish-black hair, it does not matter. There is no force that can claim you like imagination can, a force, I find, which brings nothing into something and insists that you acknowledge your authorship. Our children are not ours because we have given them our genes. They are ours because we have had the audacity to envision them.

NOVEMBER 14

The panic and deadness are back. I want to cut my arms. Benjamin gives me money to get a massage. The woman speaks little English. I take off my clothes and she puts hot compresses on my back. She pinches my waist and says, "Flubby."

I have called a doctor. Not my usual psychopharmacologist, but one of the ones I consulted prior to getting pregnant, a perinatal specialist. Everywhere I go I smell gas.

NOVEMBER 20

Her office is in the suburbs, her waiting room filled with articles on PMS, on mental illness in menopause, on postpartum psychosis and the birth control pill. She calls me in.

She is very young, and she wears braces. The braces are new; they were not there when I first consulted her, and I am not happy about their presence. As a general policy I don't take guidance from anyone who wears any kind of orthodontic device; it smacks of adolescence.

She smiles at me, and her tracks gleam. Her hair is dark, pulled back in a taut little bun, granny style, as though that might lend her the look of leadership, of wisdom.

I start to speak. I tell her the whole sorry story of my pregnancy. I tell her all about my ambivalence, going into great detail about the effects of seventies feminism on women in the eighties and nineties, how I have so purposefully structured my life to oppose the traditional motherhood role, and it is this conflict which has triggered, if not outright caused, my collapse.

As I speak she takes notes, which, narcissist that I am, makes me speak all the more and then she says, "Shhhh.

"You're speaking very quickly." She says, "When you consulted me prior to getting pregnant, you made no mention of bipolar disorder. Are you sure?"

"Look," I say. "I . . . don't have . . . to . . . speak . . . fast. It's . . . not . . . bipolar . . . it's . . . anxiety," and I smile.

She gives a small uncertain smile back and writes something down. I was just joking, I think. Shit, I think. She's going to lock me up.

So I start again. I compose myself so as not to get locked up for what would be, pathetically, the sixth time in my relatively short life span. "I have anxiety and depression," I say, "or maybe an agitated depression which seems to be rooted in my ambivalence—"

She interrupts. "Have you," she says, "ever taken the birth control pill?"

Well now, there's a question I can answer. "Yes," I say.

"And how did you tolerate it?" she asks.

"Couldn't stand it," I say. "Lasted three days. Made me cry nonstop. Gave me a nervous breakdown."

She nods, because now she has her answer. She has the answer! Her braces vanish. All I can see now are her shiny teeth, her snappy eyes.

"I don't think you should get an abortion," she says. "Some women are extremely sensitive to progesterone, which in both animal analogues and human studies can cause severe mood reactions."

And then she goes on to tell me that at this stage in my pregnancy I am ingesting the equivalent of *four hundred* birth control pills a day, so it's no wonder I'm losing my mind. "No," she says, "you're not ambivalent, or, rather, your ambivalence is hormonally driven. We see this kind of ambivalence all the time in psychiatrically vulnerable women. The good news is," she says, "once the placenta takes over and the ovaries are out of the picture, at the end of the first trimester, the psychiatric symptoms should lessen."

At this point I'm quite confused by what she's saying—placenta, ovaries, progesterone—although later I will, on my own, read about the bizarre effects sex steroids can have on the emotional pathways in a woman's brain. I will read that it is well documented, among perinatal psychiatrists, that women who have a hard time tolerating the birth control pill, or who experience depression or anxiety premenstrually, or who evidenced a mood disorder at the onset of puberty, are at especially high risk not only during the postpartum period but in the actual pregnancy itself. This is, in fact, so well documented in the perinatal psychiatric literature that I can't believe no one, NO ONE, mentioned antenatal depression to me, and to God knows how many other women who decide to carry a child. I read the statistics, that 10 to 15 percent of all pregnant women experience what's called antenatal depression, oftentimes severe, sometimes psychotic, and that these women have an 80 percent chance of developing an incapacitating postpartum reaction as well. Here's the truth, if there is such a thing. Pregnancy can be dangerous, can be deeply damaging to a woman, and it seems to be a secret. If there were a food out there that 10 to 15 percent of the population had an adverse response to, someone would put a warning on the label, but there is no warning on the label of pregnancy. If anything, there is only the opposite, the cultural myth that must be upheld, for the sake of breeding I suppose, beatific women awash and aloft. . . .

"But why——" I say, and then stop, back up. I'm confused. "At the end of the first trimester?" I say. "You mentioned the depression would go away."

"Yes," she says. "It should, or at least lessen."

"Why?" I say. "Do progesterone levels drop at the end of the first trimester?"

"Oh no," she says, "they continue to rise, right up until you give birth. Oh no. By the end of your pregnancy you'll be ingesting," and here her voice drops a tad, to add a dash of shading to her tone, "you'll be ingesting by the end the equivalent of one thousand birth control pills a day. Imagine that," she says, shaking her head. "Imagine what the liver has to process."

I do. Imagine that. I imagine standing in a blue bathroom downing fistfuls of Ortho-Novum, pink plastic packets scattered at my feet.

She continues. "Your progesterone levels rise, but the hormone, in the second and third trimesters, is produced by the placenta, not the ovaries. And the placenta makes a gentler form of progesterone."

I nod. I see. I don't. Progesterone, apparently, comes in different flavors, like chocolate and vanilla, like milk, regular, fat-free. This is how I explain it to myself, the only way I can. In the first trimester the ovaries produce a thick, clotted kind of progesterone, a kind of white gunk that clogs up the ravines in the brain, but the progesterone from the placenta is light, is skim milk, cleansing and translucent.

"Unfortunately," the doctor now says, "the depression does go away, but it can come back, at the very end of the third trimester, and your risk for a postpartum crisis is extremely high."

"And yet you're telling me," I say, "not to get an abortion."

"This is a time," she says, "of rapid advancement in the treatment of these illnesses. We have many medications, and more and more are getting developed each day. It is," she says, "an auspicious time to bring a child into the world."

I squint at her. I think she's starting to sound a little crazy herself. I can't exactly say why. Could it really be that all this turmoil is mostly hormonally driven? Is there not any significant way in which my reaction to motherhood is sociological, is psychological? I believe in a bio-psycho-social approach to many problems; she, however, seems to so much favor the bio that the psycho and social pale to zero.

"I'm already on medication," I say. "If this is just a chemical thing, then why is my medication not working?"

"You went off your medication," she says, sternly I might add, "which made your brain even more vulnerable to hormonal disregulation, and by the time you went back on, too late. It's much harder to launch a rocket than it is to keep one in the air."

Her prescription for me is to increase my Prozac dose to one hundred and twenty milligrams, plus add lithium and Klonopin into the mix. She tells me about possible risks to the fetus, but I cannot concentrate. "If you choose not to aggressively medicate," she says, "I predict, given your prior history, that you will be back in a hospital within three days. If you do choose to aggressively medicate, you have a fifty percent chance of feeling better in just a few weeks."

"Lithium?" I say.

"Lithium?" Benjamin says. "You have to go on lithium?" Because he is a chemist by trade, we have a *Physician's Desk Reference* on hand, and so we look it up—lithium . . .

In humans, lithium carbonate may cause fetal harm when administered to a pregnant woman. Data from lithium birth registries suggest an increase in cardiac and other anomalies.

We look at each other grimly. We look up Klonopin.

The effects of Klonopin in human pregnancy are unknown... When Klonopin was administered to pregnant rabbits...a non-dose-related incidence of cleft palates, open eyelids, fused sternebrae and limb defects was observed.

We call back the doctor, together. Benjamin starts with the heart.

"The cardiac abnormalities, called Ebstein's syndrome, are thought to be overplayed," the doctor says. "Of course we can't be sure, but we can be sure that your wife is ill and that she deserves proper treatment. Every woman does."

The feminist nature of her comment confuses me. Why, if she is an advocate for women, did I feel so small in her office?

"And the Klonopin," Benjamin says, "the fused sternebrae, the open eyelids . . ."

She pauses for a moment. The pause to me seems significant, a gap in which twisted things swim. "You mean the bunny studies," she says, "right?"

"Right," Benjamin says, his voice low.

"One important thing to remember," she says, "pregnant bunnies are not the same as pregnant humans. I myself have overseen several Klonopin pregnancies and the babies were fine, a little sleepy but fine."

We hang up, meet in the middle of the house. "I'm going to do it," I say.

I expect him to say no, to say, "It's my child, too, don't I have a choice?" or, "Let's consider all the risks versus all the benefits," but instead he just looks at me for a long time, and in his look I see the woman I have now become, Victorian gothic, both musty and pale, crying out with nightmares, lungs all squished, hallucinating gas. "I guess you should," he says.

And so I do. I fill the prescriptions, the scored lithium pill, the jazzy orange Klonopin, plus five bicolored bullets of Prozac, I take it all.

And we say nothing. The lithium leaves its salty aftertaste, the Klonopin careens down the dark chute of my body. I am surprised by how little we say, how we do not debate the obvious—fetal versus maternal rights, at what point personhood begins, culturally embedded ideas about drugs versus their chemical reality—no, not once do we discuss these topics, although we are, at other times, the thinking talking types. Later on, we will, I will, go over and over the path I pursued, while I watch my child sleep, her heartbeat and breathing irregular and jagged, while I pray she opens her fist for the rattle, I will see the Klonopin darting down into the darkness of my bowels, while we hope she crawls with a hope so much like that of other parents, but more, a hope underscored with anxiety and blame. Later on. When she has to be resuscitated. But not now. Are psychiatric crises so overwhelming to the mind that they inhibit the presence of ethics? Is depression at root an amoral phenomenon, its focus on the self preventing any other from really counting? Perhaps. Sometimes. Sometimes, even when we are two we are really only one; we can feel nothing but our own bones, our own difficult breaths.

DECEMBER 18

And then, of course, there's the other side to the selfish story. I go to the library and read what I can. It is snowing today, fine white crystals falling from the sky, the sky itself as hard as a block of salt except in one tiny place where the pale sun struggles to break through. I love libraries in winter. I love the steam heat hissing, the glow of burnished wood, the silence of the inside world mingling with the silence of the snow beyond the thick-paned windows. I enjoy the well-worn wooden seats and the scratched tables with lovers' initials etched in. Me and you. Self and other. Forever.

I've been on the lithium for a few weeks now, and I am noticing a difference. An appreciation of the weather. A kind of calmness that may or may not be resignation. It is in this state that I see the other side of the selfish story.

I read. Women with toddlers are the most depressed group in the United States. A woman's mental health appears to decline after she marries and bears children, whereas a man's tends to increase. Females are a whopping sixteen times more likely to experience psychosis after the birth of a child, and pregnancy for a woman with a history of depression is a known psychiatric risk.

I am almost twelve weeks pregnant now. My breasts are, depending on your point of view, either spectacular or perverse, globular and wired with veins; they glow.

I go back outside. It is nearing Christmastime and hundreds of women move through the dusk. I stand on the library steps and watch them, and I feel a new respect. Ninety-four percent of the world's women bear children, which means they agree, knowingly or not, to navigate the most difficult terrain of the brain, a journey interior but brave, even stoic, because so little is said about it. Sometimes I am ashamed of being a woman, even though the shame itself is so passé, now that we're all postfeminists. Still, sometimes the old shames come back, but not today. I like the snow, I like the salt block sky, I like how we move, en masse toward the lighted trees.

DECEMBER 28

The lithium makes me thirsty. The Klonopin helps me sleep. The thirst is tremendous and healing, gallons of cold water going in me, my heart calmed in a cool sea.

Every Christmastime I get the shopping bug, even though I'm Jewish. Every Christmastime I thank God I'm not a Christian as I watch Boston's WASPs dashing madly from store to store, their arms piled high with presents for their families, while I, safe in my Semitic roots, need only buy gifts for myself.

Not this Christmas though. I am not one but two, doubled or halved, depending on which way you look at it. Pregnancy is ambivalence incarnate—the separate selves, the separate sides—struggling to stake their claim.

I go into a store called Cherry and Webb. "A sample of our newest scent?" a woman in an apron asks, and I offer her my naked wrist. All the gas is gone. This perfume smells of laundry, of sprinklers in the evening.

I do not go to my usual spots, the petites, the cosmetics, the accessories. I go, furtively, to the children's section of the store, where infant clothes hang on racks. I look around me to make sure no one is watching, although what the secret is I can't say. I feel enormously self-conscious handling these tiny outfits, these odd hooded gowns like what a miniature monk might wear. How do you care at noon-time? I finger the frills on a little dress. There is a study that scares me. Schizophrenic mothers were compared with depressed mothers and it was found that the schizophrenic women were more effective as parents, because even though they were crazy as bats, at least they were alive, they were responsive.

And I think of that study, standing very still in a store at Christmastime, holding an infant's dress in my hand and finding it definitely not cute. The pumpkin, too, is not cute, and yet I am no longer crying, no longer thrashing about for breath. *I will design my own kind of motherhood, a different kind of motherhood,* this is what I think. *Please God, make me well enough to love whoever she is.* This is also what I think. I think the medications must be working, for my thoughts are clear, my mood even, my apprehensions deep but with a bottom.

JANUARY 15

Even-keeled. That's a sailboat in the summer. Recovering. That's a bed in a white room, a glass of fresh-squeezed lemonade on the night side table. That's me, walking about this winter world very very tentatively, stepping on frozen puddles, considering them when they crack.

I go in for my amnio today. It's early for the amnio, but because of all these medications, I want all the screenings done as soon as possible. Benjamin goes with me, of course. We ride together in the car; the snow is lumpy and dirt-streaked, and ravens rise from the plowed mounds, crying high into the sky.

First, before the needle, we meet with a counselor. We say no to Tay-Sachs, to spina bifida, to cerebral palsy, to Huntington's. I tell her, of course, about the nine pills I take each day, and as I do I think

I smell the gas again, it comes wafting back, my heart paddles fast, and then it's over. I regain my delicate balance.

Benjamin and I are taken to a room. I climb up on the table. They do the ultrasound, scanning the fetus fast for defects. "Looks good," they say, "so far," and I nod. "What's the sex?" I say. "Can you see the sex?"

"A girl," the doctor says, "probably a girl," and rain rises up in me then, a kind of drenched grieving happiness, unlike feelings I have ever had.

They are not wonderful feelings, not rosy or glowing, I would not even really recommend them, but there they are. There she is. My mother with her glittery eyes, her wants so huge and human and socially impossible they drove her down, and me, with my brown eyes, trying for both our sakes to live a largeness she could not, and she, the fetus, with her eyes sealed shut, spinning me on, spinning me out until I no longer exist. We no longer exist and yet I am not nothing today. I am with child today, powerful.

I feel the punch of the needle in my stomach, see the amniotic fluid rise into the syringe, so much they take, a pearly viscous fluid coming up. "Give me that," I want to say. I want to drink the fluid, swallow all those stem cells and grow myself, my mother young again. A second chance.

But instead there is water in a pleated little cup and then home, in my own bed, on the alert for a miscarriage. I pull out her picture, which they printed for me. Here she is. Eyes sealed shut. Spinning us out into nothing, which is everything, every risk and every benefit, every kind of collision and redemption, too much to count. Too many possibilities to hold in a single head. Why I'm going forward in the face of such ambivalence I don't know: blind faith, Benjamin, courage, conviction, conformity, stupidity, confusion. Let her escape all this. Of course she won't. I will call her Clara, for clear, and Eve, which in Hebrew means life, and I will hope the gap between her name and her life is small.

Clear life. A life without depression. That is what she means, this girl. I study her now. The picture is really good. She lies as though in a hammock, slung comfortably in the pouch of my womb. I can see a profile of her nose, one hand floating palm up as though in resignation, or acceptance. Apparently, this girl is made from me. She comes from me. She has half my genes, half my toxins, half my talents, she is in me. What of me will she shed, what will she find herself tacked to? The gift of life, what an odd expression, a still-odder gift, this box of snakes and daisies.

Now I touch her hand. She grips mine. "All right," I say. "Connected," she says, and for better or for worse that's absolutely true, connected at a level deeper and more dangerous than is wise. We want to help each other out. I feel the tiny condensed precocity of her nails, the braid of her breathing tube; she touches my eyes and I smile. This is not maternal love I'm feeling. We want to help each other out. This is not maternal love—no coos or cuteness, it's saner than that, I'm sane for now, and I am not my mother, and my name is Lauren and I look at Clara and I feel the best of what a woman has to offer. I feel friendship.

FADING TO GRAY

❧

Lee Stringer

I don't want the cheese.
I just want out of the trap.
—SPANISH PROVERB

IT WAS FRIDAY NIGHT AND I had two weeks' wages
bulging my pocket. I had gone out at lunchtime, to the company's
bank instead of my own, and changed my check rather than
deposited it. This was a new habit. Lately, I seemed to need the cold
cash right there on my hip for it to lend the least boost to my spirits.
The charge it gave me had already worn off by the time I headed for
home, but a few blocks from my apartment a neon "Wine & Spirits"
sign flagged me down, told me "I've just the thing for a sagging
mood." I stopped in to add a quart of Georgi's to my load.

It was the first thing I opened when I got home. I took my vodka
straight up on ice, no mixer. It tasted nasty this way, particularly the

cheap stuff. But there was little ceremony or ritual anymore in my
having a drink. It had taken on the form of dosage, a hedge against
the flatness lying in wait at the end of the day's momentum. Only
after I washed out a tumbler for myself, filled it with ice cubes,
drowned them with the stuff and then flicked on the TV, did I break
out the paint and brushes and posterboard I'd brought with me from
work.

I was into my second year with United Products, Inc., an
import/wholesale company that I had once counted among the
clients in the modest graphic design business I ran out of the two-
bedroom apartment of my partner, Barry. The partnership had
abruptly ended when Barry died of a heart attack and things had gotten uglier from there. There was the business of my not being on the
thirteen-year-old, rent-stabilized lease and the landlord's eagerness to
chuck me out to clear the way for more upscale tenants. There was
my brother's sudden appearance at the door looking just inches away
from death—a death which, in short order, surely came. There was
the legal battle with Barry's adopted son, who came sniffing around
for whatever payoff could be had from our business. There was the
news that throat cancer had done in my father, a surprise to me since
I had never even known he'd been ill. So when the people at United
Products proposed to set me up in-house—figuring it cheaper to buy
the cow than keep paying for milk—I didn't say no. It seemed to be
the thing to do at the time—trade off a bit of independence for security's sake.

It was going on eight when I had finally turned off the lights and
locked up the office that Friday. This was nothing new for me. I was
seldom counted among the pack that bolted for the elevator at five
o'clock. And, because of this, people generally assumed—smack in
the middle of the Go-Go Eighties as we were—that I was a driven
man. I did little to disabuse them of that notion. I walked the walk;
talked the talk; took to tooling around in Armani knockoffs; puffed
up a cloud with the odd panatela now and again. I even tacked a clip-

ping of a Porsche Cruppa to my office wall and told myself, *Soon as you're earning in the high five figures it can be yours*—an entirely ludicrous thing since I had never even bothered to learn how to drive. But all this stemmed from a long-entrenched compulsion to try to live up to everyone else's expectations. It had little to do with ambition, work ethic, or the pursuit of any dream. I had long ago disencumbered myself of ambition, for the closer I ever got to my brass rings, the less precious and more tarnished they became. As for the work ethic, I counted that among the ideals I had more or less outgrown, finding little place for them in this world. And having been more than once burned by hope and expectation, I had grown more than twice shy of chasing dreams. Overwrought with caution, I wanted nothing more than the end of all surprise. And there was refuge of a sort to be had in the Monday-to-Friday routine of the workaday world.

Weekends left me feeling marooned. Weekends busyness was all the harder to come by. And my usual Friday drill was to fly to some upscale watering hole after work, immerse myself in its false twilight, and buoy my spirits on the ready small talk and easy camaraderie there. Only, this routine had gradually grown into a sloppier, more desperate thing, invariably teetering into the dawning hours—when at last the sweet oblivion of sleep could insinuate itself.

So on this particular Friday—figuring on providing myself with a more uplifting means by which a few hours of dreaded alone time could be handily killed off—I drummed up a little take-home busywork for myself. I told myself at the last minute that our booth at the upcoming trade show could use a few hand-painted display cards, and armed myself with the necessary paraphernalia before leaving work.

Vodka at my elbow, TV spilling chatter into the room, tools of the trade spread before me on the dining table, I sailed into my weekend on the back end of a number-three lettering brush. It had been a while since I had done this sort of thing. You can't letter with a brush in the same way you use a pencil or pen. You have to break each character into a series of three or four strokes to do it successfully and you have to keep focused on what you're doing because the stakes go up with every completed letter.

I carefully laid down a pair of vertical strokes about an inch apart and connected them with a diagonal, forming a near-perfect *N*, then used three equidistant horizontals, connected with a right angle vertical stroke to form an *E*. I could hear, even over the TV, the sounds of the city bleeding in the window from the street—thunking taxi doors, groaning city buses, the screech and rumble of gridlock. This was a quirk of urban first-floor apartment living to which I had long grown accustomed. But now I particularly noticed voices above the din. Noticed, as they swelled by, their distinct flavors.

. . . Now eager and breathless.

. . . Now giddy with delight.

. . . Now low and cunning.

. . . Now shouting up the night.

. . . The bright and beautiful of boom time Gotham. Already immersed in weekend revelry. Their facility for leaping into gay abandon on so slender a premise as TGIF (a thing I had by then outlived) oppressed me. Every splash of laughter, every joyous noise sang in my ears like a Greek chorus, made me reach again for my drink.

Next thing, I caught myself, brush dangling, staring into the TV, choking back tears. Some Kodacolor feel-good movie was rolling toward its inevitable happy ending. The hero—having soldiered on for two and a half reels undaunted, every card in the deck stacked against him—was now reaping his due: an eleventh-hour orgy of human kindness from friend and foe alike. It was the kind of concoction that seldom failed to stoke whatever hope-against-hope yearnings still dimly flickered in me. It tapped into some immense reservoir of sadness and despair which had existed for longer than I cared to remember, and which I always feared would be overwhelming if ever given vent. I managed to beat it back by admonishing myself for being so pathetic as to boo-hoo over such sappy fluff. I turned back to my work and was surprised to see I had already finished the sign.

NEW THIS SUMER! it imperfectly read.

What happened next was out of all proportion to having simply misspelled a word. A blinding urge to kick, bite, scratch, claw, stomp, pound, crush, destroy, pulverize leaped through me. My teeth clenched. I slapped down the brush. Squeezed my fists into my palm. And stormed up and down the room spitting out every vile invective I could summon up. (I didn't use the "GD" word—I had ceased using that one years ago, no matter how enraged I ever got. Not because I felt I was on particularly good terms with God—I was pretty much convinced He had a berth in hell all staked out for me. But why risk provoking Him into getting ugly about the whole thing?) I went through every other profanity, though, not bothering with whole sentences, just strung them together and frothed them up until I ran out of steam, plunked down on the couch, and snatched up my drink.

The careless, too-big gulp singed my throat and stung my nostrils, but I chased it with another, smaller pull and glared at the TV. The ten o'clock news had now replaced the movie. I half listened in. Oddly, watching the day's ugliness flicker by in neatly packaged, bite-sized takes took the edge off my pique. Odder still was the feeling of abandonment that took its place. Exasperating as it was that I'd made double work for myself, going ballistic gave me a distinct wave of satisfaction that the doomed resignation with which I'd come to walk through my waking hours had never provided.

I don't remember actually doing the second sign. It felt more like I was watching it happen.

The brush dipping into the paint . . .

Hovering, for a second, above the board . . .

One glistening red letter after another sliding off the silky bristles . . .

When it was finished, when the brush laid itself to rest and the sign tilted upward to reveal itself, all I could do was wonder why, out of what sick, unfathomable need had I insisted on doing this thing to myself all over again?

NEW THIS SUMER

"GODDAMN IT!" I heard myself scream. The paint, sign, and brush went splattering against the wall with a single sweep of my arm. The vodka glass missed slamming through the window by a matter of inches. I spewed obscenities again—this time at the top of my lungs. Without the slightest thought for the neighbors. (I didn't know any of them anyway. I had been living in the building over a year—a five-story, crowded-in walk-up, people stacked one atop the other—and I hadn't so much as a nodding acquaintance with one of them.)

Pounding around the room, seeking anything upon which to unleash my rage, I turned to a rolled-up carpet leaning against the wall in the corner. I had dragged it home off the street several months ago and never gotten up the gumption to deal with it. I beat on the thing mercilessly, reveling in the all-out violence, pounding into it again and again. It was so utterly, confoundingly gratifying. When I finally spent myself, my knuckles split and raw, there was the bottomless sadness again. I had nothing left in me with which to ward it off this time. I slumped to the floor and began bawling like a wounded coyote.

The next morning, the edge of sleep still wrapped around me like a womb, I remember not wanting to open my eyes. Not wanting to see the crimson splattered, like bloodstains all over the walls. Not wanting any reminder of the night before. When Barry was alive he was fond of quoting philosophers, though he often mangled the meaning. One of his favorites, which he attributed to Schopenhauer, was *Sip not of the empyrean, drink deep, else it will kill you.* And I had always considered that what it said about heaven must be equally true regarding hell. Now, after having peered over the rim of some deep pit of undefined darkness, I discovered that part of me had been drawn to it—was strangely attracted to the sense of tragedy it held—and I was loath to acknowledge this. Heaven or hell, I was a sipper.

I reminded myself that there was something I had to do that day—visit our booth at the trade show. Gawk at the sunny packages I had designed. Assure myself they were displayed to good advantage. Maybe schmooze up a buyer or two. We had had good success the previous year with a product called Free Support, which consisted of disposable, bra-sized crescents of paper-thin, flesh-colored viscose, with self-adhesive backing. When worn under backless and strapless fashions, they gave women, for whom the war against gravity had become a losing proposition, a firmer "no bra" look. And having made my bones nursing this product onto the market—creating all of the packaging, marketing, and advertising—my prospects for further corporate glory rested firmly on the success of our new product, "Bosom Buddies," which was essentially the same item adapted for use as a bathing-suit top—the gimmick being that it enabled women to tan without incurring ugly bra-strap lines.

I did manage—on the dregs of dumb momentum—to put in an appearance at the show and meander amid the bright, optimistic, saturated hues of the summer palette. But it proved to be a parting glance. Backless gowns and lineless tans were a world to which I could no longer imagine having been connected.

I sleepwalked through my next few months with United Products—wandered in the door at casual hours, made for the door soon as the last soul had safely cleared the office, took my happy hours at more and more inglorious booze mills, put myself to bed each night with Georgi's nightcaps as my sleep tonic of choice, and each morning woke to a greater and greater need for invention in order to summon the wherewithal to nudge myself out of bed. I suppose I had resolved, without even being consciously aware of doing so, to let things play themselves out.

When the president of United Products finally turned sad eyes on

me and told me with great reluctance that there was no longer any
way he could not let me go, it seemed no great thing to simply discard
that part of my life. When I found myself upping the dosage from
alcohol shots to cocaine lines and eventually chunks of crack in a
pipe, I embraced each escalation with the same casualness with
which you might turn down a new street with no other concern but to
discover where it leads. And when my money finally ran out and the
marshal showed up to evict me, I walked out my front door for the
last time without so much as half a backward glance, anticipating
that for the first time in a long, long time, new possibilities would
definitely present themselves. I had no idea that writing—a thing I
had only dabbled in here and there—would offer that new possibility—that it would provide the means by which I could make my way
in this world doing something that is connected to who I am. Nor did
I know it would take the better part of a decade, spent drugged-out
and living on the streets, before I would stumble upon that revelation.

Had I simply sought professional help, I suppose I might have
spared myself the long hard time I had of it and gotten back on my
feet sooner. But so far as hard ways around are concerned, I can't
imagine there's much wisdom or character to be had from lying on
satin sheets. It seems to me that at least half of what life has to teach
us must come from bouncing off a few rocks. And, truth is, I never
could work up much of a passion for simply getting "back on my
feet," for being rendered, merely, functional.

I knew something was wrong with my life. I was keenly aware of
happiness becoming an increasingly elusive thing. A thing which,
more and more, I couldn't grasp for any substantial length of time.
But I didn't see anything unique about this. I simply put it down as a
symptom of the human condition.

One grows older and more knowing over time; life's more facile
charms grow dim; the soul yearns, seeking more than could ever be
had on this earth, more than could ever be wrought out of three
dimensions and five senses. We, all of us, suffer some from the limits
of living within the flesh. Our walk through this world is never

entirely without that pain. It lurks in the still, quiet hours which we, in our constant busyness, steadfastly avoid. And it has occurred to me since that perhaps what we call depression isn't really a disorder at all but, like physical pain, an alarm of sorts, alerting us that something is undoubtedly wrong; that perhaps it is time to stop, take a time-out, take as long as it takes, and attend to the unaddressed business of filling our souls.

FROM *DARKNESS VISIBLE*

~

William Styron

WHEN I WAS FIRST AWARE that I had been laid low by the disease, I felt a need, among other things, to register a strong protest against the word "depression." Depression, most people know, used to be termed "melancholia," a word which appears in English as early as the year 1303 and crops up more than once in Chaucer, who in his usage seemed to be aware of its pathological nuances. "Melancholia" would still appear to be a far more apt and evocative word for the blacker forms of the disorder, but it was usurped by a noun with a bland tonality and lacking any magisterial presence, used indifferently to describe an economic decline or a rut in the ground, a true wimp of a word for such a major illness. It may be that the scientist generally held responsible for its currency in modern times, a Johns Hopkins Medical School faculty member justly venerated—the Swiss-born psychiatrist Adolf Meyer—had a tin ear for the finer rhythms of English and therefore was unaware of the semantic damage he had inflicted by offering "depression" as a descriptive noun for such a dreadful and raging disease. Nonetheless, for over seventy-five years the word has slithered innocuously through the language like a slug, leaving little trace of its intrinsic malevolence and preventing, by its very insipidity, a general aware-ness of the horrible intensity of the disease when out of control.

As one who has suffered from the malady in extremis yet returned to tell the tale, I would lobby for a truly arresting designa-tion. "Brainstorm," for instance, has unfortunately been preempted to describe, somewhat jocularly, intellectual inspiration. But some-thing along these lines is needed. Told that someone's mood disorder has evolved into a storm—a veritable howling tempest in the brain, which is indeed what a clinical depression resembles like nothing else—even the uninformed layman might display sympathy rather than the standard reaction that "depression" evokes, something akin to "So what?" or "You'll pull out of it" or "We all have bad days." The phrase "nervous breakdown" seems to be on its way out, cer-tainly deservedly so, owing to its insinuation of a vague spinelessness, but we still seem destined to be saddled with "depression" until a better, sturdier name is created.

The depression that engulfed me was not of the manic type—the one accompanied by euphoric highs—which would have most proba-bly presented itself earlier in my life. I was sixty when the illness struck for the first time, in the "unipolar" form, which leads straight down. I shall never learn what "caused" my depression, as no one will ever learn about their own. To be able to do so will likely forever prove to be an impossibility, so complex are the intermingled factors of abnormal chemistry, behavior and genetics. Plainly, multiple com-ponents are involved—perhaps three or four, most probably more, in fathomless permutations. That is why the greatest fallacy about suicide lies in the belief that there is a single immediate answer—or perhaps combined answers—as to why the deed was done.

The inevitable question "Why did he [or she] do it?" usually leads to odd speculations, for the most part fallacies themselves. Reasons were quickly advanced for Abbie Hoffman's death: his reaction to an auto accident he had suffered, the failure of his most recent book, his mother's serious illness. With Randall Jarrell it was a declining career cruelly epitomized by a vicious book review and his consequent anguish. Primo Levi, it was rumored, had been burdened by caring for his paralytic mother, which was more onerous to his spirit than even his experience at Auschwitz. Any one of these factors may have lodged like a thorn in the sides of the three men, and been a torment. Such aggravations may be crucial and cannot be ignored. But most people quietly endure the equivalent of injuries, declining careers, nasty book reviews, family illnesses. A vast majority of the survivors of Auschwitz have borne up fairly well. Bloody and bowed by the outrages of life, most human beings still stagger on down the road, unscathed by real depression. To discover why some people plunge into the downward spiral of depression, one must search beyond the manifest crisis—and then still fail to come up with anything beyond wise conjecture.

The storm which swept me into a hospital in December began as a cloud no bigger than a wine goblet the previous June. And the cloud—the manifest crisis—involved alcohol, a substance I had been abusing for forty years. Like a great many American writers, whose sometimes lethal addiction to alcohol has become so legendary as to provide in itself a stream of studies and books, I used alcohol as the magical conduit to fantasy and euphoria, and to the enhancement of the imagination. There is no need to either rue or apologize for my use of this soothing, often sublime agent, which had contributed greatly to my writing; although I never set down a line while under its influence, I did use it—often in conjunction with music—as a means to let my mind conceive visions that the unaltered, sober brain has no access to. Alcohol was an invaluable senior partner of my intel-

lect, besides being a friend whose ministrations I sought daily—
sought also, I now see, as a means to calm the anxiety and incipient
dread that I had hidden away for so long somewhere in the dungeons
of my spirit.

The trouble was, at the beginning of this particular summer, that
I was betrayed. It struck me quite suddenly, almost overnight: I could
no longer drink. It was as if my body had risen up in protest, along
with my mind, and had conspired to reject this daily mood bath
which it had so long welcomed and, who knows? perhaps even come
to need. Many drinkers have experienced this intolerance as they
have grown older. I suspect that the crisis was at least partly metabolic—the liver rebelling, as if to say, "No more, no more"—but at
any rate I discovered that alcohol in minuscule amounts, even a
mouthful of wine, caused me nausea, a desperate and unpleasant
wooziness, a sinking sensation and ultimately a distinct revulsion.
The comforting friend had abandoned me not gradually and reluctantly, as a true friend might do, but like a shot—and I was left high
and certainly dry, and unhelmed.

Neither by will nor by choice had I become an abstainer; the situation was puzzling to me, but it was also traumatic, and I date the
onset of my depressive mood from the beginning of this deprivation.
Logically, one would be overjoyed that the body had so summarily
dismissed a substance that was undermining its health; it was as if
my system had generated a form of Antabuse, which should have
allowed me to happily go my way, satisfied that a trick of nature had
shut me off from a harmful dependence. But, instead, I began to
experience a vaguely troubling malaise, a sense of something having
gone cockeyed in the domestic universe I'd dwelt in so long, so comfortably. While depression is by no means unknown when people stop
drinking, it is usually on a scale that is not menacing. But it should be
kept in mind how idiosyncratic the faces of depression can be.

It was not really alarming at first, since the change was subtle,
but I did notice that my surroundings took on a different tone at certain times: the shadows of nightfall seemed more somber, my morn-

ings were less buoyant, walks in the woods became less zestful, and there was a moment during my working hours in the late afternoon when a kind of panic and anxiety overtook me, just for a few minutes, accompanied by a visceral queasiness—such a seizure was at least slightly alarming, after all. As I set down these recollections, I realize that it should have been plain to me that I was already in the grip of the beginning of a mood disorder, but I was ignorant of such a condition at that time.

When I reflected on this curious alteration of my consciousness—and I was baffled enough from time to time to do so—I assumed that it all had to do somehow with my enforced withdrawal from alcohol. And, of course, to a certain extent this was true. But it is my conviction now that alcohol played a perverse trick on me when we said farewell to each other: although, as everyone should know, it is a major depressant, it had never truly depressed me during my drinking career, acting instead as a shield against anxiety. Suddenly vanished, the great ally which for so long had kept my demons at bay was no longer there to prevent those demons from beginning to swarm through the subconscious, and I was emotionally naked, vulnerable as I had never been before. Doubtless depression had hovered near me for years, waiting to swoop down. Now I was in the first stage—premonitory, like a flicker of sheet lightning barely perceived—of depression's black tempest.

I was on Martha's Vineyard, where I've spent a good part of each year since the 1960s, during that exceptionally beautiful summer. But I had begun to respond indifferently to the island's pleasures. I felt a kind of numbness, an enervation, but more particularly an odd fragility—as if my body had actually become frail, hypersensitive and somehow disjointed and clumsy, lacking normal coordination. And soon I was in the throes of a pervasive hypochondria. Nothing felt quite right with my corporeal self; there were twitches and pains, sometimes intermittent, often seemingly constant, that seemed to presage all sorts of dire infirmities. (Given these signs, one can understand how, as far back as the seventeenth century—in the notes of contemporary physicians, and in the perceptions of John Dryden and others—a connection is made between melancholia and hypochondria; the words are often interchangeable, and were so used until the nineteenth century by writers as various as Sir Walter Scott and the Brontës, who also linked melancholy to a preoccupation with bodily ills.) It is easy to see how this condition is part of the psyche's apparatus of defense: unwilling to accept its own gathering deterioration, the mind announces to its indwelling consciousness that it is the body with its perhaps correctable defects—not the precious and irreplaceable mind—that is going haywire.

In my case, the overall effect was immensely disturbing, augmenting the anxiety that was by now never quite absent from my waking hours and fueling still another strange behavior pattern—a fidgety restlessness that kept me on the move, somewhat to the perplexity of my family and friends. Once, in late summer, on an airplane trip to New York, I made the reckless mistake of downing a scotch and soda—my first alcohol in months—which promptly sent me into a tailspin, causing me such a horrified sense of disease and interior doom that the very next day I rushed to a Manhattan internist, who inaugurated a long series of tests. Normally I would have been satisfied, indeed elated, when, after three weeks of high-tech and extremely expensive evaluation, the doctor pronounced me totally fit; and I *was* happy, for a day or two, until there once again began the rhythmic daily erosion of my mood—anxiety, agitation, unfocused dread.

By now I had moved back to my house in Connecticut. It was October, and one of the unforgettable features of this stage of my disorder was the way in which my old farmhouse, my beloved home for thirty years, took on for me at that point when my spirits regularly sank to their nadir an almost palpable quality of ominousness. The fading evening light—akin to that famous "slant of light" of Emily Dickinson's, which spoke to her of death, of chill extinction—had none of its familiar autumnal loveliness, but ensnared me in a suffocating gloom. I wondered how this friendly place, teeming with such memories of (again in her words) "Lads and Girls," of "laughter and ability and Sighing, / And Frocks and Curls," could almost perceptibly seem so hostile and forbidding. Physically, I was not alone. As always Rose was present and listened with unflagging patience to my complaints. But I felt an immense and aching solitude. I could no longer concentrate during those afternoon hours, which for years had been my working time, and the act of writing itself, becoming more and more difficult and exhausting, stalled, then finally ceased.

There were also dreadful, pouncing seizures of anxiety. One bright day on a walk through the woods with my dog I heard a flock of Canada geese honking high above trees ablaze with foliage; ordinarily a sight and sound that would have exhilarated me, the flight of birds caused me to stop, riveted with fear, and I stood stranded there, helpless, shivering, aware for the first time that I had been stricken by no mere pangs of withdrawal but by a serious illness whose name and actuality I was able finally to acknowledge. Going home, I couldn't rid my mind of the line of Baudelaire's, dredged up from the distant past, that for several days had been skittering around at the edge of my consciousness. "I have felt the wind of the wing of madness."

Our perhaps understandable modern need to dull the sawtooth edges of so many of the afflictions we are heir to has led us to banish the harsh old-fashioned words: madhouse, asylum, insanity, melancholia, lunatic, madness. But never let it be doubted that depression, in its extreme form, is madness. The madness results from an aberrant biochemical process. It has been established with reasonable certainty (after strong resistance from many psychiatrists, and not all that long ago) that such madness is chemically induced amid the neurotransmitters of the brain, probably as the result of systemic stress, which for unknown reasons causes a depletion of the chemicals norepinephrine and serotonin, and the increase of a hormone, cortisol. With all of this upheaval in the brain tissues, the alternate drenching and deprivation, it is no wonder that the mind begins to feel aggrieved, stricken, and the muddied thought processes register the distress of an organ in convulsion. Sometimes, though not very often, such a disturbed mind will turn to violent thoughts regarding others. But with their minds turned agonizingly inward, people with depression are usually dangerous only to themselves. The madness of depression is, generally speaking, the antithesis of violence. It is a storm indeed, but a storm of murk. Soon evident are the slowed-down responses, near paralysis, psychic energy throttled back close to zero. Ultimately, the body is affected and feels sapped, drained.

That fall, as the disorder gradually took full possession of my system, I began to conceive that my mind itself was like one of those outmoded small-town telephone exchanges, being gradually inundated by floodwaters: one by one, the normal circuits began to drown, causing some of the functions of the body and nearly all of those of instinct and intellect to slowly disconnect.

What I had begun to discover is that, mysteriously and in ways that are totally remote from normal experience, the gray drizzle of horror induced by depression takes on the quality of physical pain. But it is not an immediately identifiable pain, like that of a broken limb. It may be more accurate to say that despair, owing to some evil trick played upon the sick brain by the inhabiting psyche, comes to resemble the diabolical discomfort of being imprisoned in a fiercely overheated room. And because no breeze stirs this caldron, because there is no escape from this smothering confinement, it is entirely natural that the victim begins to think ceaselessly of oblivion.

By far the great majority of the people who go through even the severest depression survive it, and live ever afterward at least as happily as their unafflicted counterparts. Save for the awfulness of certain memories it leaves, acute depression inflicts few permanent wounds. There is a Sisyphean torment in the fact that a great number—as many as half—of those who are devastated once will be struck again; depression has the habit of recurrence. But most victims live through even these relapses, often coping better because they have become psychologically tuned by past experience to deal with the ogre. It is of great importance that those who are suffering a siege, perhaps for the first time, be told—be convinced, rather—that the illness will run its course and that they will pull through. A tough job, this; calling "Chin up!" from the safety of the shore to a drowning person is tantamount to insult, but it has been shown over and over again that if the encouragement is dogged enough—and the support equally committed and passionate—the endangered one can nearly always be saved. Most people in the grip of depression at its ghastliest are, for whatever reason, in a state of unrealistic hopelessness, torn by exaggerated ills and fatal threats that bear no resemblance to actuality. It may require on the part of friends, lovers, family, admirers, an almost religious devotion to persuade the sufferers of life's worth, which is so often in conflict with a sense of their own worthlessness, but such devotion has prevented countless suicides.

During the same summer of my decline, a close friend of mine—a celebrated newspaper columnist—was hospitalized for severe manic depression. By the time I had commenced my autumnal plunge my friend had recovered (largely due to lithium but also to psychotherapy in the aftermath), and we were in touch by telephone nearly every day. His support was untiring and priceless. It was he who kept admonishing me that suicide was "unacceptable" (he had been intensely suicidal), and it was also he who made the prospect of going to the hospital less fearsomely intimidating. I still look back on his concern with immense gratitude. The help he gave me, he later said, had been a continuing therapy for him, thus demonstrating that, if nothing else, the disease engenders lasting fellowship.

After I began to recover in the hospital it occurred to me to wonder—for the first time with any really serious concern—why I had been visited by such a calamity. The psychiatric literature on depression is enormous, with theory after theory concerning the disease's etiology proliferating as richly as theories about the death of the dinosaurs or the origin of black holes. The very number of hypotheses is testimony to the malady's all but impenetrable mystery. As for that initial triggering mechanism—what I have called the manifest crisis—can I really be satisfied with the idea that abrupt withdrawal from alcohol started the plunge downward? What about other possibilities—the dour fact, for instance, that at about the same time I was smitten I turned sixty, that hulking milestone of mortality? Or could it be that a vague dissatisfaction with the way in which my work was going—the onset of inertia which has possessed me time and time again during my writing life, and made me crabbed and discontented—had also haunted me more fiercely during that period than ever, somehow magnifying the difficulty with alcohol? Unresolvable questions, perhaps.

These matters in any case interest me less than the search for earlier origins of the disease. What are the forgotten or buried events that suggest an ultimate explanation for the evolution of depression and its later flowering into madness? Until the onslaught of my own illness and its denouement, I never gave much thought to my work in terms of its connection with the subconscious—an area of investigation belonging to literary detectives. But after I had returned to health and was able to reflect on the past in the light of my ordeal, I began to see clearly how depression had clung close to the outer edges of my life for many years. Suicide has been a persistent theme in my books—three of my major characters killed themselves. In rereading, for the first time in years, sequences from my novels—passages where my heroines have lurched down pathways toward doom—I was stunned to perceive how accurately I had created the landscape of depression in the minds of these young women, describing with what could only be instinct, out of a subconscious already roiled by disturbances of mood, the psychic imbalance that led them to destruction. Thus depression, when it finally came to me, was in fact no stranger, not even a visitor totally unannounced; it had been tapping at my door for decades.

*   *   *

Near the end of an early film of Ingmar Bergman's, *Through a Glass Darkly*, a young woman, experiencing the embrace of what appears to be profound psychotic depression, has a terrifying hallucination. Anticipating the arrival of some transcendental and saving glimpse of God, she sees instead the quivering shape of a monstrous spider that is attempting to violate her sexually. It is an instant of horror and scalding truth. Yet even in this vision of Bergman (who has suffered cruelly from depression) there is a sense that all of his accomplished artistry has somehow fallen short of a true rendition of the drowned mind's appalling phantasmagoria. Since antiquity—in the tortured lament of Job, in the choruses of Sophocles and Aeschylus—chroniclers of the human spirit have been wrestling with a vocabulary that might give proper expression to the desolation of melancholia. Through the course of literature and art the theme of depression has run like a durable thread of woe—from Hamlet's soliloquy to the verses of Emily Dickinson and Gerard Manley Hopkins, from John Donne to Hawthorne and Dostoevski and Poe, Camus and Conrad and Virginia Woolf. In many of Albrecht Dürer's engravings there are harrowing depictions of his own melancholia; the manic wheeling stars of Van Gogh are the precursors of the artist's plunge into dementia and the extinction of self. It is a suffering that often tinges the music of Beethoven, of Schumann and Mahler, and permeates the darker cantatas of Bach. The vast metaphor which most faithfully represents this fathomless ordeal, however, is that of Dante, and his all-too-familiar lines still arrest the imagination with their augury of the unknowable, the black struggle to come:

> *Nel mezzo del cammin di nostra vita*
> *Mi ritrovai per una selva oscura,*
> *Ché la diritta via era smarrita.*

In the middle of the journey of our life
I found myself in a dark wood,
For I had lost the right path.

One can be sure that these words have been more than once employed to conjure the ravages of melancholia, but their somber foreboding has often overshadowed the last lines of the best-known part of that poem, with their evocation of hope. To most of those who have experienced it, the horror of depression is so overwhelming as to be quite beyond expression, hence the frustrated sense of inadequacy found in the work of even the greatest artists. But in science and art the search will doubtless go on for a clear representation of its meaning, which sometimes, for those who have known it, is a simulacrum of all the evil of our world: of our everyday discord and chaos, our irrationality, warfare and crime, torture and violence, our impulse toward death and our flight from it held in the intolerable equipoise of history. If our lives had no other configuration but this, we should want, and perhaps deserve, to perish; if depression had no termination, then suicide would, indeed, be the only remedy. But one need not sound the false or inspirational note to stress the truth that depression is not the soul's annihilation; men and women who have recovered from the disease—and they are countless—bear witness to what is probably its only saving grace: it is conquerable.

For those who have dwelt in depression's dark wood, and known its inexplicable agony, their return from the abyss is not unlike the ascent of the poet, trudging upward and upward out of hell's black depths and at last emerging into what he saw as "the shining world." There, whoever has been restored to health has almost always been restored to the capacity for serenity and joy, and this may be indemnity enough for having endured the despair beyond despair.

E quindi uscimmo a riveder le stelle.
And so we came forth, and once again beheld the stars.

S TRANDS

❦

Rose Styron

FULL MOON. SPECTACULAR EVENING. It is the end
of summer, 1995, and gathered on their favorite white-duned
beach on Martha's Vineyard for an annual picnic to honor the night
and long friendships are ten couples. They have just watched sunset
and moonrise, taken a long walk or swim, and finished a fine potluck
picnic. Sitting on blankets by the campfire with wineglasses raised, or
standing arm in arm to harmonize, they are singing old "moon
songs," laughing and reminiscing, wanting the bright night to last
forever.

My epiphany: At least seven of the celebrants—among them,
William Styron, Mike Wallace, Art Buchwald (later dubbed "The

Blues Brothers"), a director, a professor, and two poets, all creative and successful—had been diagnosed in the preceding decade as clinically depressed.

I met Bill Styron at Johns Hopkins University in 1951, when I was a student. My professor, Louis Rubin, had persuaded his southern friend, who had just won a Prix de Rome, to come speak to our writing class about *Lie Down in Darkness*. Bill gave a shy, nervous performance. Not very impressed, I left at the end with fellow poets, barely speaking to the acclaimed author. But a year later, in Rome, finding myself on a boring date with a classicist at the Academy of Arts and Letters, I happened to pass the Fellows' mailboxes. A label with the name "Styron" reminded me that Louis had suggested I look Bill up. On a whim, I dropped a note with my phone number in his box. He called the next day and invited me to drinks at the Excelsior Bar.

When I descended the steps of the Excelsior, I discovered Bill sitting with Truman Capote (in a sailor suit, a minah bird on his shoulder). An instant three-way friendship preceded Bill's and my romance, which flowered on long walks through Rome, an Academy trip to Ravello, and a dramatic snow-and-avalanche drive through France to visit Bill's new friends (Peter Matthiesson, George Plimpton, John Marquand, Harold Humes, Billy du Bois and Tom Guinzburg) who were putting together the early issues of the *Paris Review*. We were in our twenties—literary, irreverent, energetic, able to drink and stay up all night singing hymns or lieder or classical rounds or schmaltzy country-and-western numbers. Bill had the best voice (his mother was a singer, trained in Vienna before World War I). He was very funny, with great timing and a vivid imagination. He told me he'd got by on humor at Christ Church Prep School, where he was the youngest and smallest in his class. I found him not only handsome and sexy but unusually kind, even to the persons he deftly lampooned. And vulnerable. At the Excelsior, his knees shook under the table as he described his fear of heights, put to the test that very noon as he climbed down from St. Peter's dome.

We married the next May at the Campidoglio in Rome by Marcus Aurelius on his horse. Bill's mentor Irwin Shaw persuaded the *Paris Review* gang to fly in, and with my brother and Academy friends, we dined al fresco and left for an eight-month honeymoon in Ravello. The novel Bill had begun then—*Blankenship*—did not satisfy him, so he decided we should sail home at year's end to work-ethic America. Brief months in New York were exchanged for decades in quiet Connecticut. We wrote. We started a family. Those first years together in a small, converted barn in beautiful Roxbury were near-idyllic. Bill would write in the afternoons and rewrite or reimagine late at night. Often, he would read the day's fresh prose to me, and I would type it the following morning as he slept. Our first child, Susanna, was the perfect baby, adjusting to our late schedule and becoming fast friends with our first dog, a Newfoundland named Tugwell. Our life was full of adventures: annual family visits to the James Jones' in Paris, the Carlos Fuentes' in Mexico, sailing expeditions with the Robert Brusteins in the Caribbean, and Easter breaks on the tiny, private island of Salt Cay with our *Paris Review* friends. Bill enjoyed the nightly campfire storytelling, and the antics of our collective children and surprise visitors as much as I did.

But while Bill had always cherished separate quiet time, over the decades he came to demand real solitude. He stopped allowing me to invite guests, arrange celebrations. He wrote in the afternoons and then drank tumblers of whiskey till the wee hours while he listened to certain pieces by Mozart and Beethoven over and over. He talked to me less and less, read to me not at all. Increasingly, he became irritated by noise—traffic, excessive conversation, the clatter of dropped utensils. He tried to shut out the sounds even of our four high-spirited children. Unpredictable, he would lash out at the family he loved. Having been raised by steady, affectionate parents who encouraged my independent judgment, I was baffled by my spouse's outbursts and need to control me and the children. Had he lifted a finger against any one of us I would have left, but he was—*is*—a good man with no physical violence in him. I knew his childhood had not been a happy one: his mother died when he was thirteen; he had no siblings; his sweet, distraught father soon married a nurse who was jealous and disapproving of Bill. So I made allowances for what I tagged Fear of Loss. I knew he was a genius and I considered coddling geniuses to be okay. The women's movement had not quite yet captured me. I still believed in being the dutiful wife and perhaps I had elements of cowardice, masochism, denial lurking below my so-called serene surface: I guess I thought the deepening struggle was one more stage in a long marriage, part of the unavoidably erratic liaison of two writer-activists.

Love did not prepare me for 1985. As Bill's sixtieth birthday loomed, he (a well-known, well-teased hypochondriac with a *Merck's Manual* at our bedside) became *insanely* hypochondriacal. He saw THE END on every horizon. Death was on his mind—not only for himself, but for others. When his favorite dog was sick, he was certain she would die (she lived three more years to his joy). When Polly fell off her horse and Alexandra was in a car accident, both requiring stitches in their heads, he assumed death was imminent for them both. Agonized for our daughters, Bill remonstrated *me*. I felt genuinely guilty, that it was my fault that I had not been careful enough with them. I was away a lot—I had begun a new career as a voyager for Amnesty International and traveled extensively for human rights—and, therefore, was not able to monitor Bill's moods as much as I would have liked.

Bill had also stopped his habitual drinking as suddenly and completely as he had given up smoking twenty-odd years earlier. His old pal, liquor, was making him nauseous. His insomnia—for which a careless Vineyard doctor, impressed by "William Styron," had prescribed Atavan (as often as Bill wanted) two years earlier—became far worse. A New York doctor switched him to Halcion. Bill paced in doctors' offices for this or that real or imagined physical ailment. He spent long hours lying on the bed staring at the ceiling instead of writing. Or, if he did summon the energy to write, he described characters consumed by their own fears of failing health and fortune, or approaching death. I noted, bemused, that every one of his fictional heroines was a victim of suicide or murder, but I had not understood that it was a disguise for his own apprehensions.

Over the summer of 1985, attempting to understand and keep my own balance, I convinced myself that Bill's state was caused by withdrawal from alcohol. His withdrawal from smoking in 1963 had produced a frenetic need for chocolate and the repeated theft of our children's gumdrops. But, this year, plying him with sweets did no good. Nothing did. He took pleasure in no one. His conversations—always far-ranging and spontaneous—became self-centered, labored, obsessive. Bill stopped urging me to leave him alone at home to think and work. He stopped going off without me on splendid, short trips to Paris or Moscow. He stopped railing at me for my peccadilloes and Pollyanna turns of phrase. He suddenly wanted me there all the time, didn't want me out of his sight, *wanted* to talk. He asked me to accompany him on long walks with the dogs, during which he talked about his hatred for the world and winter, his fears about work and aging.

I have to admit that on those walks, as the leaves turned in New England, when he seemed newly close and affectionate toward me, my heart was full, wifely. September was a deceptively good month for me as far as my marriage itself was concerned. I was sad for him, but I was also happy for us. I guess I believed that, when withdrawal played itself out, he'd see the colors of the leaves, the beauty of the world again.

During this time, though, I also seesawed hopelessly between bafflement and anger, between immediate compassion for Bill and despair for his future, and I began a long poem. These lines appear halfway through:

> *The man who lies beside me as he's lain*
> *night after moonless windless night*
> *this season staring at the ceiling does not*
> *feel my hand. No longer do I fear*

he'll deafen me or crush
these thinning bones. He and his
blood-red storm-black energy I've ridden
up and down the bucking hills
reveling in the sun's companionship
have left me

Whiteness
the ghost of songs
the rage beginning

We two sophisticated artists had, until now, lived comfortably in our rural world, clinging to our parents' Victorian codes of silence about any disturbing family matters.

When I finally figured out that Bill was depressed—not just moody or in withdrawal or angry at life but *clinically depressed*—I knew we needed professional help. I called Art Buchwald and Peter Matthiesson and Jean Stein, writer pals who had experienced mood swings since youth, and asked them to make this suggestion directly to Bill. When Bill's pain was at its worst, he was able to take advice from friends, who had been through something similar, more easily than from me. I became the scholar of Bill's moods and behavior, too interested and curious to turn off entirely (remember that this man I had married was never boring, always brilliantly mercurial), even when I could not reach him. I'd often thought that a marriage as long as ours was like several marriages, each partner growing and changing so often throughout. Now a delicate balancing act ensued (one thing depressives are good at is keeping you off balance) and I realized I must look around the corner to be ready for what was coming next onto our windswept, waterlogged path, if health and sanity were ever to return.

At that time our trusted family doctor had died. A local GP suggested a psychiatrist in New Haven. We went to his ugly, seedy office with the big three-quarters-dead overwatered potted tree on the damp, gray indoor-outdoor frayed carpet in the tiny waiting room. I sat on a bench two feet from the plywood door to his office. Through the wall, I could hear the psychiatrist droning at Bill about age, about lowering his creative expectations—maybe Bill shouldn't write any- more and should think of other things to do—meanwhile instructing him not to think about hospitalization because it would only stigma- tize him. Bill emerged with three prescriptions (an MAO-inhibitor, Nardil; an antianxiety pill, Xanax; and an "upper" called Desyrel which in combination with the Halcion only pushed Bill down fur- ther fast). Looking defeated, believing the prognosis, Bill insisted on being driven back at least weekly to see this doctor. "Just don't let him out of your sight," the doctor told me. Whenever I phoned him to say, "This isn't working," he prescribed more medication to Bill. I kept a diary, observing every pill, every conversation, every change in Bill's voice or gait, every doctor's order. (I've looked for the diary in vain. I remember it started with my new motto at the time: Stop. Look. Listen. Hang on.)

There *were* comic moments. Backstage at a downtown New York PEN event, Bill frantically persuaded his dear friend and editor, Bob Loomis, to taxi uptown and ransack our apartment for a pill Bill had forgotten while another author scrambled to sew a button on Bill's jacket so he would feel presentable onstage. And in Paris, Bill refused to go to a luncheon with the grandiose Madame Del Duca and crusty academicians after he received a fat check from them and had his name inscribed in marble on the Del Duca mansion wall. Bill's pub- lisher was purple with embarrassment as Madame flounced out. And flounced back. We finally persuaded him to attend briefly. And, then, at the elegant restaurant for dinner with the publisher and her fam- ily, Bill lost the check and the five of us crawled and crawled under the table to find it. All of these were much funnier scenes than Bill remembers in *Darkness Visible*. So was our last New York visit pre- hospital: *Poets & Writers* concocted a fund-raising evening where several of its premier authors performed in the Big Apple Circus, while others (like Bill) applauded from the first row. When Norman Mailer flexed his painted muscles and rolled by on a bongo board and Erica Jong, dressed as a fairy and perched atop an elephant, rode too close, the look of horror on Bill's face beat any clown's. I wonder how accurately he recalls that night.

Is it logical that a depressive's memory, even one as prodigious as Bill's, could be skewed by trauma? Surely, a novelist, prompted by the dialogue in his head and the imagination which creates and controls a story, might intuitively choose a meaningful ending. Bill's description two-thirds through *Darkness Visible* of his watching a film in the living room as I slept upstairs, hearing the gorgeous Alto Rhapsody, thinking suddenly of his children and the past joys in our house, and deciding to *live*, to wake me up so I could take him to the hospital, must be indelible in the reader's mind. In *my* mind, I never slept if Bill was not in bed beside me. And the piercing of his heart by Brahms must have taken place several hours earlier. But I am convinced that this was the moment that saved him and I'm certain his thoughts of our family did finally nullify his resolve to kill himself.

Our daughter Polly came to be with him that evening. Notes she jotted down some time later strike me as wholly accurate:

So, I guess I should write this down, or I won't believe it. I came to the house Friday evening because I'd heard Dad had had a terrible night on Thursday and that he and Mum were fairly shaken. I was prepared for a morbid gloom, but not for what the night actually turned out to be. When I went upstairs to his room he was lying there, with his long gray hair all tangled and wild. I took his hand, which was trembling. "I'm a goner, darling," he said, first thing. His eyes had a startled look, and he seemed to be not quite there. His cool, trembling hands kept fumbling over mine. "The agony's too great now, darling. I'm sorry. I'm a goner."

For the next hour, he raved about his miserable past and his sins and the waste of his life and how, when they published the scandal of his life, we should try not to hate him. "You'll hate me. You'll hate me," he said in a whisper. Everything was repeated over and over. "I love you so much. And the other children. And your mother. You'll hate me for what I am going to do to myself. My head is exploding. I can't stand the agony anymore. It's over now. I can't stand the agony. Tell the others how much I love them. I've betrayed my life. All my books have been about suicide. What a miserable waste of a life. I'm dying! I'm dying! I am dying!" And on and on, and over and over, while grabbing me to come closer, taking my head to his breast, holding me closer. My father.

When Mum finally came upstairs, as he held me next to him with his eyes closed, I mouthed the word "HOS-PI-TAL" to her.

Bill's hospital stay began agonizingly for me. Visiting each day, I would listen to hours of his nightmares, sorrows, disorientation, then watch him shuffle down the hall like a figure from *One Flew Over the Cuckoo's Nest*. When I spoke to the doctor, he warned me that electroconvulsive therapy (ECT) might be advisable. Filled with *Cuckoo* images, it didn't occur to me that techniques had been improved and I protested emphatically. Even at his most medicated, Bill begged me to keep protesting so his creative brain would not be permanently altered. I pursued this mission so annoyingly, the doctors urged me to go on vacation.

Slowly but surely, with time, therapy, and medication, Bill improved.

Polly wrote eloquently:

He survived the seven weeks there, though at times we wondered if they'd given him a lobotomy without consulting us. As his anxiety subsided, he became increasingly goofy and zombielike, but then slowly he became more coherent, more animated, and finally more willful. When his temper returned, we let out a collective sigh of relief; he was better.

In 1989, Bill wrote a version of *Darkness Visible* for *Vanity Fair*. He did not mention a second episode. Bill did have a relapse in early 1988, triggered by his acute apprehension concerning a major operation. It was being delayed a fortnight due to Mass General's busy schedule. Having persuaded a new local doctor to give him Halcion for recurring insomnia, Bill took the drug just before traveling to Claremont College to fulfill a speaking/teaching engagement. In sunny California, his gloom descended. He became alternately obsessed, distracted, or mute before the students. The Halcion had caused, in Bill's words, "a chemical commotion" in his brain. He was violently suicidal again and scared. I immediately called a psychiatrist both Bill and I admired. He said, "Get on a plane and take Bill straight to Mass General. I'll arrange for him to stay in the psychiatric wing until they operate." He was admitted days early and the whole stay was a success.

When Bill returned fully to our family and the world, I finished the poem I quoted earlier:

> *We have arrived:*
> *it is a calmer day.*
>
> *The light surf rambles with us*
> *along the fine grained sand.*
> *The sun reclines on his longest*
> *cloud-raft, glow fanning*
> *the horizon, (Curry's Line Storm*
> *turned away from rain)*
> *catching the sky-tuned gulls,*
> *smooth perched slipper shells*
> *broadside, as in late afternoon*
> *it will catch white sailboats*
> *stilled in our eastern harbor.*
>
> *Love that lay hidden under*
> *yesterday's monstrous breakers*

in the pounded dunes
walks with us. Retrievers
black and golden
chase tiptoed sanderlings
at a dead run, across the ledge
left by the last high tide.

There were no fanatasies of death for over a decade.

Almost every day, Bill is in contact with fellow depression sufferers by mail or by phone. People moved by his book write him, but
those in desperate need of help, telephone. He is invariably sympathetic, expansive, ready with crucial advice. One letter he received
was from a young professor and political activist in Nevada who had
been injured severely in an accident. The anesthesia and subsequent
drugs administered caused horrifying memories of her student days
in Chile under Pinochet to resurface. Life was an isolating nightmare, she said, until she read *Darkness Visible* and understood recovery was possible. I also recall Bill speaking on the phone for a very
long time to a man who was apparently standing outside his house
brandishing a gun, pointing it alternately at his head and at the
police trying to dissuade him from shooting. Bill literally talked the
distressed caller out of suicide. The police grabbed the phone and
thanked Bill. Another time, a woman with insomnia, ready for suicide, was put on the phone by her son, a minister at his wit's end.
Within thirty minutes, Bill had persuaded her to go to a sleep center
he knew about in Alabama.

Bill's spoken and written words of encouragement to countless
such individuals and the speeches he's given surely contribute to his
own sense of well-being, and perhaps have even stimulated his continued creativity. Thus, the vision of a writer whose premier demand
had been respect for his privacy, need for solitude and control of his
environment slowly alters while the anxieties of those around him
subside.

Looking back, I would say that sticking with the person you love through the stressful dramas of mood disorder can eventually be incredibly rewarding. Depression, Johns Hopkins psychiatrist Ray de Paulo notes, eats at the heart of every relationship. One must be sensitive, nurture the fragile connections, humor the sufferer like a baby. Do not say, "Pull up your socks, you're fine." Each "case" is as different as each person's suffering—and as different as each spousal relation—but I know from my friends that a significant number of the manifestations and underlying patterns of thought and behavior can be quite similar. Perhaps the best thing one can do is to act on intuition. And keep intuition's third eye open forever, after recovery, to note the first trembling turning leaves of a change of season.

An Unwelcome Career

∿

David Karp

IN GREATER OR LESSER DEGREE I have grappled with depression for almost twenty-five years. I suppose that even as a child my experience of life was as much characterized by anxiety as by joy and pleasure. As I look back on it, there were lots of tip-offs along the way that things weren't right. I find it difficult to remember much of my early years, but throughout high school and college I felt uncertain of myself, feared that I could not accomplish what was expected of me, and had plenty of sleepless nights. During college one of my roommates nicknamed me "weak heart," after a character type in Dostoyevsky novels, because I often seemed a bit of a lost soul. During those years, though, I had no real baseline for evaluating the "normalcy" of my feelings. At most, I had defined myself as more anxious than other people and a worrier. Even though I was always muddling along emotionally, like having a chronic low-grade fever, I was achieving well enough in school to presume that underneath it all I was okay. It wasn't until my early thirties that I was forced to conclude that something was really *wrong* with me.

People who live with depression often vividly remember the situations that forced them to have a new consciousness as a troubled person. For me, that occasion was a professional meeting of sociologists in Montreal in 1974. I should have been feeling pretty good by objective standards. I had a solid academic job at Boston College, I had just signed my first book contract, and I had a great wife, a beautiful son, and a new baby daughter at home.

The week I was in Montreal, I got virtually no sleep. It's true, I was staying in a borrowed apartment in a strange city, but I had done a fair amount of traveling and never had sleeping problems as bad as this. It occurred to me that I might be physically ill, maybe I had the flu, but I wasn't just tired and achy. Each sleepless night, my head was filled with disturbing ruminations—for example, imagining myself at a podium, frozen, frightened, unable to talk. During the day, I felt a sense of intolerable grief, as though somebody close to me had died. I couldn't concentrate, the top of my head felt like it would blow off, and the excitement of having received a book contract was replaced by the dread and certainty that I wasn't up to the task of writing it. It truly was a miserable week and the start of what I now know was an extended episode of depression. It was also the beginning of a long pilgrimage to figure out what is wrong with me, what to name it, what to do about it, and how to live with it.

Despite a progressive worsening of the feelings I first experienced in Montreal, it took me quite a while before I fully connected the word "depression" to my situation. Being depressed was not yet part of my self-description or identity. It was another prolonged and even more debilitating period of insomnia, compounded with anxiety and sadness, that pushed me to a doctor's office (an internist, not a psychiatrist). For the first time I heard someone tell me that I was clinically depressed and that I needed antidepressant medications.

I was prescribed a drug called amitriptyline (which, indeed, was a real "trip"). I began taking it in 1978 just before a family vacation in Orlando, Florida. We went to "enjoy" Disneyworld, Sea World, and Circus World. Even as I got on the plane, I knew that something was desperately wrong. My head was in a state of fantastic turmoil; I was more intensely anxious than ever before. The feelings were so awful, I should have known that the drug was a disaster, but I had no experience with these medications. I thought maybe this was supposed to happen before I became accustomed to the medicine. Things only got worse in Orlando. No sleep. I couldn't pay attention to anything. An extraordinary panic overwhelmed me.

The contrast between what you are supposed to feel at Disneyworld and what I did feel was so enormous that it engulfed me. Watching my genuinely happy children having their faces painted with exaggerated clown smiles, I felt the fraudulence of my own masklike smile. I was often on the edge of crying, but I managed to hold it together throughout the week. As we drove away from Disneyworld, however, I lost it altogether. I told my wife to stop the car in the breakdown lane and that's, in fact, what happened. I got out of the car and "broke down." My mind took over my body with huge, gulping, uncontrollable sobs. Somehow I eventually composed myself and we reached the hotel. I got in touch with a doctor in Boston who told me to get off the medication. Stopping the drug helped, but that experience was unforgettable and pivotal in my developing "career" as a depressed person.

I returned to Boston, resolved about two things. I would never again take medication and I would get to the bottom of my difficulties. I became a kind of mental-health explorer. Self-help books seemed a good place to start, but I soon realized I could not identify with the vignettes usually provided and the seven (or eight or nine or ten) surefire steps to happiness necessary for a best-seller always seemed silly to me. I started scouting around for some kind of therapy short of seeing a "shrink."

I heard about cocounseling from a colleague in another department. He was a guy I respected intellectually and was refreshingly forthcoming about the life problems that got him into this form of therapy. It may even be that he claimed cocounseling had saved his life. In any event, he'd been going to meetings for several years and gave me the name of a person to call. I was interviewed before being allowed to join the group. I never learned whether the purpose of this was to determine if I was sufficiently off balance to warrant membership or too crazy to be helped. The young woman who interviewed me was extremely appealing. She was physically attractive, warm, and empathetic. She was instantly likable and made me feel confident in her and her group.

It was called cocounseling because, along with the meetings of the group, we were expected to work independently with a partner. In both the wider group and with your partner, therapeutic success seemed to be measured by the volume of tears shed as you told your story. The theory, I guess, was that the tears somehow released all the negative energy that was keeping you down. I happened to be linked with a woman in her early twenties. We dutifully met a few times at her apartment, and along with the discomfort we both felt because of our age difference, neither of us ever succeeded in doing too much "discharging," as the group leaders put it. Although it was compelling to hear the range of problems of those in the group, I could never get with the program by weeping and quit after about six months.

Like everyone who suffers from depression, I spent a lot of time considering its causes. Throughout the early seventies, I thought I had a pretty good explanation for the problem. As they say in the academic business, 1977 was to be my "up or out year"; I would either be promoted or terminated. In short, I was under enormous pressure for six years prior—juggling the tasks of teaching, counseling students, serving on departmental and university committees, presenting papers at professional meetings, and writing two books that had to be done before I was evaluated for tenure. I thought for sure that my depression was rooted in these situational demands and that once I got tenure it would go away. In 1977, I was promoted and found that the depression actually deepened. This suggested a wholly new and more frightening interpretation of depression's locus. I had to confront the possibility that my sickness might not have arisen from social situations, but somehow from my self.

By 1980, my sleeping, which has always been the key barometer of my psychic state, was awful. I got a reasonable night's sleep here and there, but most nights followed a similar and torturous pattern. I began each night with the hope that sleep would relieve me of the misery generated by dragging myself through the day. I had tried everything at this point, short of prescribed medication to sleep— L-tryptophan from the local health-food store, warm baths, meditation, a glass or two of wine, changing bedtimes in an effort to reset my biological clock. Nothing helped. Even on my best nights, I was up every hour or so.

The loneliest moments of my life have been in the middle of the night while, as I imagined it, everybody else in the world was sleeping. Since I teach and often am standing in front of eighty students in the morning, I spent many nights obsessing over how I would pull it off the next day. I found some comfort in knowing that it had always been possible to get through my classes before, but one of the most insidious things about profound depression is the feeling that each moment in it is the worst yet. I felt angry toward those who were sleeping, especially my wife, who was right there so visibly and easily doing what I couldn't and desperately needed to do. My bad feelings intensified in the middle of the night. The volume of my personal agony reached a deafening pitch.

Sometimes, as if God was serving up a particularly ironic punishment, I would drift off to sleep shortly before I had to begin my day. The day followed, filled with obligations that felt burdensome and often impossible. I spent each day struggling to appear competent, constantly amazed that I had gotten through the last test and certain that I would shut down in the face of the next.

I felt completely alone. Everyone else—my wife, my kids, coworkers, friends, the guy who sold me my morning coffee— seemed to be moving through their days peacefully, laughing and having fun. I resented them because they were having such an easy time of it and because I felt utterly cut off from them emotionally. I felt angry because there was no way they could understand what I was experiencing. Their very presence seemed to magnify my sense of isolation. I never felt seriously suicidal, but this combination of gruesome days and sleepless nights often led me to feel that my life was not worth living. Some days were better than others, raising the elusive hope that I might be emerging from my difficulty. For the most part, though, I dragged along, feeling barely alive.

Some people experience depression primarily as a kind of mental misery. Mine has always had a physical component as well. As I saw it, my mind made a choice each day about how to torment my body. One day it was a terrible "grief knot" in my throat. Another brought chest pain that could easily be mistaken for a heart attack. Sometimes, I felt an awful heaviness in my eyes, pressure in my head, feelings of sadness in my cheeks, shaky hands and legs, or some combination of all these things. I was constantly aware of my body, monitoring from minute to minute whether things had become better or worse.

Unremitting pain gradually eroded my resolve to stay away from therapists. The first one I saw was a woman with a Ph.D. in clinical psychology. Since I am an academic and greatly value intellectual journeys of all sorts, I agreed to do an archaeological excavation of my biography. With her direction, I did some interesting exercises like going through old picture albums to stimulate reflection on various aspects of my childhood. However, our talk never generated truly illuminating connections and I concluded that this person had no special insight. Because nothing we did relieved my bad feelings, I stopped going. I tried other therapists thinking that the key to turning things around was to find the "right one." After several attempts to find a savior, I became tired of recounting my biography and fundamentally dubious about the efficacy of talking as a solution. Each new therapeutic venture began with hope and ended with disillusionment.

In 1982, I read an advertisement in the *Boston Globe* asking for volunteers for a drug study at McLean Hospital in Belmont, Massachusetts. Although I had sworn off drugs, my family and friends urged me to try the program, and once again, desperation overcame my resistance. Participation in this program, like my experience with cocounseling, required a preliminary interview, this time with the psychiatrist in charge of the study. McLean is often referred to as the Harvard of mental hospitals. In fact, with its mixture of old and new buildings and extensive greenery, McLean Hospital has the feeling of a college campus. Still, I couldn't escape the feeling that by showing up at a mental hospital, I had crossed an important identity threshold.

Next to the building where I was to have my interview was a basketball court. I remember thinking how strange that seemed since significant physical effort was impossible in my state. Could it be that the in-patients were in better shape than I was? As I climbed the three flights of stairs to the psychiatrist's office, I passed a door on each level with a small rectangular window that let me look into a locked ward. I saw some attendants, with their full key rings and white uniforms, but didn't see any patients. It was eerily quiet and there was no visible patient life. Where were they? What was being done to them? Could I end up in such a place? At that moment I felt like a mental patient, and as much as I wanted to get out of there, I imagined I had no choice. What was left for me to try?

Dr. Rosen was a pleasant-looking man in his mid-thirties who continuously puffed on a pipe and displayed a relaxed demeanor thoroughly fitting to someone in charge of his life. I was surprised to learn that Dr. Rosen was not at all interested in my relationships with my parents, my siblings, my wife, my children, or my job. He simply asked a series of questions about my symptoms. Did it feel the worst in the morning? Did I feel a mood elevation in mid-afternoon? Did I fall asleep quickly only to wake an hour later? Did I often finally fall asleep between five-thirty and seven in the morning? And so on. The questions seemed to cut to the center of my feelings and experiences. It was like going to a psychic who said things in so pertinent a way that it melted all skepticism. At the end of my twenty-five-minute interview Rosen said the magical words, "I think I can help you." I believed that science might just save me.

My association with Rosen and McLean marked a new phase in my illness journey. Despite my earlier beliefs, I committed myself to a medical model of depression. Rosen's judgment was that a trial with imipramine, then one of the most widely used and effective antidepressant medications, would set me on the right course. The whole process was clearly premised on my having a biological disorder. It was comforting to think that I might get well by controlling levels of norepinephrine in my brain, equivalent to the way diabetics monitor their insulin. As a study participant, I filled out a questionnaire once a week to determine if the depression was lifting. The imipramine, as the doctor told me it would, made my mouth feel like it was filled with cotton. This and other side effects (constipation, occasional dizziness) were troublesome to me, but I did begin to feel better. Even a slight respite in my bad feelings had a profound influence in accelerating my hope that once I got my neurotransmitters working correctly I would be home free.

I stayed on the imipramine for well over a year. Although it diminished my symptoms, imipramine was not my ticket to normality. Psychopharmacologists are very keen on trying each of a new generation of drugs that might finally do the trick for you. Consequently, I took a bewildering array of medications over the course of the next few years—Anafranil, trazodone, Halcion, lithium, Surmontil, Serax, Xanax, and the list goes on. These drugs produced terrible side effects like those I felt in Orlando. They sometimes separated me, as though behind a glass wall, from everyone else, or made me impotent, or caused rapid weight gain. Still, I felt dependent on medicines that I thought allowed me to live life somewhat more easily than in the past.

As I write these words, I am struggling emotionally after another typically lousy night of sleep. About two years ago I tried still another medication—doxepin. Once more, I did this out of a sense of desperation. Shortly after swallowing the first pill, my anxiety noticeably decreased. Within a few days my sleep patterns changed. Occasionally, I slept through the night and woke up anxiety-free, refreshed, and eager to get going with my day. I am grateful for those nights and days, but the miracle was short-lived. Within weeks I was back to status quo. Perhaps the biochemical revolution in psychiatry will eventually yield a pill—some think it is Prozac—that will permanently solve problems like mine. That would be fantastic, but I think it unlikely. Through the years my attitude toward drugs has remained steady, a mixture of hostility and dependence.

When I examine my response to medication, I realize how deeply my feelings about drugs are tied up with my views about psychiatry and its prevailing definition of depression as a biological disease. I respect the sincere impulse of medical scientists to help people, but I also wonder whether psychiatrists' willingness to embrace the use of drugs is related to their own suspect status within medicine. It certainly would affirm psychiatry as a medical specialty if it could be demonstrated that affective disorders have as clearly organic a source as diabetes, epilepsy, or heart disease. However, a plainly organic etiology has never been established in the case of unipolar depression. That people sometimes feel better after taking antidepressant medications is hardly definitive evidence that depression is caused by a physical pathology. Such logic would require us to say that the individual who feels better after a glass or two of wine with dinner is de facto suffering from some biological impairment corrected by the alcohol.

My own view—rooted in personal experience, listening to others, a lifetime of social science, and what seems commonsensically true— is that depression arises out of an enormously complicated, constantly shifting, elusive concatenation of circumstance, temperament, and biochemistry. I would never flatly declare that antidepressants should be avoided. Too many people have been helped by medication to take such a position. At the same time, though, I strongly resist an approach that systematically minimizes the role of social experience in shaping emotions, good ones and bad ones.

Every now and then I vow to "get clean" so that I might learn what my moods would be like without doxepin, Klonopin, and the self-prescribed milligram of melatonin I take every night, promptly at nine-thirty. But there's always a reason I give myself for not making the move: "I can't afford to change things with a sabbatical approaching." "If things go downhill, I'll never finish the book I'm writing." "Not now, just before our trip to Europe." "It would be unwise to stop just as I'm beginning a three-year term as department chairperson." "I can't make a change with the new semester approaching." And so on and on.

My unwillingness to embark on a new therapeutic course also influences the relationship I have with my psychiatrist. These days we meet only every few months, as the law apparently dictates when patients are prescribed "controlled" substances. Our face-to-face routine begins when she perfunctorily asks me how I'm doing. Even if things have been bad, I cheerily tell her I'm fine. To admit significant problems would inevitably initiate plans for a new medication course, something I have decided to avoid. We then spend the next half hour or so chatting amiably, usually about our work and kids, before she finally gives me what I really came for—a new prescription for old and comfortable stuff. She feels good about the value of her work and I am left alone.

Rituals, even unhappy ones, provide a measure of comfort. Like a superstitious ballplayer who will only use certain bats, my depression rituals have become a fixed, normal part of my life. I have methods for monitoring the time when I wake in the middle of the night, mood assessment questions each morning, and, as already described, regular conversations with a medical expert. My most important rit-

uals involve drug taking. I feel obliged to take my medications at precisely the same time every night, as though even a small variation
would doom me to sleeplessness. I feel an ambivalent connection to
my drugs, rather like cigarette brand loyalty or the sort of intimacy
that binds people in troubled relationships. I often discuss these drug
habits with fellow sufferers. We share a laugh about air travel and
always packing our medications in carry-on luggage. Having airlines
lose our clothing might be a considerable inconvenience, but having
our drugs lost would be an absolute catastrophe! I need rituals to prevent unnecessarily rocking my already shaky emotional boat.

Even though depression has periodically made me feel that my
life was not worth living, has created havoc in my family, and sometimes made the work of teaching and writing seem impossible, I have
not lost my family, my work, or, for that matter, my life. At age fifty-
five, I have surrendered myself to depressive illness. I do not believe I
will ever be free of it. For me, depression is a kind of mental arthritis; it is something that you just have to live with. The recognition
that the pain of depression is unlikely to disappear has provoked a
redefinition of its meaning, a reordering of its place in my life. It has
taken me more than two decades to abandon the medical language of
cure in favor of a more spiritual vocabulary of transformation.

All of us must do our best to live gracefully in the present
moment. I now see depression as akin to being tied to a chair with
restraints on my wrists. It took me a long time to realize that I only
magnify my distress by struggling for freedom. My pain diminished
when I gave up trying to escape completely from it. However, don't
interpret my current approach to depression as utterly fatalistic. I do
whatever I can to dull depression's pain, while premising my life on
its continuing presence. The theologian and philosopher Thomas
Moore puts it well with his distinction between cure and care. While
cure implies the eradication of trouble, care "appreciates the mystery
of human suffering and does not offer the illusion of a problem-free
life."

MELANCHOLY
AND THE MUSE

❧

Ann Beattie

I DON'T KNOW WHAT IT would be like not to be a writer. Part of the reason I became a writer was because in dealing with ordinary problems, my imagination is usually quite deficient. If the problem can best be solved in a way that doesn't require imagination, I'm all for tackling it through logic. Since my coping skills are not great, however, on a daily basis I tend to feel defeated. Even those times I have to deal with the mistakes made by others, coping tends to leave me feeling defeated, however successful the results. I'm not one of those crafty people who sees that the tip of a shoelace can be used as a flint. I don't improvise well. I'm decisive, but alas: my temperament does me in time after time, because my decisiveness is tempered by caution. I am not an entirely different being when I write, but because writing removes me from the world, I can at least pretend that things might be as I want them to be, if only I—I, alone— imagine correctly. In writing, I dismiss the idea of caution versus risk, because the concept of caution doesn't apply: caution is counterindicated when dealing with a rough draft. When revising, I'm capable of replacing entire pages with an asterisk and moving emphatically through time. It comes with the territory—dispensing with what's unnecessary, however much you like it. You have to trust your intuition about where you're going, and go, however unfamiliar the territory. If this sounds like some artistic version of military training, it is. But the thing is, as a writer you never get out of boot camp. All your practice, and all your resolve, to say nothing of your high standards, will not necessarily get you anywhere. In the military, you learn how to protect yourself, but being safe is the last thing that will serve you as a writer. As a writer, you spend time forgetting rules, forgetting what you know, so you can write, instead, those things your characters know. Quite often, characters serve the function of informing writers of things he or she does not know. Past writing performance—at least, in my experience—counts for little. Neither the routine, nor the triumphs that sometimes result from adhering to that routine, can be depended upon. I have sometimes taken down books I've published from the shelves and been amazed that there was a time when I apparently wrote one sentence after another, followed by even *more* sentences, to form a paragraph. Such an odd activity: needing to simultaneously remember and to forget something in order to bring into focus what did not happen, but might have.

That I've gotten used to, but the notion that I might work a more general sort of magic, making things happen, legitimizing writing, has begun to seem downright peculiar to me. I am not in a different position from any other writer who has written a number of published books, of course. In fact, it is because of our publications that we are being consulted. People in the profession ask me to endorse writing—sometimes mine, more often the writing of others. I might be asked to endorse it by teaching it. Or by explaining to a book group how I came to write a particular novel. Or I might be asked to respond, in writing, to someone's forthcoming book. This list of things is quite long, but you get the idea. The caller assumes I'm not only able to do something, but to speak clearly and reasonably about my success, or lend my success to others, like a cashmere sweater.

I once wrote a story, "Janus," about a real estate agent who believes she can make sales by placing what she considers a sort of magic bowl in the houses she is trying to sell. Until recently, I never thought of the story as analagous to my situation as a writer, but one day I realized that, in writing, of course one always brings out a magic bowl, so to speak, in order to dazzle the reader. But then I thought: Another way to look at it is that I'm not the magician, I'm the gullible audience. The other side has a bowl, too—a bigger, brighter one—and that bowl's also being used as a lure. Drink from it and you'll be complicitous. You'll be seduced: flattered to be consulted as a so-called authority, appointed as spokesperson, presumed to have influence. Even if you don't believe it, you'll be up against others who have their own reasons and need to believe it. The difficult thing, I have found, is not alienating and insulting those people as you try to protect yourself and your right to write.

Writers are such private, solitary people. They may become things other than that, but the writing almost without exception gets done because of an inwardness, a sense of privacy that you retain, even though you know that the piece you write may go public. The perspective the writer has on himself or herself seems crucially important to me, regardless of other people's perspectives. I nodded my head in agreement with Charles Simic, when he said in a recent interview: "The plain truth is that we are going to die. Here I am, a teeny speck surrounded by boundless space and time, arguing with the whole of creation, shaking my fist, sputtering, growing even eloquent at times, and then—poof! I am gone. Swept off once and for all. I think that's very, very funny." Though Simic would certainly not seem a likely "teeny speck," I like his point. At the same time, when I first read Simic's response, my impulse was not to laugh, but to admit that I'd been brought up short. It reminded me that one of the dangers of writing is taking oneself too seriously. I don't see how anyone can be a writer without being dedicated to the task, but the line between seriousness and defensiveness is difficult to distinguish. It takes real effort to step back and assess the validity of certain kinds of criticism; the most difficult criticism to take, for me, is when the reader confuses the writer—the personal psychology, or personal philosophy, or even personal habits of the writer—with the writing itself. I know that some of the time, some of these things apply. But I become depressed when I see that what I create has been misperceived as a reenactment of my life, and I become melancholy (is this the good girl's euphemism for depression?) when I realize that by agreeing to be photographed and interviewed and whatever other un-Pynchonesque things I've done, I've been complicitous.

It is a strange process one undertakes to get something written. To deflect attention from the real oddities of writing, I've joked, over the years, about the pleasure of not having to dress for the job (my T-shirts are my nightgowns, and my nightgowns get worn as tops, tucked into jeans), and about the perplexity of the UPS man, who must have fantasies about the lady he wakes up at noon. Sure, on some level it's funny. But when I talk this way, I also present myself—however ludicrous the figure I conjure up—as being in charge. Which is true, and not true. Any profession that others romanticize—which exempts very few professions—will usually continue to be seen as exciting, at the very least intensely *interesting,* even when things are looked at squarely. Of course, the truth is that it doesn't matter how the writing gets done, just that it does. If it helps the writer to be reinforced by the cynical or optimistic thoughts of another writer, or if the writer convinces himself or herself that the standards another writer sets must indeed be met, or if it helps to remember a maxim of Malraux's or to ascribe to Harry Mathew's idea that one might at least write twenty lines a day, that's fine. If, as writer, you confuse yourself with other writers, you might add to your beliefs the idea that it is necessary to keep a journal or drink to excess or to write standing up. The writers' Hippocratic oath is mumbo-jumbo, paraphrased as: Maybe this; Maybe that; Also consider; Perhaps it is true that; There are certain restrictions when writing in first person singular; Don't let the bastards get you down.

I mention these things because often, when metamorphosed for a day from worker bee to queen, I find myself behind a podium, as if I must know many truths, answering questions, or in some similar situation in a seminar room at a university, or speaking to an interviewer, or even on the rare occasions when I'm recognized by a person with a question about *The Accidental Tourist* . . . I mention these things because I romanticize writers a bit, myself, and in my romantic conception of them they are quick-thinking and astute, so that I feel it would help me to have more reflexive responses. Even now, writing this, I am searching my mind for things I might have memorized that I'm unaware of ("Friends, Romans, countrymen"— which I was long ago forced to remember—is clearly no help at all). I can paraphrase any number of what I consider extremely astute observations about writing by Flannery O'Connor (I say to students who have brought out symbol before substance: "You know what O'Connor says about symbols: 'First and foremost it has to be a wooden leg.' "). If I have read something the night before, I sometimes imply that the text contains a philosophy by which I lead my life, which I then pretend to be quoting exactly ("Proust said that 'a picture's beauty does not depend on the things portrayed in it.' "). But then I forget. I may also be unusually resistant to what others tell me to do—a condition that describes many writers, and also a number of psychopaths. Why, ultimately, do I want but not want to retain these words of wisdom? I want them, most of all, because they are just what's needed to end discussions by seeming to be furthering them.

You can easily understand that a writer gets tired of familiar questions. Some questions are interesting, and that's worth hanging in for—being surprised, and, better yet, surprising yourself by the answer you come up with. But other questions seem perfunctory or to be asking (you can only hope) a more specific question that is the hidden dark chocolate center of the Tootsie Roll pop. Thus, "Do you write every day?" may actually be the person's way of asking whether you, personally, think that she, personally, is a bad mother for writing from seven to eight A.M., even if the baby pops a hernia. In another situation—say, while a reporter is holding a tape recorder near your face, as a photographer circles to get the right angle during a windstorm atop a Chicago newspaper building—it would be nice, it would be *easy* to turn off the chaos by hiding behind the words of an eminent writer. To deflect. To seem at once well informed and deferential, well versed in the craft of writing. The bottom line with a lot of people who speak to me, who question me, is that they want the process to be demystified. And they are asking this of someone who finds it endlessly mysterious.

To the perception of certain others, I am a more or less well-known writer, and therefore important and/or interesting, while from my perspective, I am a ludicrous and cowardly—or, to give myself a break—a confused and conflicted person. Believing that certain things came with the territory, years ago, when I began my career—being told point-blank that they did—I was lured out to put one toe in the water, then my foot, and finally my entire leg. But you spend nearly twenty-five years publicizing your books, and all but the heartiest begin to feel tired, skeptical, that the showbiz aspect of writing has nothing nothing nothing to do with the act of writing, or with the worth of that writing, so that there comes a point where you find that you have the choice of wading out for the horizon line (lightning or flashbulbs?) or slogging back to the beach, wiping yourself off, and going home.

It's funny—I can see that it's funny—to be asked to read at events sponsored by liquor distributors, who pass around glasses of booze as you read. It's also possibly quite entertaining to get a freebie on some island during the winter with a bunch of other writers assembled to schmooze with rich people who are advertisers, or whatever they are—discriminating people who pick through the dish of peanuts to find the cashews, so to speak—but my letter to *Miss Lonelyhearts* asks: *What does it all mean?*

To those who romanticize the writer's life it means that you've been sent a love note, and if you complain, you're sneering at it. The argument goes: Think of all the people who'd like to be you! Look at all you have! Audience, fans, imitators (disturbingly, the latter are synonymous in some people's minds with being admired, rather than condescended to, as you are). And if you don't want to be interviewed, why didn't you stay home?

Because home is home, and if you write at home, one way to escape the writing is to escape the home, is one answer. But at this point I should remember to say that leaving the writing room and publicizing one's writing is only one aspect of the profession. Much hard work, many depleted days, and quite a heavy dose of good luck precedes it. Most times, interviewers are well informed and professional. Publicists work such long hours that their employers might do well to consider that a variation of the Libby Zion case could also come to pass on their watch, since they are running a version of a hospital. Time and again I have been moved, boistered, appreciative of the wonderful letters and endorsements of me that have come my way. There are great things about being a writer. But I'm not writing the ray-of-sunshine essay, I'm writing the gray-cloud one. I'm writing the one about one writer's only partially successful attempt to keep the world at bay, as well as some of the bizarre and unwanted perceptions held by people in that world that haven't exactly helped me along. I screen calls (double protection: unlisted number); I have no lecture bureau (my line on that is: *It can be bad enough dealing with those who went to the trouble of tracking you down because they ostensibly wanted you*). I will generalize here and say that writers often have that one-toe-in, one-toe-out ambivalence about the act of writing, though if they are compelled somehow, some way, they will do it. But ask these same conflicted creatures to go public with what they've done, and all but the boldest will hang back, wishing to avoid eye contact, hoping that they'll be spared and that no one will ask them to dance. Writing is such a private activity that going public with it later can be doubly difficult for someone who has spent long periods listening to voices in his or her head, correcting and amending those voices, letting those voices out, and bringing them back again. Writers know that this has nothing to do with ordinary social intercourse. The whole process is antithetical to being sociable. What people outside the profession rarely recognize is that writers' contradictory and/or self-destructive behavior (getting rid of obligations and other impediments to writing, then staring out the window) can be deliberately contrived to build tension, rather than to dissipate it.

To get in shape for writing, many writers do exactly the opposite of what athletes do: they get as out of shape as they can, through as many depressing and unsavory ways as anyone can imagine. It's understandable, on some level, because the writer is convinced— rightly or wrongly—that whatever the writer may have discovered in her previously completed writing will almost certainly have deserted her. If she remembers it, it's tainted by being predictable, or worse yet, a *device;* on the other hand—surely she remembers *something?* Athletes don't have to flex their muscles and feel them before swimming or throwing a javelin because they know that their body is in shape. It's taken effort and discipline, and things are never perfect, but in theory, considering the size of that bicep . . . I know athletes have bad days, but they can train, while generally speaking, I don't think there are ways writers can train to be better writers. Discipline, I suppose, is common to both athlete and writer, but with writers, sadly, it doesn't necessarily result in anything usable. No, the writer is a good stereotype of the ninety-eight pound weakling—the girl or guy who's terrifically out of shape because he or she has taken pains to be that way. I mention this because the sneaky truth is that while some writers are in great physical shape, writers in general have almost been forced to make a mind-body split because of the time put in sitting on one's ass. Yes, some go right from the poem to the treadmill, but I don't think I'm wrong in noticing that much of the time exercise, conducive to the release of endorphins, is counterindicated when one is trying to have inspirations.

For writers, a certain amount of pressure is necessary before beginning, and one of the ways of building that pressure is to become dismayed with oneself. Many writers most vivid writing has been devoted to deriding themselves for their faults. I can't count the times I've had writers explain that they're starting a diet when they finish their manuscript, or that the light at the end of the tunnel is the annual end-of-summer softball game, which they're going to (vague threat; don't believe it) whether they've finished that book or not. Conventional advice is that when one is about to do something difficult, one should take a deep breath, let it out, and then begin. Writing, however, is not analogous to being stretched out on a massage table. It's probably slightly analogous to being the masseuse: seeing what muscles are tight and going after them; considering the whole body, and then considering it incrementally; proceeding on the basis of the thoughts in one's brain, but also through the thoughts in one's fingertips.

At this point in my writing life, writing is much harder than it used to be. I can mention several factors, outside factors, that I think have influenced my feelings about this, and I *will* mention them, even though I am embarrassed that I know better, yet I have let them intrude. They include, but are by no means restricted to: negative reviews of my work in which the reviewer did not like a book I also did not write; requests for blurbs of other people's books that are sent to me, sometimes three or four a day; my trips to chain bookstores, where inevitably the book I am looking for is misshelved, and the greatest ingenuity is required to find it, regardless of where the computer erroneously says it is to be located (I recommend searching, yourself, for Geoff Dyer's *Out of Sheer Rage*). To be less polite about what makes me weary, I could have spoken of the three things above that bother me as (1) stupid people who can't read the text in front of them; (2) desperate (nice) people perpetuating desperation by routine acts of desperation; and (3) Barnes & Noble. However these things are named, they are here to stay.

No matter. I am not alone in bearing grudges against reviewers who have doomed a book's chances because they've missed the point, the tone, *everything*; I am more inundated than some writers with galleys, and less inundated than others. Lighten up, Beattie—you've had many a good cappuccino at a Barnes & Noble. I have to realize (I'm talking to myself, trying to make it register by writing it down, since it hasn't helped to keep it in my head) that it's a different world than it was when I began. I know that. So why am I having so much trouble adjusting? In part, because I'm not the only dinosaur. The things I've complained about and am largely at a loss to explain are subjects that come up with other writers I speak to. They, too, are annoyed, saddened, upset, confused, and maybe—one writer wouldn't ask another writer this—writing less because of it. (Cardinal rule: You *never* say anything that could whammy another writer.) (I anticipate a few letters from my writer friends saying, No, no, writing *more* because of it, and you can, too!)

Maybe some of the problem is that I was too effective, years go, at keeping things at bay, and it gave me a sense of false security that's been intruded upon, now, because of the sheer number of things going on, and going on so publicly. Who would have believed ten years ago that there would be a column on publishing in *The New York Times*? Maybe some of it has to do with so many more MFA programs that have become pitching machines for writers coming at us in far greater numbers—maybe because of things like that, Yours Truly, Sensitive Spirit has become exposed to the reality that writing is a business, a burgeoning business filled with problems (read the column) of such magnitude that I can't help but be reminded of my vulnerability within this system constantly—reminded that, increasingly, I'm more and more helpless.

In retrospect, I see that I had an advantage when I started out, and that advantage was that I didn't know what I was up against, didn't think of the business of writing at all, never suspected that so many manuscripts were vying for so few positions. So, with the good fortune to be ignorant, I proceeded. I'm not saying that numbers, if I'd known them, would have deterred me. Or that I succeeded only because of good fortune. But what I'll never know is whether there was, in those days, anything that corresponded to the amount of desperation that's floating around now: sincere and serious people's desperation in the face of what seems to be some unconquerable monster. That preoccupies me, but more than that I wonder whether, back then, there was so much burning desire. For a lack of what else to call it, I'll call it burning desire: people getting degree after degree in writing; people eager to pay to schmooze on mountaintops in summer; people who ruin their own lives and the lives of others by relentlessly pursuing their dream of being a writer, which, in this culture, is quite different from being a person who writes. In some ways, I'd be relieved to know that things were the same: that there were more degrees, more mailings, more of everything than I knew. That would stop me from feeling that I'm standing still while an avalanche is happening. It would make me see how silly I was, not to realize that the stakes were so high, and so very very meaningful, apparently. It might make me less confused about why writers are considered stars. Surely some of it is necessary forgetting, because I can remember complaining to my sort-of neighbor Donald Barthelme that the postman had rung my bell one day, and I'd gone down three floors to receive what turned out to be his novel. Donald listened with slight sympathy. When I pressed the point, he explained to me that he had recently been given a manuscript by his exterminator. So maybe it was always, all of it, precarious beyond reason and a circus I mistook for one spotlit act. Some days, the sheer amount of desire and longing to publish, succeed, publish some more begins to seem that all the world is in adolescence, with its heightened sense of urgency, while I become the flip side of the cliché: the parent—in any case, the older person—who does, but does not quite understand.

Which takes me back to those moments when you're totally involved in what you're writing, on a roll, delighted enough to thank any deity you believe in that you thought of the right word or the *wrong* word, better yet the *wrong* word, but that wrong word brought forth such expansive possibilities. You have to love writing for the thing itself, not for its yellow hair. I know that. And when I'm involved, those times things are going right, I'm undistractible, unflinching, unhinged by exhilaration. I remember that. It's just that after being at this for so long, okay, I didn't expect it to be easy, that would have been nuts, to expect it would become easy when it never was . . . it was just that a certain naïveté I had then more easily permeated the cell walls of my sentences, and I saw—not with regularity, but I did see—things I didn't know I knew. Maybe those things are still there, but I'm confused; I now think, *Hmm—I might have known that.* Then, when I didn't know something, I didn't know it. I didn't question whether I might have known and forgotten, or whether what emerged might be just a momentary, jaded thought about something about which I might otherwise have equilibrium. Then I knew a mystery to be a mystery: it was a surprise, if it was therefore something new, something I didn't know I knew until I wrote it, and wrote it *that* way.

As you get older, fortunately—and unfortunately—the pressure builds. As I've said before, it can be a wonderful incendiary force. The fire can come from without or from within, and if you're an imaginative enough person, you can sometimes manage to pretend that one thing is the other. So while I do believe that many of the things that come along with being a writer are worrisome and call one's attention to the huge numbers of books in the world and to the high hurdles one is expected to jump (all photographers absent until you jump them, and then you're asked to jump for a re-creation). The greater concern is whether talent will hold, and if so, what can be done with it so that the writing is not merely excellent, but something more. Something which, paradoxically, has to do—if it isn't too much to hope for—with staying naive.

The middle-aged muse is malcontent. Where before she whispered the strangest fragments, now she clears her throat and presents, almost audibly, too many recognizable statements. There's ambient sound, too, saying, *It's the World's Fault*. Which it is, damn it, sometimes, to some extent—but it's also your fault (I'm talking about myself, but I'm a fiction writer, so I can pretend it's you), because when you were young, the muse came and you didn't realize that the deal was that it had to go both ways: you had to fend things off and keep a private, silent, mind-easy place for the muse; you had to care for the muse, as well as she cared for you, or she'd become strident, rather than inspirational. It is an occasion for melancholy, realizing that you might have gone a little too public, being diverted by what you construed as writerly obligations, listening to too much chatter, letting those seemingly important but ultimately very unimportant things infiltrate where once the muse had time and space to alight.

GHOST IN THE HOUSE

❧

Donald Hall

FOR TWENTY-THREE YEARS, UNTIL SHE died of leukemia in 1995, I was married to the poet Jane Kenyon. When I first met her, Jane was moody. Laughing extravagantly with other student poets, she was funny, outrageous, and smart. Then she would go silent, withdraw, her mouth curved down, her forehead knotted. Most of the time when she felt low, she kept to herself. She consulted a university doctor who prescribed a drug that appeared to deepen her depression. When we were first married, she spent two years in psychoanalytical therapy, which did not cure depression but which helped her to interpret feelings, to avoid the emotional erratum slips that most of us should wear on our foreheads: "For 'compassion' read 'anger' throughout."

Three years after we married, Jane and I moved to the isolation of a New Hampshire farmhouse, largely at Jane's urging. For twenty years we lived in the same house, inhabiting a double solitude. We thrived in cohabitation and in boundaries. Each leaving her/his separate hive of writing, we would meet in the kitchen for another coffee, mid-morning, without speaking; we would pat each other's bottom. In our silence, we were utterly aware of each other's presence. In our devotion to poetry and each other, our marriage was intimate and content.

And nothing is simple. By temperament, I was impatient, always eager, as Jane said, for "the next thing, the next thing." Often she sank into speechless discontent while I remained energetic. Then in her poems I encountered depression that was more than moodiness. Old harness in the barn suggested itself as a noose. There were poems of blankness and lethargy:

> *I had to ask two times*
> *before my hand would scratch my ear.*

In another she wrote:

> *—The days are bright*
> *and free, bright and free.*
>
> *Then why did I cry today*
> *for an hour, with my whole*
> *body, the way babies cry?*

In time, Jane was diagnosed with a bipolar mood disorder.

> *... the soul's bliss*
> *and suffering are bound together*
> *like the grasses ...*

She was never delusional; her mania was notable but God never telephoned her. On the other hand, her depression ranged from deep sadness to agony, and Jane was more frequently depressed than manic.

Psychiatrists have documented the high incidence of bipolarity among artists. Writers are the most bipolar—and among writers, poets. See "Manic-Depressive Illness and Creativity" by Kay Redfield Jamison in *Scientific American*, February 1995. One percent "of the general population suffer from manic-depression." Jamison cites figures for mood disorders in artists, depending on different models of sampling, that go upward from 38 percent.

No one can induce bipolarity in order to make poems. Does the *practice* of the art exacerbate a tendency? Surely for the artist the disorder is creative in its manic form—excitement, confidence, the rush of energy and invention. Maybe DNA perpetuates bipolarity because mania or hypomania benefits the whole tribe, inventing the wheel and Balzac's *Cousine Bette*, while depression harms only the depressive and those close to the depressive.

Ten years after we married, I watched Jane lower into the blackest place. She had been a principal caregiver for her father, and she was with him when he died. She stayed up all night with him when morphine confused him and, with her mother, tended him twenty-four hours a day. The cancer that wasted him, his collapse in mind and tissue, commanded her asleep or awake. In 1982, six months after the death, we drank a beer one night in the small town of Bristol. As we drove back, Jane sank under a torment and torrent of wild crying. At home she curled on the sofa in the fetal position and wept for three days. I wanted to hold and comfort her, as I had earlier done when she was low, but now I could not touch her. If I touched her, she would want to scream.

She spoke little, in gasps, but she told me that she was not angry at me, that she loved me, that her despair had nothing to do with me. It was heartbreaking not to touch her, not to be able to give comfort.

Doubtless my anxious presence across the room was another burden. I understood and believed that I was not responsible for her melancholia. In later returns of her sickness, she continued to worry that I would misinterpret her feelings. She persuaded two doctors to tell me that her depression was caused by the chemistry of her brain, that it was endogenous and unrelated to our life together.

That first black time, she gradually stopped weeping and her mood rose slightly. She saw our internist, who recognized clinical depression and prescribed drugs; I'm not sure which drug he began with but it must have been a tricyclic. The Prozac class of drugs (which didn't help Jane) was not yet available. For advice on treatment, our doctor spoke with Dr. Charles Solow, head of psychiatry at Dartmouth-Hitchcock Hospital. Later, Jane visited Dr. Solow regularly, and relied on him for treatment until she died. He prescribed a variety of drugs, and talked with her continually—kind, supportive, sympathetic. Jane was medicated most of the rest of her life. She kept wanting to survive without pharmaceutical help, and in 1992 tried the experiment of going naked. A precipitate plunge returned her to medication.

In "Having it Out with Melancholy," she makes a stanza:

> *Elavil, Ludiomil, Doxepin,*
> *Norpramin, Prozac, lithium, Xanax,*
> *Wellbutrin, Parnate, Nardil, Zoloft.*
> *The coated ones smell sweet or have*
> *no smell; the powdery ones smell*
> *like the chemistry lab at school*
> *that made me hold my breath.*

The tricyclic Doxepin helped her for three years, the longest stretch without a deep trough. During these years she had her ups and downs, she was sad and she was gay, but Doxepin appeared to prevent deep depression. As she inhabited a fragile comfort, she could work on her poems. Then her body learned how to metabolize the drug and she needed larger doses, until it was no longer safe to increase the dose.

This drug, like others, gave her a dry mouth, but the side effects were not miserable. Some drugs did nothing for her, or reduced the intensity of orgasm, or included side effects nasty enough to disqualify them. When she was manic in 1984, she took lithium, which she hated. Lithium is known to suppress creativity. After that year, she was never manic for long episodes. Often she dosed daily on a combination of drugs—Wellbutrin maybe, a tricyclic or two, a trace of lithium. Another drug that helped was an old MOA-inhibitor, Nardil, which kept her from depression for almost a year, but limited her sleep so much that she became exhausted and had to stop taking it. Despite her energy and relief from dolor, I didn't like some side effects of Nardil, nor did her closest friends. She seemed much as she seemed in mania: dogmatic, combative, sometimes querulous, abrasive sometimes—without her characteristic alertness to the feelings of others. But Nardil held depression off.

She described herself in a section of "Having it Out with Melancholy":

9   WOOD   THRUSH
High on Nardil and June light
I wake at four,
waiting greedily for the first
notes of the wood thrush. Easeful air
presses through the screen
with the wild, complex song
of the bird, and I am overcome

by ordinary contentment.
What hurt me so terribly
all my life until this moment?
How I love the small, swiftly

beating heart of the bird
singing in the great maples;
its bright, unequivocal eye.

With Dr. Solow's help, Jane avoided deepest depression much of the time, but its misery lurked at the edges of her daily life, and sometimes sprang from the shadows. I remember Jane on the bathroom floor banging her head against toilet and pipes. Another time she arrived trembling after driving back from Concord: she had fought all the way the impulse or desire to drive off the road into a boulder or a stone wall. And I remember a terrible Christmas Day, when I gave her as usual too many presents, each of which depressed her further. Someone who is stupid, bad, ugly, fat, and hateful does not deserve presents; gifts mock her. After this bout lapsed, the presents I had given her always retained the tint of misery. The counterpart can be true: recollections of a manic experience may cheer you up, even though you know that the joy was endogenous and ended in depression.

Despite her thoughts about hanging herself with a horse's harness, despite her fear of driving into walls, I did not think that Jane would kill herself. Maybe her treatment kept her from the extremes that lead to suicide. Surely her Christianity helped: she knew that self-destruction would be an insult to God. There was also her sensitivity to pain and her fear of it. This woman, who dreaded pain so much, suffered fifteen months of physical agony in her attempt to survive leukemia. Her desire to live, when she knew that her chances were poor, astonished her. Only at one moment during her illness did she seem depressed in the old way (she was *not* cheerful about leukemia) and it was while her mother lay dying three thousand miles away—the daughter unable to nurse, herself requiring intense care. The hospital psychiatrist in Seattle noted "suicidal ideation without intent," which may well describe her earlier thoughts and images of self-destruction.

Much of the time, during her last twelve years of physical

health, Jane dropped low, she suffered, but she functioned; she wrote poems especially as she climbed out of depression. Her most direct account is "Having it Out with Melancholy." It pained her to write this poem. It pained her to expose herself. But writing the poem also helped her to set depression out, as she knew it—depression and its joyful tentative departure. She wanted the poem to help others who were afflicted. The first time she read it aloud, at the Frost Place in Franconia, she paused during her reading, resisting tears. When she ended, a line of people waited to talk with her: depressives, people from the families of depressives.

When Jane was mildly depressed, medium-depressed, supported by drugs but weary and fatigued and without serenity, she found a way to raise her spirits and energy for a few hours. In her worst blackness, I could not touch her, but in grayness an orgasm would make her happy and eager to work. She leaped out of bed to write or garden. Therefore, we made love whether we felt like it or not. Endorphins restored, for a moment, energy and the desire to work. Sometimes her climax was merely distant thunder. Such a side effect banished Paxil to the wastebasket.

Mania became obvious first in 1984, but looking back I can recall earlier moments, including a prolonged mystical experience in 1980. She felt the presence of the Holy Ghost, and felt that the spirit was female. The presence passed but its memory remained. Mystics are bipolar: Gerard Manley Hopkins wrote sonnets of ecstasy and sonnets of despair; Saint John of the Cross described the dark night of the soul. If God enters the human spirit, why should He not use the brain's wiring?

Of her 1984 mania I remember most clearly two or three months, spring and summer of that year. During this first extended elation, I did not know what I confronted. I thought: I must learn to live with an entirely changed woman; I was married to someone I had never known. Frugal Jane *had* to buy a peridot ring; indecisive Jane, who always asked me to make choices—what restaurant to go to, which night to see the play, what book to read aloud—knew *exactly* what we should do, when and where. In her superabundant energy she was bossy: before, she had hidden in my shadow; now she charged forward as bright as the sun of June. She was consumed by desire; on her thirty-seventh birthday we seemed to make love all day long.

The radical change confused and upset me. When Jane went manic I fell into depression. She soared up and I plunged down—a moody seesaw. I felt "suicidal ideation without intent." Then I understood, with shame, that for years I had used her depression to think well of myself: I was the rock, unchanging in all weathers; I was the protector. Now her manic elation and her certainty cast me down. After this first episode of her mania and my response, I put away my complacent self-congratulation.

She fell into depression after mania ceased. Six months later she turned manic again, weeks not months, and spoke carelessly, hurtfully, without malicious intent—in ways she would not have done without mania. By this time I knew what was happening. Thereafter, mania was brief.

Her friends sympathized entirely with her depression but also suffered. Although we were relatively reclusive, we had friends at our church, poet friends who came for weekends, old friends from Ann Arbor, our families. Jane when she was well spent more time in company than I did, lunching with women friends in New London twelve miles away. Her closest friends were two other writers, Alice Mattison and Joyce Peseroff. They saw each other when they could, and workshopped together several times a year. The excitement of their meetings exhausted and elevated Jane. Depression never canceled a workshop, but once she asked Alice not to come calling from a summer place in Vermont. Every month Jane and I drove to Connecticut to see my mother, in her eighties, to shop for her and to visit. (Jane used the opportunity to see Alice, who lived nearby.) Several times, when she was depressed, I had to drive down alone. Sometimes I put visitors off at Jane's urging. I telephoned a dying friend to tell him he could not visit. I canceled a skiing visit from my son and friends because Jane could not see anyone. Every summer Jane's brother, sister-in-law, and niece visited from Ann Arbor. Once I had to telephone and ask them not to come. It was generally I who telephoned, at Jane's request, because she could not herself make the call. On occasion when acquaintances made briefer visits, Jane remained in the bedroom with the door closed while I sat talking with them elsewhere.

One of the hardest things, if you are depressed, is to try to hold yourself up in the presence of others, especially others whom you love. I remember a birthday for granddaughters at my daughter's house. Jane stood looking on, wretched, hardly able to speak. She was quiet, there were many people, and she practiced invisibility. My daughter looked at her and said, "You're *miserable*, aren't you?" When Jane nodded Philippa spoke with sympathy and left her alone. You do not try to cheer up depressives; the worst thing you can do is to count their blessings for them.

Depression was a third party in our marriage. There were many happy third parties: poetry, lovemaking, the church, reading Henry James aloud, watching baseball, afternoons spent swimming and sunbathing by Eagle Pond. There were evenings of raucous laughter with friends, not mania but gaiety. Yet depression's ghost was omnipresent for both of us, in dread if not in actuality. She was obdurate in the face of it, trying to be well, writing out of depression to exorcise the illness for her own sake and for the sake of others. Then listlessness and sorrow and self-loathing would overcome her again; then with new medication she would return again to her daily life.

BACK

We try a new drug, a new combination
of drugs, and suddenly
I fall into my life again

like a vole picked up by a storm
then dropped three valleys
and two mountains away from home.

I can find my way back. I know
I will recognize the store
where I used to buy milk and gas.

I remember the house and barn,
the rake, the blue cups and plates,
the Russian novels I loved so much,

and the black silk nightgown
that he once thrust
into the toe of my Christmas stocking.

Jane always understood that her melancholia was inherited, present from birth, but she did not go on medication until after her father's death. Maybe long-term caregivers are more prone to subsequent depression, or to exacerbation of depression—even more prone than people shocked by a sudden unexpected death, who grieve for words unspoken. (With a long illness, everything can be said—if anything can be said.) Trauma affects the chemistry of the brain. The death of the cared-for one—as well as the desperate prolonged caregiving itself, which failed in its purpose—may make changes in the brain like the changes of posttraumatic stress syndrome. For fifteen months I sat by Jane's side, obsessed by her leukemia and her suffering. In the hospital I fetched warm blankets and made lists of questions for our hematologist. At home I saw to her pills, and infused her with food and drink and chemicals. I helped her walk and cleaned up after her.

After she died, I was miserable in my grief. I screamed, I spoke to her pictures and at her grave, I wrote her letters in verse. I dreamed that she had run off with another man; I could not sleep because I dreaded dreaming. But I was not depressed in the way that Jane had been depressed.

It has been observed that the survivor often takes on characteristics of the dead. To embody them? To fill the vacancy? Six months after Jane's death I found myself standing near the birdfeeder with

Peterson's *Guide* in my hand. The birds had been Jane's preserve for twenty years at the farm. I thought birds were just fine, I loved their song, but I didn't know one from another. With Jane gone I was taking her place. Among her other symptoms, Jane was affected by the growing darkness of October, November, December. I had always enjoyed the short days: they felt cozy. Late autumn in the year of her death, something like seasonal affective disorder overcame me. I brought her light box from her study to the top of my desk.

Thirteen months after her death I became manic for three months: I lost twenty pounds, slept two or three hours a night, and pursued women boldly. Perhaps my sexual need was a response to nightmares of Jane's adulterous abandonment. Perhaps it was eros doing combat with thanatos. (I think of how lovemaking lifted Jane for a moment from gray depression.) Perhaps it was only the familiar symptom of mania. Amazed at my elderly energy, I never considered that I was manic or hypomanic until I crashed into despair and murderous rage, rapidly cycling. (I sought help, and have been helped.) Maybe I perpetuated Jane by imitating her. Maybe inherent bipolarity became activated, the brain altered because of caregiving, failure, and loss.

WRITING THE WRONGS OF IDENTITY

Meri Nana-Ama Danquah

FOR A PERIOD OF TIME after clinical depression became the literary topic du jour, it seemed as if most of the work I read about the illness was written by white Jewish women from Boston who had, at some point in their lives, been treated at McLean. I must admit, I always thought it rather odd that one city could contain so much sadness, that one hospital could contain so many talented and successful people among its roster of former patients. Nevertheless, I would search for these books. I would purchase each and every one as soon as they were published, take them home, and sit barefoot and cross-legged on my couch, with a box of Kleenex at my side, while I read about the lives of these people in this city that systematically manufactured great writers and even greater misery.

As a reader, what I cherish most about literature is the permission it grants me to escape the confines of my own life. No matter who or what I am, have been, or want to be, I am able, for the length of a book, to inhabit a new reality, one that the author constructs. My relationship to the literature of depression, however, is somewhat different. It is based not on a desire to lose myself in the pages of a book, but on a relentless need to find, and define, a very specific part of myself through the book. That part which melancholy stalks like a jealous lover. For many years, the only place in this huge world of words where it appeared as if I was welcome to carry out that search was inside the narratives of these women. These white Jewish women from Boston.

Of course, not all of the work on depression was written by them. During the period of time to which I am referring, a number of authors were writing of madness, of disorders and moods. There were a few books and essays by men and other women, some of whom were not Jewish and did not come from or live anywhere near New England. Regardless of their gender or place of origin, these writers did have one thing in common: they were white. All of them. Which placed me in the peculiar position of having very little choice but to look to these white people for some sense of validation, some basic understanding of who I am as a depressive and, ultimately, as a person underneath this illness.

There are times when I feel like I've known depression longer than I've known myself. It has been with me since the beginning, I think. Long before I learned to spell my name. No, even longer than that. I'm sure that before I could even speak my own name or learn to love the color of my skin, this hollow heartache was following me, patiently awaiting the inevitable crossing of our paths, planning my future unhappiness. I've always been aware that something in my life was not quite right, if not totally wrong. My scales were never balanced. For every twelve joys, I had twenty-five sorrows. And each sorrow was like a song. A melodious seduction bringing me closer and closer to this terrible sickness which has cost me lovers and friendships, money and opportunities, time and more time. So much wasted time.

At first, I had a hard time figuring out why there were no glossy magazine articles or literary books about depression by black people. I've never thought of myself as average, but I've also never thought of myself as an anomaly. Surely there were other black women suffering from depression, questioning their sanity, searching for an affirmation, if not an answer. Why were they not coming forward or writing about it like their white counterparts?

In deciding exactly what it was that I wanted to share in this essay about my experiences with clinical depression, I realized that mental illness and race are topics that can not be divorced from one another. Not easily. Not for me. You see, the mask of depression is not all that different from the mask of race. So much of clinical depression has to do with identity, with images, with how those of us who suffer from the disease perceive ourselves and how, based on these oftentimes grossly distorted perceptions, we interact with others. So much of racism has to do with the same. It, too, barrages its prey with groundless images; it concerns itself more with the fiction of a prescribed identity than with the notion of any true individuality. It, too, seeks to blur a person's vision of herself, and her place in the world. Racism is also an illness. Perhaps not in the same way as depression, but an illness nonetheless. To contend with either one is bad enough. To grapple with both at the same time . . . that's enough to drive a person—pardon the expression—"crazy." Welcome to my insanity.

As a black woman struggling with depression, I don't know which I fear more: the identity of illness or the identity of wellness. One might imagine that the identity of wellness would, naturally, be the most desirable of the two. But that's usually the problem with desire: what you see is not necessarily what you get. The societal images of black female wellness, as evidenced (still) in present-day popular culture, have nothing at all to do with being well. Far from it. They have everything to do with the lies of history—a history that, invariably, has been shaped, created, or informed by the poisonous ideology of racism.

In these lies black women are strong. Strong enough to work two jobs while single-handedly raising twice as many children. Black women can cook, they can clean, they can sew, they can type, they can sweep, they can scrub, they can mop, and they can pray. Black women can fuck, too. They are rarely romanticized, just oversexualized. Hookers, whores, Thursday-night concubines, and sultry-voiced back-alley blues club singers with Venus Hottentot hips. Either that or they are desexualized, just straight-up masculinized, mean-faced and hardened. Whatever the case, black women are always doing. They are always servicing everyone's needs, except their own. Their doing is what defines their being. And this is supposed to be wellness?

Not that the identity of illness is any better. Its only appeal is the allowance for vulnerability. You are able to need others, to invite their assistance, to accept their love—the catch is that you also have to be fragile. Anybody who's ever *really* been sick knows that the tolerance level for illness is low. Once the get-well roses begin to wilt, everything changes. Compassion and caretaking turn into burdens and vulnerability becomes weakness.

If the illness is something as nebulous as depression, folks begin to treat it like a character flaw: you are lazy, incapable, selfish, self-absorbed. The list is pretty much the same regardless of one's race. But race cannot and should not be disregarded; there is no room in the black female identity for weakness, laziness, incapability, selfishness, self-absorption, or even depression.

If I were to say that reading all the books by those depressed white people did not have a profound impact on my ability to come to terms with my own battle against depression, it would be disingenuous. Each one was like a mirror. Even if the external reflection looked nothing at all like me, what I saw of the internal reality was an accurate representation. The disease was the same, the symptoms were the same. The resulting confusion and hurt were the same.

None of that was enough though. I craved wholeness. I wanted to recognize *all* of me. Yet no matter how much these authors' confessions assuaged the discomfort I felt within, their stories could only meet the marrow and bone. They could never move outward and touch the flesh, the blackness that dictated the world in which I existed. What they could, and did, do was inspire me to write my own story. In writing that story I began, finally, to see why voices like mine were all but absent in discussions about depression. Let me show you what I mean:

Anecdote #1: While I was in the process of writing what would eventually become a memoir about my journey through depression, I was invited to a dinner party. It was a rather boring affair, the type that's full of old blue-haired women with fake teeth, fake fur, and real pearls. Not only was I one of the few people in the room under fifty, I was the only nonwhite person there as well. It wasn't my scene, so I didn't have much to offer by way of conversation, but the friend who brought me was, for some reason, determined to have me meet and make nice with the other guests, probably under the misguided assumption that they could help my career as an emerging writer. With great pride, he told one woman that I was writing a book.

The woman asked about the topic of my book. My friend took it upon himself to answer. "A book about black women and depression." The woman chuckled. "Black women and depression?" she asked. "Isn't that kinda redundant?" Everybody who heard this comment, including my friend, found humor in it. They laughed and laughed. Their obvious approval encouraged the woman. "Don't get me wrong," she continued. "It's just that when black women start going on Prozac, you know the whole world is falling apart."

Anecdote #2: Another dinner party. This time everyone in attendance was black and under forty. I was only casually acquainted with most of the people there. There were several clusters of conversation, including one being held by a group of women huddled in the kitchen. I joined them, figuring their conversation would be the most interesting. At parties, talk that takes place in the kitchen is usually simmering with colloquialism and candor. They were discussing pregnancy and childbirth. Two of the women were expecting, and everyone was taking turns telling tales of their own delivery dramas and dispensing wisdom that they'd heard or overheard from somebody who knew somebody who was an expert on these matters. Statements like, "Cocoa butter will make the stretch marks disappear," and, "They say that if you only breast-feed for three months, they won't sag after your milk is gone." Then someone other than me dropped the "d" word. "Hey, do you guys know anything about postpartum depression? I've been hearing about it a lot lately."

"Depression? I don't think they were talking about us. That is not a luxury we can afford."

"I'm telling you," another woman added. "That's all about white folks who don't have any real problems, so they have to create stuff to complain about. If black women started taking to their beds and crying about postpartum depression, who'd be left to play nanny to all those little white babies?"

Anecdote #3: When I was a creative-writing MFA student at Bennington College, I met Robert Bly, Mr. Iron John himself, the epitome of white male sensitivity. He was a guest faculty member. I was in the cafeteria searching for a place to park my tray when I noticed that Liam Rector, the director of the program, was having lunch with Bly. I decided to sit with them. I was introduced to Bly as a nonfiction student. He glanced in my direction and said hello. Then Liam added, "Meri is writing a book about black women and depression." Robert Bly looked over at me again and said, without hesitation, sarcasm, or irony, "Whew. That's going to be one really long book."

There is a lesson in each of these encounters, a soft sinew of truth connecting pain to power. It's always alarming to hear such opinions. They never fail to shock me, render me speechless. I don't believe that anyone actually thinks black women are, in some way, immune to clinical depression. I think it's simply that the black female identity of wellness—and all its silences—is ultimately preferable to the loud revelations that lie beyond the black female identity of wellness. After all, the women at both dinner parties were right. When black women fall apart, the world as we know it also falls apart. The myth of Mammy comes tumbling down.

Based on his frank reaction, Robert Bly obviously had some idea of what is hidden behind that myth. He was right when he suggested that the despair which generations of black women have had to endure could fill volumes. And, in fact, it has. From folklore to old wives' tales to contemporary novels, we have attempted to write the wrongs of our identity, to claim a humanity. Yet by and large, this documentation has been relegated to the pages of fiction. Which still positions our stories under the label of a lie, the invention of an artful imagination. Which prevents us from being able to distinguish diagnosable illnesses, like depression, from adaptive responses to the inequity of our circumstances, like despair. Which keeps us feeling fraudulent— as if we're not "keeping it real"—when we are not able to get out of bed on any given morning, let alone rise up to the challenge of life's hardships. What will it take to heal us of this legacy?

There is strength in numbers. It's hard to be the only one of anything—the only disabled student in a school, the only single mother in a community, the only immigrant on the job. You are perpetually aware of your difference. After I met two other black women who were willing to openly admit that they were also dealing with depression, the sense of helplessness I had been feeling when I thought I was all alone turned into a sense of hopefulness. They were walking, talking, breathing people—not well-crafted characters. Their experiences authenticated mine in a way that nothing else could. Their presence addressed all of the questions and issues I had about what it means to be a black woman living with a psychological disorder. It means seeing yourself in a way that is often inconsistent with the way the world sees you. It means seeing yourself as a human being who is entitled to a wide range of human emotions and conditions, including illness and wellness.

By the time my memoir, *Willow Weep for Me*, was published, I had undergone various methods of treatment for my depression. Therapy, antidepressants, mood stabilizers—some of which were ineffective and others of which worked marvelously. I had become unashamed of the illness and unafraid of its stigma. Moreover, I had moved past the tendency to view my life against the blinding background of whiteness, the need to paint it with predetermined images of blackness. Every now and then, I find myself thinking about those white Jewish women from Boston. I find myself wondering about their reaction to *my* story. Do they read my work and see more than race? Can they enter my world and recognize something of themselves in my reflection?

ON LIVING BEHIND BARS

⌥

Nancy Mairs

IN TRUTH, THE WINDOWS AND doors were not barred. The windows were made of very small panes of glass sashed with heavy metal, so that although it was possible to break the glass (my friend Ed once smashed his hand through a pane, bloodying his arm from knuckles to shoulder), no opening was large enough to permit egress. The door to the ward was locked at all times, but with a doctor's permission one could get the staff to open it and thus could come and go almost at will. More important, for me at least, no one could enter the ward unless invited. Thus, the terrible, complicated, demanding world, fear of which made me flush and tremble with feverish nausea, was kept at bay. The only person who came through that door to see me was George, who arrived every night I lived there with a Brigham's chocolate ice cream soda, the only nourishment I would willingly take.

I lived for more than six months there, at Metropolitan State Hospital in Waltham, Massachusetts, most of that time on R2, the admitting ward for nonviolent patients; R3, a locked ward, was upstairs. There was also an R1, for geriatric patients, I think, and possibly an R4, but maybe I made these up. This narrative will be full of such gaps and lapses, because during the latter part of my stay my brain was zapped twenty-one times. No one seems sure how electroconvulsive therapy acts therapeutically, but everyone knows that it wreaks havoc with the short-term memory. What I have left are mostly random images, some in remarkable detail and clarity, but few embedded in any logically continuous context. I had once, many years later, a string of black clay Mexican beads on a nylon thread that snapped suddenly, in the middle of a class I was teaching, scattering little fish and birds and balls every which way. My students scrambled, retrieving many of them, and my foster son restrung them, in a new pattern necessitated by the missing pieces, into a shorter necklace. One can, to some extent, recover one's losses, but the bits that roll under the shelves, into the corners, out the door are gone for good.

I signed myself into Met State on an evening late in August 1967. Earlier in the day I had gone to my psychotherapist in a state of panic so overwhelming that I had lost all control over it. It was not a new condition—Dr. Levine had been treating me (for symptoms of depression and anxiety, I later learned) for months, as had several others before him—but by this time I was too debilitated to function at all; and he suggested that ten days of hospitalization, the standard term of commitment, might calm me enough so that I could try to resume my life. Was he lying to me? Did he know from the outset that ten days in a mental hospital, at least the first time, is only enough for coming apart altogether, and that the putting back together, if it gets done at all, will be prolonged and in some ways more dangerous than the collapse itself? Perhaps not. He can't have been many years older than I was, still in training as a psychiatrist, his head chock full of hysteria and vaginal orgasm, no doubt, and I think *he* panicked. He knew that he couldn't cope with me, that I was likely to die if left to my own devices, so he turned me over to the keepers of madwomen where whatever trouble I might cause could be closely contained.

After he, George, and I had agreed on this solution, he had some arrangements to make, so George and I left, returning later to pick up some paperwork. I think Anne may have been with us at least part of the day, but I'm not sure. She, like everyone else around me, had long since ceased to seem real; only George was left to populate my world. But I recall stopping at a park filled with play equipment which Anne particularly loved, and I don't think we'd have gone there without her. The day, hot and bright, took place in slow motion, under water. I wore flat sandals, a dress of blue cotton sprigged with lavender flowers, long-sleeved, high-waisted, and full, which my mother had made me as a maternity dress but which, thanks to the whim of fashion, remained serviceable. I cried a good deal. I knew no one who had been in a mental hospital. I couldn't believe that within a few hours I'd enter one myself. Here was failure—of nerve, of breeding—more drastic than I'd ever dreamed.

I was admitted to the hospital at night. I don't know why. It was a poor arrangement because it gave the whole transaction the flavor of an emergency, and I was quite panic-stricken enough without any extra theatrical effects. By this time I was sobbing reflexively, inconsolably, without cease. The admitting psychiatrist was a small Indian man (almost all the doctors there were foreigners working their way into the American system; if they were any good they quickly moved on to better hospitals or private practice). Dr. Haque. His accent was so strong that I couldn't understand most of what he said. "Why are you here? Why are you here?" he asked. I kept shaking my head and choking on tears. The silliness of this scene, both of us strangled, one on the English language and the other on grief, escaped me for sev-

eral years. Before long, Dr. Haque abandoned attempts at communication, wrote several prescriptions, and sent me upstairs. An attendant
locked the door behind me and set me in a chair in the small day-
room, where a number of patients were watching television. One of
them asked me if I had a match and, through an oversight in security,
I did. I sat among them, now dry-eyed, until someone shouted,
"Meds." I queued up, as I would four times a day in the months
ahead, and was given three tablets—one yellow, one blue, one
white—and a little translucent green football. Then I went to bed.

I hadn't been able to explain to Dr. Haque what brought me to Met
State, but I had no doubt that I was where I belonged. I had no doubt
that I was mad. How else account for the anguish I felt in the midst of
a life in every way satisfactory: marriage to an intelligent, loving
man; graduation with honors from a prestigious women's college; the
birth of a healthy and charming daughter; a lively job in which I'd
received a significant promotion within months of my hiring. How
account for the fact that I could no longer cross the threshold of my
apartment without George beside me, could not swallow food in anyone's presence but George's, and not always then. Not for many years
would I learn that both my situation and my symptoms made me a
prime candidate for matriculation at Met State. Not for even longer
would I glimpse the possibility that, though I have often been in terrible trouble, I have never been insane.

Only recently have I begun to concatenate my experiences into
patterns distinct from the narrative ground in which they are embedded: This process I call essay-writing. In doing so, I have been startled
at the durability of the terrible trouble I've been in. My earliest
memories are anxiety-ridden: While I sit in a high chair in the
kitchen of my grandmother Garm, I throw up into the dish painted
with red and blue morning glories on the tray; later, I've been crying
inconsolably for my lost blue blanket and a woman, Garm or perhaps
her mother, Buntie, rocks me in a darkened room as I stare out into

the lighted hall; my mother is nowhere around. I don't know when these incidents took place—if indeed I haven't made them up entirely—but it may have been during my three-week visit to Garm when my sister Sally was born. I was then not quite two. A few months earlier I had been hospitalized for rheumatic fever and had nearly died, not of the illness but of the sulfa used to treat me. I have no memories of this event, but it seems a likely root of the terror I felt at separation, especially from my mother.

As I got older, my distress grew greater, not less. The wider my horizons, the more space in my world for disaster, dreaded in the diaries I kept from the age of ten through my freshman year in college. The early diaries have disappeared, along with a string of pearls, a silver chain, my high-school yearbook, and a couple of dozen worn-out diapers I was going to use for dustrags, in one of my many moves. Thus, the first record I have of the patterns of being that would force me one day to commit myself to Met State occurs in 1957, a few months after the dissolution of my first true love affair and shortly after I entered a high school of about fifteen hundred students from a junior high of fewer than a hundred. Thrown entirely off balance, I wrote, "All is wrong. I don't understand *anything*. I'm completely upset, and tired, and numb. I hate so much, am indifferent to so much, and what love is left goes to the wrong places." I was, as usual, in the throes of an inappropriate crush: "Sometimes I wish I was still going with James. I was so happy. Now it seems I have nothing to live for except someone who doesn't live for me. Ah, my standards are all mixed up. Maybe if I understood algebra it would help. I'm bored. No, I'm just so very, very tired." I love the remark about algebra, both because it's funny and because it's true. My failure to understand algebra represented a failure to control my enlarging world, from which arose my confusion and panic, so that in a queer way my existence has been shaped by my inability to solve quadratic equations. One New Year's Eve, reflecting on the year just past, I spoke with an insight it has taken me most of the rest of my life to grasp: "I close this diary with something akin to tenderness. On its

pages are the bright, happy days in my little world. And then comes
the deep depression I have now, because I left this world, & it locked
me out." Any transition, any separation from the past, any movement
from a "little world" into a larger one resulted for me only in dread
and despair.

I lived in unutterable loneliness though seldom in solitude, since
my family was growing with Mother's remarriage and the birth of
my little brother and sister and I was heavily involved in academic
and social activities. My loneliness, in fact, only grew sharper when I
was in the presence of others, especially my peers. One of my earliest
school memories is of my "best friend," Susan Fowler, turning on me
and leading a band of children in taunting shouts—"Smitty Spider!
Smitty Spider!"—the mocking of my name landing like lacerations
in my flesh. From then on I felt tangential to any group, fearful of
outright exclusion yet ignorant of the rules of admission, of the
magic words that would let me all the way in. Gradually I learned a
bit of the language, enough to pose as a member of the group, but
the conflict I felt between the pose and my inward experience only
increased my sense of alienation.

Wearing the human mask, I stumbled ahead into life, tripping
time after time over my own terror. "I want so desperately to express
myself," I wrote in May 1958. "I can't stand this suppression. I want
to write, to act, to sing, anything. I can't. I can't." I railed against
myself for being lazy and disorganized. Heartsick over my failure to
have the highest marks in my class, I wrote at the beginning of 1959,
"I feel so inadequate, so small," and more than a year later, "If something doesn't happen, I'll scream. I am so empty, so hungering. I
know that deep within me lies something but I see it in comparison
with the talents of others & it is so pitifully small." By the time I got
to college, I was nearly paralyzed by dread of my inadequacy: "Why
can't I study? Today I put in only 2–3 hours of studying, when 6 hours
are required & I have this history exam tomorrow. I see the others
buried in their books & I know I have to be like them to succeed but I
don't do anything about it. I want to know but I don't want to learn.

I've got to settle down or I'll not be in Wheaton long and then oh God what will become of me?"

What will become of me? What will become of me? That question grew to be the ground of my mental existence, against which the details of my joys and sorrows were picked out. And the answer was always terrible. Never mind the successes I'd had in the past (and successes did keep popping up: publications and writing awards, honor roll, acceptance into college, elected offices in school and church organizations, a long-term love affair). They were quirks of fate. I achieved each one with the last reserves of my energy and abilities. I lived at the edge of catastrophe. Certain that the next step would pitch me over, I hung back emotionally even though I took each step as it was expected of me: "I'm afraid, too, in a vague, uneasy way. Afraid of what I can do. . . . I am afraid to grow. I am afraid that when the time comes that I am grown, I will not be able to face life for fear it will not be as beautiful as it is in my private existence."

I had some inchoate sense as I was leaving for college of the way in which, as future moves through present into past, one revises the raw material into an orderly whole, but I could not yet extrapolate that the past (not to mention the present or future) is *always* purely a construct, intrinsically uninhabitable by the builder, who must live outside time in order to make time. I wanted to live in a fairy house: "Ten more days. Ten more days until I step off the edge of this bright bittersweet world into oh God into what? Surely there have been other times when I have felt like this, that I was leaving the sunny shelter of my reality to enter something inconceivable. Junior high. High school. They, dear memories, must once have been strange & frightening. But to leave, to say with finality, goodbye, old life that I have always known, goodbye house, town, family, love—oh this is pain & panic & bewilderment far wilder than I have ever known." Dragging my heels and howling like a Sabine, I inched forward into a future fraught with danger, the more so as I had to take fuller responsibility for it. "I'm scared. So constantly scared," I wrote after my first day of college classes. "I want to cry, to run from the fact that I am on my own, that everything is up to me."

Years of living in fear took their toll. I felt "sick & exhausted" all the time. By March 1958 I was recording episodes of depression, using the term in a clinically correct manner, though I would not begin to know that for another decade. "Every so often I get so deeply depressed that it is physical," I noted in June 1960. "I sit bleakly, unable to notice what goes on around me, unable to shake off a smothering apathy. . . . It is a wearing, terrifying experience." Because I could not, through strength of will or intellect, control the symptoms, I felt helpless, and I began to believe that I was going mad. In July 1959 I wrote, "The depression was worse instead of better. I suppose it is my fault. I suppose I could destroy it if I tried. But I don't know how to go about it. I just get more tense & frantic. . . . I know this sounds like a 3rd rate philosophical science fiction novel, but you have no idea what is happening to me, how near the breaking point I am. If only I did not have to live with myself, within the tortured confines of my own mind. I am going insane."

A life of entrapment within the "tortured confines" of one's mind becomes hard to cherish. I began to long to be rid of it. Two days after my fifteenth birthday I wrote, "For the 1st time in my life I asked God to take my life & meant it." I soon made this prayer an almost daily habit. I felt helpless to sustain a life churned into ceaseless waves of pain.

"I am so depressed," I wrote shortly after beginning college. "I wish I knew why so I could stop it. I'm alone & afraid always. Yet I don't know what I can do. There is no other place for me but here, & if I'm unhappy here, then I must die." Until this time death was something I awaited, a prince to wake with a kiss the sleeping beauty behind her hedge of thorns. But in December 1960 I wrote, "I wish I could break my life in half & drop it down a grate." A month after thus taking my life into my own hands, I attempted suicide for the first time. A small gesture, interrupted by the casual arrival of a friend, which left only a pale faint pucker inside my left wrist. But a quick kiss of the prince all the same.

Not long after, I stopped keeping a diary, and have kept a journal only sporadically ever since. No matter. The patterns I have just examined in some detail persisted, I know. I fell in love with a man who was willing and able to marry me, and near the end of my junior year in college we were married, but he failed to make me happy as I had expected. In my senior year, when George was away a great deal in the Navy, I consulted the college physician about my relentless anxiety. He put me on meprobamate and advised me to get pregnant (read your *Physician's Desk Reference* and then try to figure that one out), even if I had to trick George in order to do so. I took the medication, though not the advice, but it did me no good. In December 1964, in a letter I never mailed, I wrote to George, "Well, whatever the cause, I have certainly turned your life (and mine) into hell." I started psychotherapy, and I held out for rescue: "When you come home to live I hope to be a real wife again. Next summer should be good. You working like a normal person with me home keeping house." Actually the next summer was good. We were making a mutually agreed upon baby, who arrived in September. The following spring, George's stint in the Navy at an end, I went to work to put him through graduate school. A few months later I began to have agoraphobic attacks, which grew so severe that I quit work in June 1967. In August I committed myself to Met State.

But why? But why? Dr. Haque wanted to know and never found out; I'm not sure I ever spoke with him again. Once I calmed down, I thought I knew: I was crazy. I have presented my early experiences at some length, however, because I believe now that they reveal that I was not crazy at all. I never heard voices or saw visions; I never confabulated; my affect, though often mournful, was never inappropriate; I often wished but never believed myself someone else; I never feared that objects or people were trying to harm me; I was neither violent and abusive nor totally withdrawn. My failure was not in perceiving reality; I perceived it full well, and despised it. In it my father was dead, friendships were difficult and romances impossible to sustain, my efforts at writing were clumsy, and each day was pretty well indistinguishable from every other. Life was a ramshackle structure, and I was a painstaking architect with outraged sensibilities.

Such a person is not mad, though she may, as I did, take to scribbling. The raw materials of my life seemed sluggish, entropic, and I labored to give them definition. Hence the diaries, I think, though I didn't understand their function at the time. In fact, it seems not to have occurred to me that I was writing my life until shortly after that first suicide attempt, when my college roommate commanded me to stop living in a dream world and I reflected, "Poo is right about the dream world. I don't know when it started—the game which is a constant story. I seem always to have lived in my imagination. At first I suppose it was just for pleasure; then it became a habit, a way of living. Now everything I see or experience becomes part of a pattern. It is rather a beautiful way to live, for I am acutely sensitive to the things I hear or see or do, to moods & colors & perceptions. Perhaps that is why I don't want to move out of it." Here was a potentially useful insight into my existential mode, but with the same breath I reached it I judged and rejected it: "But lately I have been so afraid that I know it is a torturous way to live also. It's dangerous to live alone in a pleasant world of shadows, unaware of unpleasantness. Not that I don't know that ugliness & pain & hate exist, for I have seen them and felt them. It is just that, finding them insupportable, I exclude them, replacing them with my own unreality which has begun to haunt me. It has made me self-centered, over-dramatic, callous to others. Yet even tho' I see these things, I don't know whether I'll be able to leave it. I've got to try, tho'—I've got to try to save my life."

Clearly I believed that the "dream world" was in every way *separate from* "reality" instead of *constituting* my reality, all that I would ever get. I saw two worlds, the "wrong" one in which I lived and the "right" one occupied by everyone else, and I battered my fists and face and knees trying to break through from one to the other. The "right" world was a mirror trick, of course, a true dream world, played by a culture that creates and then taunts outsiders: "Smitty Spider! Smitty Spider!" I really had no place else to go. Thus, in order to "save" my life I could only leave it. The paradox was insoluble.

I went to Met State to get cured not of madness but of being me.

If in fact I was, as I now believe, not crazy but a sort of cultural prisoner, Met State certainly made a madwoman of me. The label realizes the condition: Call a woman crazy, and she'll justify your faith. Especially if you lock her into a drab and dirty space with dozens of other wayward souls, make sure that she is never alone, feed her oatmeal and bananas until her bowels are starched solid, drug her to the eyeballs so that she can scarcely read or speak, and threaten to shoot bolts of electricity through her brain.

Met State may have been, as reputed, the best of the state hospitals in Massachusetts. It was not a good place. I spent most of my sojourn on the "best" ward, the one for short-term patients. Located on the second floor of a modern box of brick, it contained sleeping wings for men and for women, made up of several pavilions of four beds each separated by chest-high partitions, as well as a laundry room, a shower room, and a toilet room. The three toilets had neither seats nor handles; one squatted over them, then flushed by pressing a button. They were separated only by low partitions with no doors. Men, I suppose, grow used to communal elimination, but I never did.

Between the sleeping wings was a common area holding two recreation rooms, one large and one small, the meds station, and a cafeteria-style dining room. We were discouraged from crawling into our beds during the day, so I spent most of my time in the large recreation room, staring out of the small-paned windows at the green, then gold, then brown, then white of the wide hospital grounds. I was so heavily drugged, especially at the beginning when I was being given antipsychotics, that I couldn't read or write much, but I worked on an intricate piece of crewel embroidery some of the time, and listened to the Red Sox in the World Series on a tiny portable radio with an ear plug. Every time the Sox made a good play, I clapped in glee, and since the radio was all but invisible in my lap, I suppose that my outbursts complicated my psychiatric diagnosis. Three times a day I was forced into the dining room, but I couldn't swallow food when people were around, so I ate almost nothing and lost weight steadily. When I got down to ninety-three pounds, I was given the choice of being put onto the medical ward for intravenous feeding or taking a horrid, lumpy dietary supplement, like liquid oatmeal, called Liprotein, which I was promised I could drink alone. I was still made to go to meals, but after each one I was escorted into the laundry and left with my Liprotein.

The ten days of my voluntary commitment came and went, and I signed a new form, for an indefinite time. I had yet to see a doctor, though I did attend a couple of sessions of group therapy, which left me frightened and upset. Dr. Levine came once, but I felt too panicky to talk to him, and he never returned. Finally, on the eighth of September, I was assigned to Dr. Julian, an Austrian woman. I refused to see her ("Not sure why—," I jotted in the journal I'd begun to keep erratically, "don't want to be intimate with a woman, perhaps"), and wound up being carried into her office because I wouldn't walk, but once there I found her "tough and perceptive and intelligent." Today I can hardly remember her, but she worked with me regularly, and occasionally also with George, and I suppose that she saved my life, a gift for which I have sometimes been grateful.

Shortly thereafter I was given a battery of tests—IQ, TAT, Rorschach—perhaps on Dr. Julian's orders. I don't know why. No one ever explained any aspect of my condition to me. At the time I took the tests, I was very disheartened about my lack of progress, and my discouragement made me sullen and uncooperative. My responses were terse and disjointed. A few days later another psychiatrist, also a woman, came to the ward to tell me that I was schizophrenic and would have to have insulin-shock therapy. I knew about insulin shock. My grandmother had died in a diabetic coma. And the patients under treatment were housed on R2 because they needed constant supervision. They disappeared each morning. When they returned they sat drowsily in their bathrobes, sipping chocolate milk heavily sweetened with corn syrup. Every so often one would nod off, and then their nurse would slap her face and shout at her until she roused. They were as fat as slugs, as slow, almost as silent. And the treatment lasted months. I had come for a few days, and now I was to be incarcerated for months. At the risk of being thought crazier than ever, I threw a fit.

Dr. Julian was furious when she heard what had happened. She assured me that the tests had not revealed schizophrenia and that she would never permit me to be treated with insulin shock. She was true to her word. She wanted me instead to have electroconvulsive therapy. I wasn't much happier with that suggestion. I refused to sign the necessary paper, and we reached a stalemate.

For the first month or so, I never left the ward, though I was soon permitted to do so, except accompanied by George for awkward visits home. In late September the whole ward was herded out for a picnic, and in my journal I recorded, "I didn't want to go, but I did go. Terribly anxious at first, then calm enough to eat a hot dog, finally enjoying lying alone on the grass in the sun." Wearing a black turtleneck and yellow jeans printed with tiny red and black flowers, I lay in the last of the summer's heat, belly full, in a brief moment of ease. "Maybe I'll try to go out a bit from now on," I wrote that night. And thanks to a new companion, I did start leaving the ward.

At this point I did something so predictable that I can almost (but only almost, mind you, only almost) laugh at it: I fell in love with one of the other inmates, a young man named Ed who was part of the emerging drug culture. On R2 about half of us were under twenty-five, and of that number I was the only one who had never done any drugs, except alcohol and the pills in the little paper cups that were handed to me four times a day. Part of the reason I fell in love with Ed was that I was lonely and bored. I had always vaguely thought that it was the brilliant who were unstable, especially artists, of which I had once fancied myself one; and perhaps if I'd gone to McLean Hospital, the elegant buildings and grounds of which I could glimpse on the next hill, with the likes of Robert Lowell and Sylvia Plath, my glamorous fantasy would have been validated. But at Met State I learned about the tedium of madness: "It's that there's no one here to talk with intelligently. Each patient has a theme that is repeated over and over—Ruth bragging about her cleaning, her house, her ability to earn money as a waitress, all in loud, rough, ungrammatical language; Anne preaching Holy Roller religion; Muriel complaining that someone disturbed her sleep; etc., etc. I'm sick of it. It didn't matter at 1st—everything was new and strange then, and I didn't pay much attention to others anyway." The men were no more promising companions: John, a big soft boy terrified that he was gay, who was himself some days, dressed in jeans and an oxford-cloth shirt, and others was Jesus Christ, naked but for one of the striped spreads that covered all our beds; David, who had been in mental institutions since he was four, rocking and humming and flapping one hand in front of his face for hours on end; sweet Homer, a small round gray man in his fifties who yearned wistfully and fixedly for death as for a beautiful woman. Ed was intelligent, educated, usually lucid. He liked to write poetry and to listen to music. I tried to attract him, I noted, "telling myself the whole time, of course, that I wasn't doing any such thing. Because I'm not sure I want him. It seems sometimes like an exercise, a test of my charm, and something to do during these long, boring days."

But I also fell in love with him because being "in love" was, as it had always been, the only condition that promised me any hope of rescue from myself: "The effect is, at least, exhilarating. I feel more alive, more in touch than I have in a while." I was by this time drowning in domesticity. "Me home keeping house" hadn't turned out to be what I needed after all, and getting a job had only exacerbated my situation by providing one more arena for potential failure. "I have the feeling that Dr. Julian and George and everyone who's trying to 'help' is just cramming a way of life down my throat," I wrote. "I'm not sure I want it—to be sober and stolid and settled. I like to play. I want to play. What a drag the real world seems. Full of dustrags and shrieking babies, of meals to cook, evenings of bridge with nice young couples. Ugh." No wonder my throat tightened and my stomach heaved in the face of food. I couldn't swallow anything more.

With Ed I played: two irresponsible loonies in a legally drugged haze. We listened to Tim Buckley and The Beatles' *Magical Mystery Tour* and the Jefferson Airplane on the ward's tinny portable phonograph. We wandered for hours hand in hand around the hospital grounds. We headed into the woods and made love. One afternoon I remember going to my bed, taking off my underclothes and knit stockings, pulling on my woolen coat with muted green and purple stripes known in my family as the horse blanket, all under the sour suspicious gaze of a woman in a nearby bed, then running bare-legged from the ward into the woods to meet Ed and fall onto a snow-covered heap of leaves in a clumsy, shivering embrace. For some reason, this really did seem better than the "real world" of warm wide beds.

We did one another no good, of course, and possibly a fair amount of harm. I think now that I prolonged my stay because I was too obsessed to leave him. Toward the end, when I went home on a trial basis, I returned after five days "suffering attacks of nausea, unpredictable and unmanageable." As soon as I saw Ed again, "I nearly fainted. The old romantic swoon. The gladness at being with him again, at finding him happy to see me—it's so powerful. But so are the fear and sadness and despair. And I suspect that they are very important to me. It's been so long since I really suffered in love. And as Ed pointed out in group meeting this morning, sadness can be in a strange way enjoyable—it can be creative, productive." The old romantic swoon indeed. The old romantic swindle. And I was still buying whatever shares came on the market.

Despite my claims of exhilaration and happiness after I met Ed, my condition continued to deteriorate, though not visibly, I assume, since some time late in October I was allowed to make plans for leaving the hospital. I drove into Cambridge one day to ask Mr. Tillinghast, my boss at the Smithsonian Astrophysical Observatory, if I could return to work. He accepted me warmly. In a seamless movement I then drove home instead of back to Met State. In the bathroom I stood in front of the marble sink and swallowed one Darvon after another. When I had taken them all, I drove back to the hospital, undressed, and got into bed. Just before drifting off, I recall telling another patient what I had done. I came to the next morning in the Intensive Care Unit of the Waltham City Hospital, lungs aflame from a bronchoscopy necessitated by my aspirating vomit while unconscious, wired like the Bride of Frankenstein. In a while I was moved to a regular room, and a couple of days later I went back to Met State in an ambulance. The men who drove were glad to see me and praised the improvement in my looks. I didn't remember them from my earlier ride, but I was touched that they were clearly happy that I hadn't died.

The next entry in my journal, headed simply "Monday," begins, "I don't know the date. I've been here so long now. Summer has gone and much of autumn. The weather is cold enough that Anne needs her snowsuit." A little further on, "There's much more to me than I knew. And the parts that I didn't know are the ones on top now, coming out strangely, controlling me. It's still *me*, I'm sure, no one else, but I don't know this person. I'm not frightened, am I? I guess I am. I surely must know of what; they keep asking what? what? what? I feel crazy now. I've never been crazy before. I wish I were dead." The following one, dated 7 November, restates my dread: "I'm not at all dead. But I'm so afraid that I'm going mad. I've had a lot of medicine, so it's probably just that. I hope. I wonder if Dr. Julian would let me go mad. I wonder if she could stop me."

She certainly wanted to stop me, and she continued to insist that shock treatments would help, but I still refused. Late in November,

she transferred me to Continuing Therapy and Guidance—CTG—
the wonderfully euphemistic title of the heart of Met State, the
chronic wards, which held seven hundred men and seven hundred
women with one psychiatrist for each sex. I lasted there about a week.
Then I revolted. "I mean to leave this place," I wrote. "It is unbeliev-
ably dismal—and I'm on the *best* ward in CTG. There is everywhere
a sense of age and decrepitude about both the buildings and the
patients. Everywhere grime and the sour stench of sweat and urine.
The 'day room' is a wide hall littered with old, garishly painted
Windsor chairs and lit by a few low-watt bulbs. At night nowhere in
the ward is there light enough to read by. I sleep in a large dormitory
with about 16 beds—the bed sags and groans with the slightest
movement. Worst of all are the meals, served in a cavernous dining
hall reached by a circuitous route I still haven't figured out. No question of eating in those surroundings. So I am in every sense uncomfortable—sleepless, hungry, and oppressed.

"I do not believe that this is 'better' for me than R2; and I don't
think the whole damned hospital is doing me much good. I'll ask
Julian this afternoon to make me a day patient; if she won't, I'll try to
sign myself out. I'll admit to being frightened, but also eager to show
some initiative."

I know now that Dr. Julian had done just what she set out to do: to
scare the wits out of me. She agreed instantly to my becoming a day
patient. My rapid departure from CTG was something of a miracle:
The shortest stay I heard of while there was that of a young woman
who'd been there two years, the next shortest, of a man who'd been
there six. I found that I had limits to what I'd do, even for craziness. I
bolted.

Within two weeks I failed as a day patient, disintegrating into
"unbearable depression. Indescribable really. I can only say that I
now know what it is like to exist from minute to minute—and that
just barely. Tonight, free of it, I find myself praying that I shall never
go there again." Now, as Dr. Julian must have known, I had reached a

crux: I could either kill myself, as I had demonstrated, or return to the dim halls of CTG. Once again she offered me shock treatment. I signed the papers without hesitation and returned to R2.

Between the middle of December and the middle of February I had twenty-one treatments, at the rate of three, two, and then one a week. They were painless yet vaguely dreadful. Each time, my fluid intake was restricted and I was given shots to dry up my secretions and relax my muscles. With a group I was led downstairs; we waited lined up on straight chairs in the dim light behind screens until our names were called one at a time. When I heard mine, I walked around the screens and lay on a bed while a nurse jabbed sodium amytal into my arm. Almost immediately, lovely waves of sleep, later groggy consciousness, finally a reward of dessert and coffee. Sometimes I had a headache, but otherwise felt no physical effects.

Mentally I felt very peculiar. "I feel as tho' I am in a dream," I wrote after the second treatment; a month later, "I feel very strange the last couple of days—things even smell funny to me"; a few days after that, "*I* have gone as mad as a hatter. I don't know what has happened. But for several days now I have felt really crazy. And badly frightened." But on the twenty-eighth of January I wrote, "Sitting here this morning, I suddenly felt stronger and more competent than I have been feeling. Perhaps one day I will be capable of handling life on the outside by myself," and on the eighth of February I recorded that I weighed a hundred and eight pounds. I began to go home for a few hours each evening; I invited my sister and her husband to dinner; on the eleventh of February George and I went to a movie; I spent one day at home with Anne on my own, then two. On the twenty-third I went home "for as long as I want," and although I fled back to the hospital after five days, I didn't stay long. The next time I left, I didn't return.

Much earlier, I referred to myself as a "cultural prisoner" in Met State. If that phrase is to be more than radical rhetoric, then I must confront and explore the terms of my incarceration. I do not believe that I was not "sick" at the time I was locked up, or even necessarily that I was badly treated while I was there. On the contrary, today I believe in my illness more purely as illness—rather than mental weakness or moral flaw—than I could ever have done then; and since I left the hospital after only six months, my treatment seems to have been unusually effective in view of the rather primitive conditions under which it took place. I was sick, all right, but what I see now is that sickness forms only in relation to some standard of health which does not exist of itself in some fictional objective other world but which is created from the observations, responses, values, and beliefs of those "healthy" subjects who seek to articulate it.

Dr. Julian told me that my "life became troubled when men entered it," and I accepted her Freudian-tinged explanation at its face value: that I had failed to adapt my personal existence to the presence of James and Fred and Caleb and Adam and George and Ed in it. I did not think of my experiences as in any way typical rather than idiosyncratic; and I never believed my responses to them any-thing but problematic. The possibility that those responses, though maladaptive, might have been in a curious way the saving of me— the life ring that kept me from going down in a sea of womanly graces—I have only just begun to explore.

Indeed my life became troubled, not when individual men entered it, but when I emerged from the long undifferentiated dream of my female-supported childhood into the Real/Male World, an environment defined and dominated by the masculine principles of effectiveness, power, and success, an environment containing a ready-made niche for me which happened to be the wrong size and shape. Some days I longed to smash the entire hideous alien structure, but I had no tools. Other days I wanted nothing more than to fit into my niche, even if I had to whack off my hands and my feet and my head to do so. Empty-handed, contemplating self-mutilation, of course I grew depressed. I believe now that my depression was—and still is— my response to the struggle not to go under, not to go down for the last time, sinking into acceptance of that space which crabbed and cramped me. I will not be the little woman, my depression cried, even while I was hunching and squeezing, cracking my bones and scraping my knuckles and knees. I will die first. For this reason I call it the saving of me.

It was not entirely coincidental, I suppose, that my depression grew prominent after my mother remarried when I was eleven. Then, for the first time in seven years, a man literally entered my life to stay, though he did so with exceptional gentleness. My stepfather's rare calm, together with his capacity for accepting and cherishing people just as they are, certainly eased the upheaval his sudden presence caused. Even so, he separated my mother from me, calling from her a new kind of attention. And through her experiences I observed the contours of a grown woman's life up close. She quit her part-time job at Stepping Stones School for Exceptional Children. And then she made babies: Nathan and Barbara. I adored the babies, who came at just the right time to thrill me to my early-adolescent core. But I must have found their effects on Mother tiresome, for I remember complaining to Aunt Jean while visiting her in the Boston house, which was filled with books and modern paintings, not to mention writers and musicians and curious strays both human and feline, that I was sick of conversations about diapers and feedings.

I both wanted and didn't want the normalcy my mother's new life conferred. As soon as I began to perceive the traits of a womanly existence, I longed for them: "I want to be normal. Not average, normal. I want to be witty & charming & *popular*, especially with boys. I don't want to be different." Yet I relentlessly subverted my own desires: "I have no one to talk to. Sometimes I know I am aloof, but I'm not stuck-up. It's just that I have too much to think about. I don't want to think about clothes and boys. What's wrong with me?" A couple of years later I seem to have improved my conversational techniques, though without increasing my satisfaction: "I am easier with the kids now—I can joke with them & chat informally. But always I feel so isolated, so awkward, so alone." Uneasy among my peers, I groped for friendship with older women, like my drama coach. "I try—I really think I do try to be close to the kids my own age," I reflected. "It is no good. I am awkward & uncertain. With Miss Hare it is different. I am still very young & ungainly but it is not so important that I do not say what I am expected or do the logical thing. I can be me—sulky if I want, or blithe; temperamental or gay or pensive. There is not the same pressure to be typical." But of course such relationships—pashes, I think the British call them—were too unequal to erase my loneliness.

I finally found out what was "wrong" with me years and years later in a conversation with my present therapist. I had been bemoaning—still—my inability to make friends when Ken asked me how I had liked to spend my time when I was young. After I described, with considerable enthusiasm, the long walks I took in all weathers through the woods behind my house, he said, "There's a term for people like you." "What?" I perked up, always eager to pick up a new bit of psychological jargon. "It's called being introverted," he said. Introverted, for God's sake. Some new jargon. Yet, familiar though the word was, I'd never applied it to myself. And suddenly, trying it on, I understood that my loneliness was not an aberration but an existential choice. "I think I *ought* to want friends," I jotted in my journal after our conversation. "But by and large people don't exist for me unless they're present or built into my interior landscape. And I certainly don't want to spend time with them."

Introversion is no illness. It's simply a habit of mind. Why then did I view it as the doom of my happiness and fulfillment? I could have done so only by believing that the one avenue to that happiness and fulfillment was laid not with my own insights and actions but with my relationships to others. And there, of course, is the paving stone of a womanly existence: to create and elaborate the social bonds that sustain community. Church fairs. Choir picnics. PTA. Summer playground programs. Covered-dish suppers. Christmas pageants. The men may leave the community regularly—in a village the size of the one I grew up in, all but a handful had to work elsewhere—

but they leave their women behind with their telephones and their morning coffees and their bridge luncheons and their afternoon teas, all talking a mile a minute, their words like needles and patches and thread, their lives one long quilting bee of human bonding. Gossip is not idle. It is an exercise in design, the picking out of patterns in the social fabric. The fingers of every woman strengthen and embellish the whole.

A woman clumsy with a needle can thus be a serious liability, as can one who shirks the task. I kept meandering off, both literally, on those long solitary wooded ambles, and figuratively, plunging into inward thickets because I had "too much to think about." My mother moderated and socialized my behavior as best she could. She frowned at, though she did not forbid, my jaunts. She paid for, though she could ill afford, ballroom-dancing lessons, summer camp, Fellowship retreats. She discouraged those too-passionate single attachments I formed desperately time and again, those fascinations with one other which disrupt the warp and woof of social intercourse. Instead she approved of group activities, and these I plowed into compulsively, taking on more and more responsibility, until the race from stage to printer to pulpit to meeting hall left me more than half dead with exhaustion.

None of this gave me any less to think about, only less time in which to do the thinking. Why then did I do it? I was a genuinely good child, a typical first-child/girl, who liked to please others. My mother conveyed to me, for the most part tacitly, that my natural way of being—solemn, solitary, reflective—was neither wholesome nor attractive; and my experience certainly bore her out. I was in a hopeless bind: to do as I would—to please others—I could not be as I was. And the greed for thinking: What does that signify? Simply, I think now, that I was a writer, which is not so dreadful a fate when you think about some of its alternatives. I could, for example, have been a certified public accountant. But from this distance I can see that, for that girl in that small town in the late 1950s, it set up some insoluble conflicts that turned it into quite a dreadful fate indeed.

I loved to write. It was in this yearning that I located—probably pretty accurately—that difference which generated my isolation. Do others, I wondered, "see things as I do? I do not think so, for if they did they would not still be alive." And, life-threatening though my vision seemed, I would not repudiate it: "Sometimes I think I shall die from being different even as I cling to the difference fiercely." In short, I believed myself—not unusually for an adolescent—possessed of a special gift that could transform life from the drudgery of French assignments and allergy shots and arguments with my disappointingly ordinary boyfriend into a valiant quest: "Sometimes, vaguely, in the murkiness which is my mind, my creativity, my genius, flashes a glimpse of this greatness which is pure pain & pure joy. Yet I do not know what it is or where to find it. I do know this— that when I find it, if I find it, I will discard all else as meaningless & follow it for the rest of my life." Out of the kitchen and onto the steed.

But I never made it. I never became a writer. Instead I became The Gifted Girl with Lots of Potential, as I christened her twenty years and more later. I never got one foot into the stirrup, let alone sat astride the beast. And because I failed to do so, I almost died of sorrow.

I believed my failure the result of my personal shortcomings. The gift was simply not good enough. "I know that deep within me lies something," I had written, "but I see it in comparison with the talents of others & it is so pitifully small." After typing up some poems, I commented, "It is disheartening that so few have the slightest merit. But some show what I hope is promise."

Much more damaging than my disgust at my work, however, was my self-repugnance. The gift might be pitifully small, but worse yet, I failed to use it. "Something in me is crying out," I wrote. "The desire to create. I cannot. My brain is frayed with the need to produce, but I am paralyzed. I keep saying—when I have time. Yet when I do have a free moment, I waste it. I feel pent up, desperate. My ability rides me. My lack of it tortures me. I am torn apart." This paralysis would lie at the core of my depression ever after. But I now think it worthwhile to look at the context in which I wrote that passage, because it reveals not a lazy wastrel, as I believed, but a woman trapped in the manifold webs of female duty and expectation.

I had just graduated from high school and planned to go to a very expensive college in the fall, so I had to go to work for the first time in my life. Since my only experience was baby-sitting, I logically took a job as a mother's helper for an affluent couple with three small children. The woman was a version of what I would become in a few years, all resentment and raw nerves; her particular fixation (rather different from mine) was cleanliness. Every day I washed floors, vacuumed and dusted, did mountains of laundry (no towel could be used twice, and the children had to have clean clothes three times a day) and ironed it all, even the children's T-shirts and the man's boxer shorts. I also attended the children, of course, and since I wasn't allowed to leave them for a moment, I had to postpone many chores till after they were asleep. I tumbled exhausted each night into a cot in the baby's room and woke with him each morning at 5:30. In short, I was initiated into female adulthood with a rigor that made my mother's efforts in this direction seem feeble. To make matters worse, I was bitterly homesick, fearful of going to college, and lonely for my boyfriend, who'd gone on a cross-country camping trip. In this setting, depleted both physically and emotionally, I flagellated myself for failing to create. As well ask poetry of a paper bag.

And yet, when the time came three years later, I chose the depletion rather than the poetry. Unable to believe in greatness, I could not discard all else as meaningless and follow it for the rest of my life. On the contrary, I discarded greatness as meaningless and opted for a man and his child. That I was miserable in marriage and motherhood did not reflect on my choice. It merely indicated that something was still—interminably—wrong with me. So wrong that at last I had to go to the hospital to get fixed.

My choice did not change while I was there. Only once in my hospital journal did I mention writing, toward the end of my stay: "I can't write poetry. I'm afraid I'll never be able to." My concern was not with writing but with relationships, especially my relationships with George and Anne. Indeed, I can trace the progress of my therapy and my satisfaction with it through my attitude toward Anne and my duties to her. Early on, in reflecting about her, I grasped and stated my central problem: "I want to see her but I don't want to take care of her. I wonder if I want her at all in any adult fashion. I'm not very grown up."

I certainly wasn't very grown up. Transitions had always been problematic for me, remember. When I was fifteen I had written, "I'm afraid to grow. I am afraid that when the time comes that I am grown, I will not be able to face life for fear it will not be so beautiful as it is in my private existence." And I'd sure as hell been right. The transition into female adulthood had been impossible. Thinking back on that summer as a mother's helper, I'm not exactly surprised. So the task I set for myself while I was at Met State was to turn myself into a grown woman; and the gauge of my maturity was my ability to want to mother my daughter.

It wasn't easy. "It seems unspeakable that I should not want and love my child," I wrote. "But she seems to represent to me everything I rebel against—being tied to the house, following dull routine, and above all accepting responsibility." Getting well to me meant ending my rebellion. Gradually I yearned to do so: "I feel so sad—especially toward Anne. I miss her so and feel so ashamed that I can't take care of her like a real mother. She is beautiful, so sweet and bright. Why can't I be an ordinary woman. We visited the Maxons on Saturday and I envied Judy bitterly—caring for David, keeping her own house, ready to have another baby. I want to be like that." And, "I want to be well. I want to be like Sally, like Judy, like my mother. Not that they are living in a state of bliss—that would be a drag, I should think. But they cope with their lives and get joy out of them. I should be able to do that, too. I have everything going for me—intelligence; education; a loving, understanding, patient husband; a bright, charming daughter. Why am I sick and frightened? How can I get well?" And, "I would give almost anything to be Judy Maxon, settled in her

ordinary little ranch house, busy with her 2 little children, etc."
Finally, "I miss George and Anne. Even tho' yesterday was frightening and exhausting, it was promising. I want to live at home. I want to
be well." Shortly thereafter I went home to live.

I did not, however, get well. I got functional, which is another condition altogether (though not, on the whole, one to be sneezed at). My
ignorance of the difference, which almost cost me my life, I attribute
to my doctors, none of whom taught me the first thing about depression. Not one told me that I had quite a common illness, of which dis-
rupted sleeping patterns and loss of weight are clear-cut symptoms,
and which tends to respond readily to drug therapy. When, after my
release from the hospital, I fretted to Dr. Levine about a possible
recurrence, he assured me that there was no reason to believe that I
would ever have one. I suppose he was adopting the typical medical
stance, especially toward hysterical females: If you tell them about a
symptom, they're sure to develop it, so the less said the better. He'd
have done me better service to warn me that nearly half the people
who experience one depressive episode will experience another, and
that as a woman I was at an especially high risk. Instead, he gave me
to believe that I'd paid my dues and could now get on with my life.

I never did go back to the hospital, at least. In that escape I was
luckier than most women at Met State. Agnes had come back, leaving
her year-old baby and several other children, for her fourth series of
shock treatments. Shelly, who had slid from McLean down to Met
State when the frequency of her hospitalizations became too expensive even for her advertising-executive husband, tallied and
recounted her suicide attempts with rhapsodic vigor. Their families
had evolved systems for accommodating mother's absence with as little disruption as feasible. And then there were those seven hundred
women in CTG, many of whom had lived longer at Met State than
anywhere else, with their faded hair and eyes, shuffling through the
dim corridors in soft house slippers, fingers plucking at the pale flow-

ers on their limp cotton shifts. Their families, if they had any, must long since have grown disheartened, perhaps even moved away, for no one ever came for them. In any case, the incarceration of these women became a structural component—whether as presence or as absence—in the lives connected with theirs. Mine never did.

One of my greatest fears about having been hospitalized was that I'd never be given a job again. But in truth I found my re-entry into the world remarkably easy. Shortly after my suicide attempt, I had a note from my boss at the Smithsonian Astrophysical Observatory: "Please don't worry about your job at SAO. I think it will be here when you get back. Come when you're ready. I can always use your kind of help. If you want, you can try a little part-time work later on. Remember that, while I appreciate your responsible attitude, it won't matter if you miss an occasional appointment here." This calm man, who would be dead himself within a couple of years at the age of thirty-six of lung cancer, rescued my shambled life. Shortly after my release I did go back, at first part-time, soon full-time. I discovered then that Mr. Tillinghast had never accepted my resignation but had put me on leave without pay, so that my service was continuous and there's no awkward gap in my résumé.

In fact, however, I've never had to conceal that gap. From the beginning I've been able to tell people about my hospitalization without catastrophe. I've encountered puzzlement, even skepticism— after all, when you meet me, in my conservative clothes, with my face carefully made up, wearing the poise bequeathed me by my paternal grandmother, you're more likely to think you're seeing Mrs. Middle America than a madwoman, though in truth Mrs. Middle America is, very often, a madwoman—but seldom suspicion and never rejection. I've never been denied anything I wanted on the grounds of mental instability. In this I am no doubt fortunate, ironically, in being female. Women, because they have been viewed by their culture, embodied in the last century or so not in priests but in scientists, especially psychologists, as deviating from the white male bourgeois norm that culture imposes, have been permitted, indeed expected, to

manifest a certain amount of mental and emotional dis-ease. So six
months in a mental hospital in an odd way has rendered me normal.
Too, I never tried to do anything my culture considers particularly
responsible. I worked at low-paying jobs without authority in nonprofit organizations, and I confined myself to culturally devalued
activities. Child-rearing, editing, writing, teaching: What real harm
could I do? No one had to force me, as they did Thomas Eagleton in
1972, to withdraw from candidacy for vice president of the United
States because I'd been treated in a mental hospital for depression.

And yet, though I learned to function, however modestly, on "the
outside," as we used to call it in the hospital, I never got well. I didn't
know that I was still depressed. Remember, no one had ever taught
me about depression, so I came to associate it with the episode that
put me into the hospital. I didn't know that it could, in its chronic
permutation, twist itself into the fibers of my existence, a continuous
strand of unusual tensility so woven into my way of looking at the
world as to constitute, together with the grayish cast of my eyes and
my laboring limp and my fondness for Reese's Peanut Butter Cups
and my fear of all spiders except tarantulas, my self. Maggie Scarf in
Unfinished Business: Pressure Points in the Lives of Women suggests
that my depression might really be analogous to my eye color, that is,
that it has a genetic basis. Depressive episodes are often triggered by
ruptures in relationships, and females appear from the moment of
birth to form, sustain, and rely upon relationships more readily than
males; thus, she reasons, females are genetically predisposed toward
relatedness as one of the species' survival mechanisms, and consequently predisposed as well toward depression.

Until a relational and/or depressive gene is discovered, I remain
skeptical about such an explanation, smacking as it does of the biological determinism which has forced women to bear children
because they have the necessary equipment, telling them that they
must fulfill their maternal instinct (as Betty Rollin points out in
"Motherhood: Who Needs It?" an instinct is something you die from
not obeying, and no woman has ever died from not having a baby,

though plenty have died in childbirth); and which has forbidden them education because their brains are too small, telling them that knowledge leads to madness. But I don't think we need such a gene anyway. Acculturation is quite powerful enough to emplace the parameters that will yield, time after time, female derangement. I do not deny, however, that depression, whatever its etiology, manifests a physiological component, most often in eating and sleeping disorders that, because they are clearly controlled with medication, suggest some sort of biochemical imbalance in the depressive's system.

In the summer of 1980, almost exactly thirteen years after my commitment to Met State, I slid precipitously into another acute depressive episode. Because I had not understood that I could have such a breakdown again, I did not recognize what was happening to me, and by the time one of my neurologists did, it was almost too late. I took the antidepressant medication he gave me all at once instead of in the measured doses he'd prescribed. I was lucky that the psychiatrist who interviewed me in the emergency room chose to send me home rather than commit me to the hospital, because I think, on the basis of my earlier experience, that in the hospital I'd have gotten much worse before I began to get better. As it was, I had a pretty bad time of it for a few months, but I survived intact.

And at last I began to learn about depression. I had, finally, a therapist who was willing to teach me and also to be taught by me as I began to explore the significance of my illness, and who could see that, even though I was a woman, my adjustment to marriage and motherhood was not, somehow, quite the point. I turned back and back into my experience, not to seek the origins of my illness in that experience, because I had stopped believing that any event or series of events had made me sick, but to find the structure of my dis-ease, the ways in which I had shaped my desires and disappointments into the depression that frames my way of being. What, I wanted to know, were the terms of my existence?

Although I had stopped being a diarist twenty years earlier, I had felt driven ever after—in fits and starts—to keep a journal of some sort, so I have a sketch, however spotty and faded, mapping my interior landscape. It has taken me a long time to learn to reread the signs. About five years ago I reread the early diaries and noted, "The me-ness of the diaries that disturbs me most is their now-ness—that is, the familiarity that I feel which arises not from memory but from currency. That Nancy all too often sounds like this Nancy, and I find myself thinking, Jesus, haven't I made any progress at all? I'm still falling in love, still thinking of death (tho' I don't wish for it so much any more, perhaps because I'm so much closer to it)." And just a few months ago, after reading them again: "That young woman strikes me thru' with horror and pity—her raw nerves, her clear-cut tho' undiagnosed depression, her sexual fears and frenzy. And I know that if I turned to my journal of 3 years ago, tho' the prose would be plainer I would still hear her shrieks and wails. . . . The diaries shriek fear. And a sense of failure. Things that are with me yet."

Things that will be, I see now, scrutinizing these texts that span more than a quarter of a century, with me forever. The terms of my existence: sickness, isolation, timidity, desire for death. They lie black as bars across the amazingly sunny landscape of a privileged life: good family, good education, good marriage, good jobs, good children. Since I don't believe in a depressive gene or genie, I must have chosen these terms myself. But who would make such a choice? Only a madwoman. But I'm not mad. You can take that as axiomatic. I've spent many years arriving at it, and it works. However comfortable an explanation madness might be, I can't have it.

Now that I've let go of madness, I can think about depression with more curiosity and less fear. It happens to an enormous number of us—millions and millions at any given moment. Most of us it happens to are women. Anything that strikes on such a massive scale cannot be purely idiosyncratic. Despite the personal features on some of my symptoms, my incarceration in Met State, emblematic of this wider prison of my life, was less a personal than a cultural event. I got there/here not because I am the one and only Nancy Mairs but because, in being Nancy Mairs, I reify—however idiosyncratically—the privileges, permissions, and denials that mold my type.

I am a kind of paralytic, my paralysis very characteristic of the depressed state. I don't dare move. "I am always afraid of losing things," I write in my journal. "What if I forget the names of the men I've slept with?" What if indeed. I don't know. But I catalogue these men and, at other points, all my past addresses, the cats who have lived with me, the poems I've published, my current blessings. Lists and lists, lest I forget. In one of Anaïs Nin's early diaries I come upon and jot down a quotation from E. Graham Howe: "The expression which is known as depression can be more clearly understood as coming to those who are not willing to be depressed, i.e.: to fall down according to the falling rhythm, or to let go when the time has come to lose. Depression is characteristically associated with over-conscientiousness, and so it is particularly liable to befall virtuous people. This is because they feel it is their moral duty to hang on to all good things, fixing them forever against the moving law of time."

Here I am: fixed in a graceful pose, my head thrown back, at the top of the field behind the house I was raised in, looking down the long slope across the greening, boggy bottom to the woods bronzed with last year's oak leaves still clinging, reddened with the new tips of maples, bearing bunches of my past like branches of lilacs, reeling at the fragrance, my arms pricked by the gray twigs, aching under the wet weight. But who am I, who am I, frozen in this pale light?

"I've never considered myself ordinary, average—," I write in my journal, "have always considered myself special in some way, destined for something—never sure what. But it would make a difference to the world somehow. Now I'm 33 years old, and it occurs to me that I probably won't ever do anything distinguished or lasting. I try to think of my raising my own children and educating others in those terms, but it won't do—that's not what I had in mind; the gestures are too small." I'm on my trail at last, though not for several more years will I recognize myself: The Gifted Girl with Lots of Potential.

Sure enough, still here. Only, as everyone knows, you can't at thirty-seven get away with what you got away with at seventeen. And after twenty years, the poor child is considerably the worse for wear.

She'd been an authentic creature once, though. What had happened to keep her hanging around so long after her time, frazzled, frayed, though with still an occasional quick grin of her girlish charm? From Patricia Meyer Spack's *The Female Imagination* I copy an insight into my journal: "Preservation of the feeling that one is set apart by special gifts depends often on failure to test those gifts, but the reluctance to test oneself generates guilt and disappointment. Unchallenged capacities fade away; it's harder and harder to believe in them. The world allows women not to use themselves, then denies their value because they fail to function fully." By the time I find it, I am too far gone into depression for any new understanding to brake my slide; but after I survive, and begin to emerge, it is still there, dated 4 September 1980, reminding me sternly that my time is up.

No more Gifted Girl with Lots of Potential. No more grandiose intentions of being a writer when I grow up, never realized because the products never come right and so I'm safer to sit still than to start the inevitable failure. This is all the grown up I get to be. No more "dream" world, more perfect than the "real" world, waiting if only I can find the small golden key: in which I love and rear my children without pain; in which I gratify my husband's slenderest desire; in which I dust all the surfaces in my room every morning instead of at Christmas and Easter; in which I understand how to solve a basic quadratic equation; in which someone discovers all the poems I haven't written and publishes them one after another in *The New Yorker*. There is one world—this world—and I have made it. No hope of a cure, ever, for being me.

In many ways these recognitions have been freeing. But nothing I know can free me from depression, which is, by now at least, my existential style. It has infected me at the level of my nerve endings, and I will likely need, I am told, three tiny yellow pills with a glass of water at bedtime ever after if I am to survive. All the bars are in place, and the cement of guilt and disappointment is harder than any of the tools that I've found in here with me have been able to chip.

Still, of late I've felt a difference. I've begun to notice how large the space that encloses me seems to be. It's not a bad place really. The floors are polished, and the windows let in wide bands of light. I've put up no curtains but I've hung some tapestries on the walls into which are woven many fair women and many rhododendrons but no unicorns. I am mostly alone here, but occasional visitors float in and out bringing me chocolate ice cream sodas and fresh jokes. In the precise center of the room is a desk holding a black fountain pen, a bottle of black ink, and a stack of yellow legal-size pads, some of which are inscribed in a round black hand.

This place is real. I can live here. Come by, and I'll make you a cup of almond tea.

FROM *THE SAVAGE GOD*

∽

A. Alvarez

I HAVE TO ADMIT THAT I am a failed suicide. It is a dismal confession to make, since nothing, really, would seem to be easier than to take your own life. Seneca, the final authority on the subject, pointed out disdainfully that the exits are everywhere: each precipice and river, each branch of each tree, every vein in your body will set you free. But in the event, this isn't so. No one is promiscuous in his way of dying. A man who has decided to hang himself will never jump in front of a train. And the more sophisticated and painless the method, the greater the chance of failure. I can vouch, at least, for that. I built up to the act carefully and for a long time, with a kind of blank pertinacity. It was the one constant focus of my life, making everything else irrelevant, a diversion. Each sporadic burst of work, each minor success and disappointment, each moment of calm and relaxation, seemed merely a temporary halt on my steady descent through layer after layer of depression, like a lift stopping for a moment on the way down to the basement. At no point was there any question of getting off or of changing the direction of the journey. Yet, despite all that, I never quite made it.

I see now that I had been incubating this death far longer than I recognized at the time. When I was a child, both my parents had half-heartedly put their heads in the gas-oven. Or so they claimed. It seemed to me then a rather splendid gesture, though shrouded in mystery, a little area of veiled intensity, revealed only by hints and unexplained, swiftly suppressed outbursts. It was something hidden, attractive and not for the children, like sex. But it was also something that undoubtedly did happen to grown-ups. However hysterical or comic the behaviour involved—and to a child it seemed more ludicrous than tragic to lay your head in the greasy gas-oven, like the Sunday joint—suicide was a fact, a subject that couldn't be denied; it was something, however awful, that people did. When my own time came, I did not have to discover it for myself.

Maybe that is why, when I grew up and things went particularly badly, I used to say to myself, over and over, like some latter-day Mariana in the Moated Grange, "I wish I were dead." It was an echo from the past, joining me to my tempestuous childhood. I muttered it unthinkingly, as automatically as a Catholic priest tells his rosary. It was my special magic ritual for warding off devils, a verbal nervous tic. Dwight Macdonald once said that when you don't know what to do with your hands you light a cigarette, and when you don't know what to do with your mind you read *Time* magazine. My equivalent was this one sentence repeated until it seemingly lost all meaning: "Iwishiweredead, Iwishiweredead. Iwishiweredead..." Then one day I understood what I was saying. I was walking along the edge of Hampstead Heath after some standard domestic squabble, and suddenly I heard the phrase as though for the first time. I stood still to attend to the words. I repeated them slowly, listening. And realized that I meant it. It seemed so obvious, an answer I had known for years and never allowed myself to acknowledge. I couldn't understand how I could have been so obtuse for so long.

After that, there was only one way out, although it took a long time—many months, in fact—to get there. We moved to America— wife, child, *au pair* girl, myself, and trunk-upon-trunk-load of luggage. I had a term's appointment at a New England university and had rented a great professorial mansion in a respectably dead suburb, ten miles from the campus, two from the nearest shop. It was Germanic, gloomy and far too expensive. For my wife, who didn't drive, it was also as lonely as Siberia. The neighbours were mostly twice her age, the university mostly ignored us, the action was nil. There wasn't even a television set in the house. So I rented one and she sat disconsolately in front of it for two months. Then she gave up, packed her bags, and took the child back to England. I didn't even blame her. But I stayed on in a daze of misery. The last slide down the ice-slope had begun and there was no way of stopping it.

My wife was not to blame. The hostility and despair that poor girl provoked in me—and I in her—came from some pure, infantile source, as any disinterested outsider could have told me. I even recognized this for myself in my clear moments. I was using her as an excuse for troubles that had their roots deep in the past. But mere intellectual recognition did no good and, anyway, my clear moments were few. My life felt so cluttered and obstructed that I could hardly breathe. I inhabited a closed, concentrated world, airless and without exits. I doubt if any of this was noticeable socially: I was simply tenser, more nervous than usual, and I drank more. But underneath I was going a bit mad. I had entered the closed world of suicide and my life was being lived for me by forces I couldn't control.

When the Christmas break came at the university, I decided to spend the fortnight in London. Maybe, I told myself, things would be easier, at least I would see the child. So I loaded myself up with presents and climbed on a jet, dead drunk. I passed out as soon as I reached my seat and woke to a brilliant sunrise. There were dark islands below—the Hebrides, I suppose—and the eastern sea was on fire. From that altitude, the world looked calm and vivid and possible. But by the time we landed at Prestwick the clouds were down like the black cap on a hanging judge. We waited and waited hopelessly on the runway, the rain drumming on the fuselage, until the soaking fog lifted at the London airport.

When I finally got home, hours late, no one was there. The fires were blazing, the clocks were ticking, the telephone was still. I wandered round the empty house touching things, frightened, expectant. Fifteen minutes later, there was a noise at the front door and my child plunged shouting up the stairs into my arms. Over his shoulder I could see my wife standing tentatively in the hall. She, too, looked scared.

"We thought you were lost," she said. "We went down to the terminal and you didn't come."

"I got a lift straight from the airport. I phoned but you must have left. I'm sorry."

Chilly and uncertain, she presented her cheek to be kissed. I obliged, holding my son in my arms. There was still a week until Christmas.

We didn't stand a chance. Within hours we were at each other again, and that night I started drinking. Mostly, I'm a social drinker. Like everyone else, I've been drunk in my time but it's not really my style: I value my control too highly. This time, however, I went at the bottle with a pure need, as though parched. I drank before I got out of bed, almost before my eyes were open. I continued steadily throughout the morning until, by lunch-time, I had half a bottle of whiskey inside me and was beginning to feel human. Not drunk: the first half-bottle simply brought me to that point of calm where I usually began. Which was not particularly calm. Around lunch-time a friend—also depressed, also drinking—joined me at the pub and we boozed until closing time. Back home with our wives, we kept at it steadily through the afternoon and evening, late into the night. The important thing was not to stop. In this way, I got through a bottle of whiskey a day, and a good deal of wine and beer. Yet it had little effect. Towards evening, when the child was in bed, I suppose I was a little tipsy, but the drinking was merely part of a more jagged frenzy which possessed us all. We kept the hi-fi booming pop, we danced, we had trials of strength: one-arm press-ups, handstands, somersaults; we balanced pint pots of beer on our foreheads, and tried to lie down and stand up again without spilling them. Anything not to stop, think, feel. The tension was so great that, without the booze, we would have splintered into sharp fragments.

On Christmas Eve, the other couple went off on a skiing holiday. My wife and I were left staring at each other. Silently and meticulously, we decorated the Christmas tree and piled the presents, waiting. There was nothing left to say.

Late that afternoon I had sneaked off and phoned the psychotherapist whom I had been seeing, on and off, before I left for the States.

"I'm feeling pretty bad," I said. "Could I possibly see you?"

There was a pause. "It's rather difficult," he said at last. "Are you really desperate, or could you wait till Boxing Day?"

Poor bastard, I thought, he's got his Christmas, too. Let it go. "I can wait."

"Are you sure?" He sounded relieved. "You could come round at 6:30, if it's urgent."

That was the child's bed-time; I wanted to be there. "It's all right," I said. "I'll phone later. Happy Christmas." What did it matter? I went back downstairs.

All my life I have hated Christmas: the unnecessary presents and obligatory cheerfulness, the grinding expense, the anti-climax. It is a day to be negotiated with infinite care, like a minefield. So I fortified myself with a stiff shot of whiskey before I got up. It combined with my child's excitement to put a glow of hope on the day. The boy sat among the gaudy wrapping paper, ribbons and bows, positively crowing with delight. At three years old, Christmas can still be a pleasure.

Maybe, I began to feel, this thing could be survived. After all, hadn't I flown all the way from the States to pull my marriage from the fire? Or had I? Perhaps I knew it was unsavable and didn't want it to be otherwise. Perhaps I was merely seeking a plausible excuse for doing myself in. Perhaps that was why, even before all the presents were unwrapped, I had started it all up again: silent rages (not in front of the child), muted recriminations, withdrawals. The marriage was just one aspect of a whole life I had decided, months before, to have done with.

I remember little of what happened later. There was the usual family turkey for the child and my parents-in-law. In the evening we went out to a smart and subdued dinner party, and on from there I think, to something wilder. But I'm not sure, I recall only two trivial but vivid scenes. The first is very late at night. We are back home with another couple whom I know only slightly. He is small, dapper, cheerful, an unsuccessful poet turned successful journalist. His wife is faceless now but him I still see sometimes on television, reporting expertly from the more elegant foreign capitals. I remember him sitting at our old piano, playing 1930s dance tunes; his wife stands behind him, singing the words; I lean on the piano, humming tunelessly; my wife is stretched, glowering, on the sofa. We are all very drunk.

Later still, I remember standing at the front door, joking with them as they negotiate the icy steps. As they go through the gate, they turn and wave. I wave back. "Happy Christmas," we call to each other. I close the door and turn back to my wife.

After that, I remember nothing at all until I woke up in the hospital and saw my wife's face swimming vaguely towards me through a yellowish fog. She was crying. But that was three days later, three days of oblivion, a hole in my head.

It happened ten years ago now, and only gradually have I been able to piece together the facts from hints and snippets, recalled reluctantly and with apologies. Nobody wants to remind an attempted suicide of his folly, or to be reminded of it. Tact and taste forbid. Or is it the failure itself which is embarrassing? Certainly, a successful suicide inspires no delicacy at all; everybody is in on the act at once with his own exclusive inside story. In my own case, my knowledge of what happened is partial and secondhand: the only accurate details are in the gloomy shorthand of the medical reports. Not that it matters, since none of it now means much to me personally. It is as though it had all happened to another person in another world.

It seems that when the poet-journalist left with his wife, we had one final, terrible quarrel, more bitter than anything we had managed before, and savage enough to be heard through his sleep by whoever it was who was staying the night in the guest-room above. At the end of it, my wife marched out. When she had returned prematurely from the States, our own house was still let out to temporary tenants. So she had rented a dingy flat in a florid but battered Victorian mansion nearby. Since she still had the key to the place, she went to spend the night there. In my sodden despair, I suppose her departure seemed like the final nail. More likely, it was the unequivocal excuse I had been waiting for. I went upstairs to the bathroom and swallowed forty-five sleeping pills.

I had been collecting the things for months obsessionally, like Green Shield Stamps, from doctors on both sides of the Atlantic. This was an almost legitimate activity since, in all that time, I rarely got more than two consecutive hours of sleep a night. But I had always made sure of having more than I needed. Weeks before I left America, I stopped taking the things and began hoarding them in preparation for the time I knew was coming. When it finally arrived, a box was waiting stuffed with pills of all colours, like Smarties. I gobbled the lot.

The following morning the guest brought me a cup of tea. The bedroom curtains were drawn, so he could not see me properly in the gloom. He heard me breathing in an odd way but thought it was probably a hangover. So he left me alone. My wife got back at noon, took one look and called the ambulance. When they got me to the hospital I was, the report says, "deeply unconscious, slightly cyanosed, vomit in mouth, pulse rapid, poor volume." I looked up "cyanosis" in the dictionary: "A morbid condition in which the surface of the body becomes blue because of insufficient aeration of the blood." Apparently, I had vomited in my coma and swallowed the stuff; it was now blocking my right lung, turning my face blue. As they say, a morbid condition. When they pumped the barbiturates out of my stomach, I vomited again, much more heavily, and again the muck went down to my lungs, blocking them badly. At that point I became—that word again—"deeply cyanosed": I turned Tory blue. They tried to suck the stuff out, and gave me oxygen and an injection, but neither had much effect. I suppose it was about this time that they told my wife there wasn't much hope. This was all she ever told me of the whole incident; it was a source of great bitterness to her. Since my lungs were still blocked, they performed a bronchoscopy. This time they sucked out a "large amount of mucus." They stuck an airpipe down my throat and I began to breathe more deeply. The crisis, for the moment was over.

This was on Boxing Day, 26 December. I was still unconscious the next day and most of the day after that, though all the time less and less deeply. Since my lungs remained obstructed, they continued to give me air through a pipe: they fed me intravenously through a drip-tube. The shallower my coma, the more restless I became. On the evening of the third day, 28 December, I came to. I felt them pull a tube from my arm. In a fog I saw my wife smiling hesitantly and in tears. It was all very vague. I slept.

I spent most of the next day weeping quietly and seeing everything double. Two women doctors gently cross-questioned me. Two chunky physiotherapists, with beautiful, blooming, double complexions, put me through exercises—it seems my lungs were still in a bad state. I got two trays of uneatable food at a time and tried, on and off and unsuccessfully, to do two crossword puzzles. The ward was thronged with elderly twins.

At some point, the police came, since in those days suicide was still a criminal offense. They sat heavily but rather sympathetically by my bed and asked me questions they clearly didn't want me to answer. When I tried to explain, they shushed me politely. "It was an accident, wasn't it, sir?" Dimly, I agreed. They went away.

I woke during the night and heard someone cry out weakly. A nurse bustled down the aisle in the obscure light. From the other side of the ward came more weak moaning. It was taken up faintly from somewhere else in the dimness. None of it was desperate with the pain and sharpness you hear after operations or accidents. Instead, the note was enervated, wan, beyond feeling. And then I understood why, even to my double vision, the patients had all seemed so old: I was in a terminal ward. All around me, old men were trying feebly not to die; I was thirty-one years old, and, despite everything, still alive. When I stirred in bed I felt, for the first time, a rubber sheet beneath me. I must have peed myself, like a small child, while I was unconscious. My whole world was shamed.

The following morning my double vision had gone. The ward was filthy yellow and seemed foggy in the corners. I tottered to the lavatory: it, too, was filthy and evil-smelling. I tottered back to bed, rested a little and then phoned my wife. Since the pills and the booze hadn't killed me, nothing would. I told her I was coming home. I wasn't dead, so I wasn't going to die. There was no point in staying.

The doctors didn't see it that way. I was scarcely off the danger-list: my lungs were in a bad state; I had a temperature; I could relapse at any time; it was dangerous; it was stupid; they would not be responsible. I lay there dumbly, as weak as a new-born infant, and let the arguments flow over me. Finally, I signed a sheaf of forms acknowledging that I left against advice, and absolving them from responsibility. A friend drove me home.

It took all my strength and concentration to climb the one flight of stairs to the bedroom. I felt fragile and almost transparent, as though I were made of tissue paper. But when I got into pajamas and settled into bed, I found I smelled bad to myself: of illness, urine, and a thin, sour death-sweat. So I rested for a while and then took a bath.

Meanwhile my wife, on orders from the hospital, phoned our National Health doctor. He listened to her explanation without a word and then refused, point blank, to come. Clearly, he thought I was going to die and didn't want me added to his, no doubt, already prodigious score. She banged down the receiver on him in a rage, but my green face and utter debility frightened her. Someone had to be sent for. Finally, the friend who had driven me home from the hospital called in his private family doctor. Authoritative, distinguished, unflappable, he came immediately and soothed everyone down.

This was on the evening of Thursday the 29th. All Friday and Saturday I lay vaguely in bed. Occasionally, I raised myself to perform the exercises which were supposed to help my lungs. I talked a little to my child, tried to read, dozed. But mostly, I did nothing. My mind was blank. At times I listened to my breath coming and going; at times I was dimly aware of my heart beating. It filled me with distaste. I did not want to be alive.

On Friday night I had a terrible dream. I was dancing a savage, stamping dance with my wife, full of anger and mutual threat. Gradually, the movements became more and more frenzied, until every nerve and muscle in my body was stretched taut and vibrating, as though on some fierce, ungoverned electrical machine which, fraction by fraction, was pulling me apart. When I woke, I was wet with sweat but my teeth were chattering as if I were freezing. I dozed off almost at once and again went through a similar dream: this time I was being hunted down; when the creature, whatever it was, caught me, it shook me as a dog shakes a rat, and once again every joint and nerve and muscle seemed to be rattling apart. Finally, I came awake completely and lay staring at the curtains. I was wide-eyed and shuddering with fear. I felt I had tasted in my dreams the death which had been denied me in my coma. My wife was sleeping in the same bed with me, yet she was utterly beyond my reach. I lay there for a long time, sweating and trembling. I have never felt so lonely.

Saturday night was New Year's Eve. Before I even arrived back from the States, we had arranged a party; there seemed no point now, despite everything, in calling it off. I had promised the doctor to spend it in bed, so for a while I held court regally in pajamas and dressing-gown. But this was an irritating, self-important posture. Friends came up to see me out of a sense of duty—they had been told I had had pneumonia. Obviously, they were bored. The music and voices below were enticing and, anyway, I had nothing now to lose. At 10:30 I got up, just to see in the New Year, I said. I got back to bed at six the following morning. At 10 A.M. I was up again and went down to help clean the house while my wife slept on. The debris of that New Year's binge seemed to me like the debris of the monstrous life I had been leading. I set to work cheerfully and with a will, mopping up, polishing, throwing things away. At lunch-time, when my wife staggered down hung over, the house was sparkling.

A week later, I returned to the States to finish the university term. While I was packing, I found, in the ticket pocket of my favourite jacket, a large, bright yellow, torpedo-shaped pill, which I had conned off a heavily insomniac American the day I left. I stared at the thing, turning it over and over on my palm, wondering how I'd missed it on the night. It looked lethal. I had survived forty-five pills. Would forty-six have done it? I flushed the thing down the lavatory.

And that was that. Of course, my marriage was finished. We hung on a few months more for decency's sake, but neither of us could continue in the shadow of such blackmail. By the time we parted, there was nothing left. Inevitably, I went through the expected motions of distress. But in my heart, I no longer cared.

The truth is, in some way I *had* died. The over-intensity, the tiresome excess of sensitivity and self-consciousness, of arrogance and idealism, which came in adolescence and stayed on and on beyond their due time, like some visiting bore, had not survived the coma. It was as though I had finally, and sadly late in the day, lost my innocence. Like all young people, I had been high-minded and apologetic, full of enthusiasms I didn't quite mean and guilts I didn't understand. Because of them, I had forced my poor wife, who was far too young to know what was happening, into a spoiling, destructive role she had never sought. We had spent five years thrashing around in confusion, as drowning men pull each other under. Then I had lain for three days in abeyance, and woken to feel nothing but a faint revulsion from everything and everyone. My weakened body, my thin breath, the slightest flicker of emotion filled me with distaste. I wanted only to be left to myself. Then, as the months passed, I began gradually to stir into another style of life, less theoretical, less optimistic, less vulnerable. I was ready for an insentient middle age.

Above all, I was disappointed. Somehow, I felt, death had let me down; I had expected more of it. I had looked for something overwhelming, an experience which would clarify all my confusions. But it turned out to be simply a denial of experience. All I knew of death was the terrifying dreams which came later. Blame it, perhaps, on my delayed adolescence: adolescents always expect too much; they want solutions to be immediate and neat, instead of gradual and incomplete. Or blame it on the cinema: secretly, I had thought death would be like the last reel of one of those old Hitchcock thrillers, when the hero relives as an adult that traumatic moment in childhood when the horror and splitting-off took place; and thereby becomes free and at peace with himself. It is a well-established, much imitated and persuasive formula. Hitchcock does it best but he himself did not invent it; he was simply popularizing a new tradition of half-digested psychoanalytic talk about "abreaction," that crucial moment of cathartic truth when the complex is removed. Behind that is the old belief in last-moment revelations, death-bed conversions, and all those old wives' tales of the drowning man reliving his life as he goes down for the last time. Behind that again is an older tradition still: that of the Last Judgement and the after-life. We all expect something of death, even if it's only damnation.

But all I had got was oblivion. To all intents and purposes, I had died: my face had been blue, my pulse erratic, my breathing ineffectual; the doctors had given me up. I went to the edge and most of the way over; then gradually, unwillingly and despite everything, I inched my way back. And now I knew nothing at all about it. I felt cheated.

Why had I been so sure of finding some kind of answer? There are always special reasons why a man should choose to die in one way rather than in another, and my own reasons for taking barbiturates were cogent enough, although I did not recognize them at the time. As a small baby, I had been given a general anaesthetic when a major operation was performed on my ankle. The surgery had not been a great success and regularly throughout my childhood the thing gave me trouble. Always the attacks were heralded by the same dream: I had to work out a complicated mathematical problem which involved my whole family; their well-being depended on my finding the right answer. The sum changed as I grew, becoming more sophisticated as I learned more mathematics, always keeping one step ahead of me, like the carrot and the donkey. Yet I knew that however complex the problem, the answer would be simple. It merely eluded me. Then, when I was fourteen, my appendix was removed and I was once again put under a general anaesthetic. The dream, by then, had not recurred for a year or two. But as I began to breathe in the ether, the whole thing happened again. When the first sharp draught of gas entered my lungs, I saw the problem, this time in calculus, glowing like a neon sign, with all my family crowding around, dangling, as it were, from the terms. I breathed out and then, as I drew in the next lungful of ether, the figures whirred like the circuits of a computer, the stages of the equation raced in front of me, and I had the answer: a simple two-figure number. I had known it all along. For three days after I came round, I still knew that simple solution, and why and how it was so. I didn't have a care in the world. Then gradually it faded. But the dream never returned.

I thought death would be like that: a synoptic vision of life, crisis by crisis, all suddenly explained, justified, redeemed, a Last Judgement in the coils and circuits of the brain. Instead, all I got was a hole in the head, a round zero, nothing. I'd been swindled.

Months later, I began to understand that I had had my answer, after all. The despair that had led me to try to kill myself had been pure and unadulterated, like the final, unanswerable despair a child feels, with no before or after. And, childishly, I had expected death not merely to end it but also to explain it. Then, when death let me down, I gradually saw that I had been using the wrong language; I had translated the thing into Americanese. Too many movies, too many novels, too many trips to the States had switched my understanding into a hopeful, alien tongue. I no longer thought of myself as unhappy; instead, I had "problems." Which is an optimistic way of putting it since problems imply solutions, whereas unhappiness is merely a condition of life which you must live with, like the weather. Once I had accepted that there weren't ever going to be any answers, even in death, I found to my surprise that I didn't much care whether I was happy or unhappy; "problems" and "the problem of problems" no longer existed. And that in itself is already the beginning of happiness.

It seems ludicrous now to have learned something so obvious in such a hard way, to have had to go almost the whole way into death in order to grow up. Somewhere, I still feel cheated and aggrieved, and also ashamed of my stupidity. Yet, in the end, even oblivion was an experience of a kind. Certainly, nothing has been quite the same since I discovered for myself, in my own body and on my own nerves, that death is simply an end, a dead end, no more, no less. And I wonder if that piece of knowledge isn't in itself a form of death. After all, the youth who swallowed the sleeping pills and the man who survived are so utterly different that someone or something must have died. Before the pills was another life, another person altogether, whom I scarcely recognize and don't much like—although I suspect that he was, in his priggish way, far more likeable than I could ever be. Meanwhile, his fury and despair seem improbable now, sad and oddly diminished.

The hole in my head lasted a long time. For five years after the event I had periods of sheer blankness, as though some vital center had been knocked out of action. For days on end I went round like a zombie, a walking corpse. And I used to wonder, in a vague, numb way, if maybe I had died, after all. But if so, how could I ever tell?

In time, even that passed. Years later, when the house where it had happened was finally sold, I felt a sharp pang of regret for all the exorbitant pain and waste. After that, the episode lost its power. It became just so much dead history, a gossipy, mildly interesting anecdote about someone half-forgotten. As Coriolanus said, "There is a world elsewhere."

As for suicide: the sociologists and psychologists who talk of it as a disease puzzle me now as much as the Catholics and Muslims who call it the most deadly of mortal sins. It seems to me to be somehow as much beyond social or psychic prophylaxis as it is beyond morality, a terrible but utterly natural reaction to the strained, narrow, unnatural necessities we sometimes create for ourselves. And it is not for me. Perhaps I am no longer optimistic enough. I assume now that death, when it finally comes, will probably be nastier than suicide, and certainly a great deal less convenient.

PLANET NO

❧

Lesley Dormen

IN THE BICENTENNIAL MANHATTAN SUMMER of 1976, with the Tall Ships showing off in New York Harbor and the streets crowded with knowing city girls in tank tops, with open-faced sailors lifted straight from some old Hollywood musical, two losses sent my life into crisis. An architect I'd loved for under a year left me for a woman he met in a supermarket parking lot. And my best friend, Tessa, a woman as central to my understanding of myself as my own brown eyes and small feet, disappeared into marriage and withdrew from our friendship completely.

"Come with me to the seaport," my friend Jerry urged me that Fourth of July weekend from a pay phone. I was a few months shy of my thirtieth birthday. He was the married man I'd fallen in love with at twenty-five, twice my age, my introduction to a New York I was drawn to but couldn't seem to locate through my own generation's experiences. Jerry was no longer my lover (I'd left him for the architect), no longer married, and therefore no longer required to conduct our relationship from public phones, but the habit lingered.

"I'll take you to a party on a Romanian yacht. Norman Mailer will be there. Abbie Hoffman will be there. We'll drink lousy wine and flirt with each other."

"No," I said, "I can't." This was my answer to everything that summer. I can't. I don't think so. Not today. I'm sorry. No.

My heart pumped dread. It was an actual substance I could feel coursing through my bloodstream—some days a barely-there awareness, other days a carbonated liquid that seemed to have replaced my blood. At the same time I was aware of something large and dark that pushed up against—and was possibly worse than—the dread.

It was an out-of-time summer to begin with, the summer of 1976, an improbably silly (all those ships and sailors) time bookended between the tabloid sourness of FORD TO CITY: DROP DEAD and the following year's summer of Sam, a period that punctuated the still-recent twin disgraces of Vietnam and Watergate. Although for me it had begun as hopeful (I was a single woman in love and therefore temporarily excused from having to worry about my future), by summer's end the darkness had crashed through the dread and my life had narrowed down to a single life-or-death struggle.

I'd come to New York in 1968, the year I graduated from college in the midwest. I'd been an English major looking for a job "in publishing." Helen Gurley Brown was reinventing *Cosmopolitan* and Germaine Greer was about to roar into bad-girl fame with *The Female Eunuch.* I tied a silk scarf to my purse and, trying to pretend I wasn't afraid of everything, reported to a job at *American Girl,* a teen magazine published by the Girl Scouts. It was my mother who had found the want ad in *The New York Times,* bought my interview suit at Bonwit Teller, and cheerleaded me out the door of her Westchester home. Newly graduated, I was still sleeping late and hoping to idle, safe from my future, a few weeks more. But like a good daughter, I went. She was irresistible, my mother, glamorous and warm, ironic and naive—the kind of mother all your friends wish were their own.

As the sixties turned into 1970 and became The Sixties, I carefully measured columns of type with my big yellow pica ruler, copyedited manuscripts, and proofread long galley sheets. In the evenings I took the subway home to the apartment Tessa and I rented together on the Upper East Side. We smoked joints, listened to Janis Joplin, and hung out with the boys on the third floor. We trained binoculars on the masturbator in the building across the courtyard, ordered in Chinese food, and talked about what was wrong with all the people we knew. We did all the things people do in their twenties when life is still an extension of college, and of childhood really. Mostly we laughed. It seems amazing how much we laughed considering how terrified we both were.

Those were the years when you were likely as not to sleep with every man who so much as caught your eye across a party, when you didn't see a single baby or toddler on the street. Where were all the families? Maybe on the Upper West Side. We took leaves of absences from our jobs and traveled through Europe, plotted our love affairs, and abruptly left the city to share a house with our college friend David in a picturesque Connecticut town.

I took a job in the town's library. I tap-danced in a community production of *Anything Goes*. I wrote the first paragraphs of a few short stories. Tessa commuted to her job in New York and David and I collected her at the train station each evening. One night she got off the train with three top hats and canes and we lip-synched our way through Sondheim's *Follies*. But there were other evenings when Tessa's after-work face in that crowd of rumpled family men held a fierce and unnamed turbulence. "Uh-oh, we're in for it," David would say, reaching behind him to unlock the back door of the Toyota.

"Sometimes when I close my eyes at night to go to sleep," Tessa told me, "I feel I'm getting smaller and smaller and that by the time I wake up I'll have disappeared." It was 1972. All three of us had begun to see therapists.

"I had a sexual relationship with my stepfather," I told the psychologist whose office I drove to once a week in an adjacent picturesque Connecticut town. It was the first time I had said those words out loud, and having said them, I had nothing to add. At least, in the stalemated silence that followed, I neither offered nor perceived an invitation to elaborate. We returned to more fertile ground: my unreciprocated romantic feelings for David, my general feeling of purposelessness. If I were a girl in a story, how would I see myself, the doctor wanted to know. "Like an orphan," I answered, instantly ashamed to have said something so mawkish.

By then, the specific memories that added up to whatever it was I meant by "sexual relationship" had distilled themselves into a black dot that occupied a familiar place in my mind and that I could visit or not at will. The dot stood for the sexual play my mother's second husband had begun with me the year I was twelve. The dot stood for the sexual pleasure I felt. The dot stood for the shame I felt to recall the pleasure. The dot stood for the groan that came from my stepfather's throat the day he tore himself away from me in my narrow bed and said aloud the five spell-shattering words: "Oh, Lesley, this isn't good." The dot stood for my pity for him and my humiliation by him. The dot was a seed grown around me into a thick, obscuring forest of betrayal and guilt. The forest hid me in plain sight. First from my mother. Then from myself. Oh, yes, I'd think, when my mind touched that dot, that old friend, my precocious knowledge of illicit pleasure, my duplicity, my longing, my guilt. Reaching for the dot was a repetitive exercise my mind mindlessly performed, finding the dot and refinding it in a burlesque of reassurance—would it be there, yes, there it was, it was always there—and then moving away, leaving me with the vague uneasiness that was a familiar part of my internal landscape.

David and I also attended group therapy. This weekly session was held on the grounds of Silver Hill, a private sanatorium in another leafy town near ours. When David and I drove away from the hospital after group and down the curving drive, I was aware of a small sinking inside myself. I didn't articulate the feeling, but if I had it would have gone something like this: Wouldn't it be nice if a person could just stay in such a place for a while? As if it were a vacation resort. As if it were a future.

This wasn't romanticism. Until I met David and Tessa, I'd never known anyone who saw a psychiatrist, had no leanings (save for one unforgettable night seeing Judy Garland play the Palace) toward the mythology of breakdown. I'd never read or even heard of Sylvia Plath or Anne Sexton. I knew Holden Caulfield and *Tender Is the Night* and I'd memorized the odd Emily Dickinson poem, but I don't recall an adolescent fascination with anyone, literary or otherwise, whose showy demons spoke specifically to me.

I was drawn to Silver Hill because it was a mental hospital. But what would mental illness have to do with me? On the one hand, I was a "normal girl," an ordinary young woman whose "decision" to see a psychotherapist was influenced by friendship and casual intellectual curiosity. *The Interpretation of Dreams* sat in the pile of books on my bedside table, but so did *I'm Okay, You're Okay*. On the other hand, as accustomed as I was to feeling I stood on the sidelines of ordinary life, my uneasiness was growing more insistent; it felt like doom. Still, I could no more open my mouth and conjure words to describe my guilty yearning for a Silver Hill than I could describe the dot or my ambivalent love for my mother. I was the dot. My mother was the atmosphere I breathed, the oxygen that gave me life—even if it was an uneasily suspended life.

Instead of Silver Hill, I returned to my mother herself, again and again—weekends in Westchester, dinner and theater in New York. Once there, in my mother's orbit, the dread alchemized into a memory-sapping malaise that bled me of all purpose. The chilled air of her beautiful house was dream water in which I could barely move a limb and barely wanted to. Furthermore, whatever it might take on

my part to look for and find release from that benumbing atmosphere, that spell, seemed beyond the power of will, the strength of
hope.

Except when I was with Tessa. Her bell-jar remove from feeling
mirrored my own. But I had never named it, never described it even
to myself. Internally I had come to see myself as if I were a doubled
photographic image of a young woman: out of focus and unrecognizable. Tessa's comic distance—her verbal authority extended enter-
tainingly to her body, her family, her hometown, her lovers, and her
own self-lacerating despair—reliably reflected back to me my own
unreliable self. Unlike my mother's sunny optimism, which came at
me with the disregard of a wild pitch, Tessa's droll deadpan described
a neighborhood where I already lived. In my friend's voice I heard
the universal laws I knew: life is absurd, hilarious, and hopeless. It is
full of longings and unimaginable fireworks, fated to give up gigantic
helpings of disappointment and pain for every tiny speck of joy. In
Tessa's orbit, the dread quieted and the despair was beat back. Someone I recognized from the bottom of my soul recognized me. It felt
like happiness.

Tessa returned to Manhattan within a year, wanting the world.
In her desire for it all I saw was my own failure of desire. "It's okay to
work in a library—or to be a receptionist or a clerk in a store," the
group-therapy doctor told us one afternoon at Silver Hill. "It's okay
to want a smaller life." But when Tessa's U-Haul passed by the
library and she tooted the horn, I felt amazingly alone. It wasn't okay
with me.

Almost two years passed before I followed her back to the city. My
mother's third husband had begun to publish a men's magazine, a
Playboy clone formerly owned by F. Lee Bailey, and he needed editors. I brought Tessa on staff, and the two of us assigned articles,
lunched with agents, interviewed minor celebrities, and wrote the
sexy "girl copy" that went alongside pictures of naked women in
fuzzy boas and frilly garter belts.

How do you date the beginning of despair? It is true, I think, that as Kierkegaard wrote, "the specific character of despair is precisely this: it is unaware of being despair." I date the beginning of what I would later understand to be major depression to Tessa's marriage and to being dumped by the architect, but I do it the way you locate the spirit of a decade in some vivid, attention-focusing event: Woodstock, say, or Watergate. As 1973 slipped into 1975 and the seventies became a stage where Amazon women noisily insisted on themselves, my nerve faltered and sputtered out. No distractions or devotions— not love, not sex, not Tessa, not my mother—buffered me. Yes, the summer of 1976 was in fact the summer I started seeing a second therapist, the summer I began to attach a narrative story to my dread, the summer I did something. But I had been falling toward this one bone-shattering, trance-obliterating place, the psychic scenery shifting and changing as I tumbled, for a long time.

Certain moments stand out: a warm Manhattan posttheater evening on the corner of Broadway and Forty-fifth when I found myself unable to kiss my mother good night. Weeping in the arms of the architect in an Ohio Holiday Inn the weekend I was a bridesmaid in Tessa's wedding. A late summer night in bed at my mother's house, hearing the house humming efficiently around me and not being able to breathe, the bedroom walls coming in on me, waking my brother to tell him I didn't know what was happening but that I thought I couldn't breathe and did he think I could be dying? I didn't die. I waited until morning and took the train back to my Manhattan apartment.

The great good gift in my life in the summer of 1976 was a one-bedroom walk-up on one of the most beautiful blocks in Greenwich Village. I'd inherited the apartment from Tessa's new husband, who had lived there for many years. I moved in almost as an afterthought, assuming it would be what my other two New York apartments had been, a waiting room for marriage. Then, after the architect left me, and then Tessa—absorbed into her married apartment with its reassuring china cabinet and triumphant spice rack—retreated, for the longest time I thought those small rooms would be where I vanished or died, where I would never find comfort, where I would live a life erased by despair, failed at love and work and happiness and all the things I hadn't come to know there were to want.

One of the many things I hate about the word "depression" is the assumption of blankness attached to it, as if the experience of depression is as absent on the inside as it looks to be from the outside. That is wrong. Depression is a place that teems with nightmarish activity. It's a one-industry town, a psychic megalopolis devoted to a single twenty-four-hour-we-never-close product. You work misery as a teeth-grinding muscle-straining job (is that why it's so physically exhausting?), proving your shameful failures to yourself over and over again. Depression says you can get blood from a stone, and so that's what you do. Competing voices are an irritating distraction from the work. No wonder depression doesn't get invited out much. Not because it's not the life of the party, it knows it's not that, but because self-absorption as a work ethic is so prickly and one-eyed. That's okay with depression—it figures, who'd want to be friends with it, anyway?

But certain voices, written ones, did penetrate the windows and walls of my small rooms and thinned skin. Reading was my one dependable addiction. I vividly remember sitting on my sofa and coming across an essay by Karen Durbin in *The Village Voice*, "On Being a Woman Alone." I see myself there in the menacing drift of the afternoon, feeling more alone I was sure than any woman who could write about being a woman alone could ever fathom being, and reading words that spoke so directly to my struggle that they felt like code. My dreams that summer were filled with water. In her essay, Durbin relates an experience of a near drowning to illuminate her own dangerous solitude. "What I felt was a slow, dull dying, as the water deadened my legs, turning them to lead, pulling me down deeper each time . . . I felt no hope. I couldn't save myself, but it seemed insane to die without at least trying to call for help." I must have read that essay fifty times. Sometimes I quieted the dread just by touching the sentences on the newsprint.

When Jerry gave me the number of a clinic and insisted I call for an appointment, he sounded frightened for me, and so I did. Therapy, at the very least, would be an activity related to my primary work—fright and failure—and so it seemed possible to get on the subway and take the work there.

I sat in the reception room at the clinic, waiting for my name to be called—I had arrived well ahead of my appointment time—feeling the way you do before a test, nervous and eager to perform well. But I couldn't imagine what that performance would consist of, much less the point of it. I felt wrong. I felt baffled by and ashamed of my passivity and the flatness of my imagination. I assumed these were failings of character, not conditions that could be cured. Yet the wrongness and the flatness and the passivity produced such inexpressible pain. Surely that couldn't be right. But what words could I come up with to describe the bitterness I felt toward myself for my failings? Words were too small.

A slim, blond-haired woman in a jeans skirt and sandals came out to get me. I followed her into a room with a clattery air conditioner. She seemed to have faith in the words I spoke, and so I tried to have faith in them, too. I began at the beginning. I told her about the father I lost through divorce at six and the stepfather who seduced me at twelve and David who couldn't love me and the architect who'd stopped loving me. These men received top billing in my account of myself. They were larger than my complicated mother and my best friend, who were the ocean I swam in and therefore seemingly separate from my pain.

"And then he said. So I said. I thought. And he didn't even . . ." This wasn't what I meant to be telling, this wasn't it. "I'm sorry, I sound like Dear Abby," I said, then launched into the next round of lovesick details in the same dumb incantation of the story-without-an-ending. And though this story, the wrong story, didn't seem to reach into the hard heart of the despair, I didn't know what else to tell.

"Go on," she said kindly. She was too new to be away in August.

In October, she tried holding me, the two of us sitting side by side on the sofa in her office.

"You'd better not kill yourself," she told me in January when I let her know I was hoarding Valium, that just the idea of suicide was a comfort to me. "I don't want that on my conscience."

By March, I was beginning to think I could find comfort, or at least a resting place, in the idea that perhaps I really was "sick." But she wouldn't let me think of myself that way. "You're not dissociating," she crisply explained.

I wasn't telling stories anymore, that's for sure. They had all dried up and disappeared. I was just showing up in her office once or twice a week, always desperate to get there but out of words once I did, sometimes crying, other times silent and stony, something self-pitying and choked in my throat. I was terrified to meet anyone's eyes on the subway, especially the older women, the ones with too much makeup who couldn't meet anyone's eyes themselves. Except for the occasional Valium, there were no drugs then, not for me. Antidepressants weren't widely prescribed yet. And at any rate, it didn't occur to me to ask for other medication. I got to know depression the old way, by taking it uptown to a therapist's room.

It became obvious to me in that room—during the talking, dreaming years of my thirties—that my stepfather's use of me was the curve in my depression story. His touch had caused the spine of the story to veer off into a new direction, had reconfigured the terms of my loves and longings to be. (Sometime during my thirteenth year, my mother ran her hand across my back and discovered that my actual spine *was* curved: I had scoliosis.) It was in that therapist's room that I first heard my story, and its curve, as something separate from the dot. Something happened—something that was separate from me. There was a me that existed before the something and a me that existed after. Before and after were separate, not the same. Not the dot. Furthermore, it was possible to stand outside those events, to observe them and draw a conclusion about them. It was possible to not just be them.

It was impossible at first. I worried that maybe the curve itself was theoretical. I knew the facts of what happened, just not how I felt about them. How could a therapist take my word for my emotions? Yet here I was expecting that same therapist to base her treatment of me on what I told her. I didn't know which was worse—feeling like a fraud or feeling totally alone. (Maybe she was the fraud.) I made her tell me my story again and again. I became a student of it, crammed it, turned it this way and that way, peered at it through the available seductive theories and popular prisms—Freud! Donahue! *The Drama of the Gifted Child!* I rubbernecked the accident site as if it were, to borrow Walker Percy's words, my own "sweet center of bad news." Variously, I clung to my story's curve as a shipwrecked person would to a piece of ocean wreckage and held on—waving and drowning both.

Did depression find me because of my stepfather's touch? Did depression rush to fill the shocked space left when he withdrew his touch? Or was depression a consequence of my essential chemical constitution? Or did events themselves create the chemistry? I don't know. But I do know that there wasn't much then or now in the popular conversation about incest and depression that describes what felt truest about my experience. I wasn't angry at my mother because she failed to protect me. I was preoccupied with my mother. My stepfather's touch had not only reshaped me, it had also reshaped her in my eyes. Incest made my mother larger and my stepfather smaller. My stepfather's touch did not leave me either suspicious of men and sex or self-destructively promiscuous. My sexuality was as robust, imperfect, and mysterious as the next woman's. What I distrusted was the act of desiring—the excitement of my own imagination at play. I was frozen in a girlhood made curiously old.

Knowing these things didn't impress depression much. Depression is wilier than that. The big question was what I was going to do—how was I to live a meaningful and unafraid life outside of that room? Back in the dead air of my little apartment where even the objects around me seemed concrete forms of my nothingness, what good was knowing my story? And even as the months passed and some of the bleakness lifted and I ventured beyond the Chinese take-out on the corner, knowing the story of my past seemed scant protection from the insistent turmoil of my present.

During those years of therapy, I found myself thrown back into an adolescence I'd never experienced. My standoff with my mother continued to erupt in small, hurtful dramas. (Would I or would I not accept her hand-me-down raccoon coat? Two months worth of therapy on that.) My love affairs were tumultuous, complete with angry scenes on street corners and abrupt exits from restaurants, like women I had seen in movies. I grieved obsessively when they ended. Tessa, spooked by my depression and disapproving of the men I fell in love with, told me she couldn't see me at all. I brought each small story to that therapist, all the evidence that I was becoming a woman who made mistakes, who hurt other people, who insisted on herself. Terrifying. But also joyful: I fell in love with New York, with the giddy green of the first spring after the worst of the depression lifted, with new friends, travel, and wonderful books. I looked around my apartment and saw that there was pleasure in things, in their colors and shapes, and that one did not actually need a marriage certificate to buy good pots. I found the courage to enroll in a fiction workshop. Now that I could separate out the voices inside my own head, I knew my continued survival depended on the pleasure I felt when I played with them. I began to become a writer.

As time passed and I moved from seat to seat in the theater of my own psyche, my perspective shifted along with my sight lines. I came to see my story as an ordinary story. I was and always would be a woman with a curve. I no longer live on the planet of depression, but I am angled toward it. Some years ago a difficult love affair ended, and I felt my body lurch toward the same atmospheric pull of despair—all the metabolic refusals of sleep, food, pleasure. I told myself: Okay, I will grieve, but I will not give in to depression's undertow. By then, Prozac had insinuated itself into the culture's vocabulary. When I called my therapist to ask her about antidepressants, she didn't hesitate to send me to a psychopharmacologist. I liked the fact that the psychopharmacologist was less interested in the curve of my particular story than he was in the straightforward narrative of my body's responses to events. I've been taking antidepressants since. Will I always? I don't know. When a recent work setback startled me into that familiar state of mourning, breaking through whatever net the antidepressant provided, I was amazed to realize that my body didn't distinguish between work loss and love loss. I temporarily upped the Zoloft. It's as if the secrets of the universe have been revealed to me—and they turn out to be based on a formula no more complicated than the recipe for Jell-O.

I met my husband ten years ago, when I was finally making my living as a writer. He's never known me as a woman living on Planet No, but I've described my life there. I want him to know where I come from. I have lived longer now without depression than at any other time of my life. I marvel at my ability to move in and out of ordinary feelings like sadness and disappointment and worry. I continue to be stunned by the purity of these feelings, by the beauty of their rightful proportions to actual life events. I'm hardly carefree—I still scan myself for depression as if checking for broken bones. But I consider my ability to participate at last in the everyday a gift. I don't know where depression comes from or where it goes. I do know that it was the crucible, the rite of passage, that allowed me to create my life.

A MELANCHOLY OF MINE OWN

❧

Joshua Wolf Shenk

AFTER HE HAS AWOKEN, FROM uneasy dreams, to find himself transformed in his bed into a giant insect, Gregor Samsa's first encounter with the world outside his bedroom comes in the form of his mother's voice. "Gregor," she says. "It's a quarter to seven. Hadn't you a train to catch?" When he opens his mouth to answer, Gregor hears a peculiar sound. The voice is "unmistakably his own" but has a "persistent horrible twittering squeak behind it like an undertone that left the words in their clear shape only for the first moment and then rose up reverberating round them to destroy their sense." And so, having at first thought that he would "explain everything," Gregor says only this: "Yes, yes, thank you Mother, I'm getting up now."

In *The Metamorphosis,* a story about alienation, the first rupture is one of language. Words emerge true from Gregor Samsa's mouth, but they soon ring false. Just as his body has become unrecognizable, inexplicably Other, so has his voice. "I am constantly trying to communicate something incommunicable, to explain something inexplicable," Kafka wrote of himself. He was alienated from language, and even felt trapped by it. Words, metaphors, and stories were his only way out.

W o r d

When I was a small child, about eight I think, I ripped apart my bedroom in a frenzy. I threw the pencil sharpener off my desk. I pulled the sheets and blankets off my bed and turned over the mattress. I pulled clothes out of their drawers, drawers out of the bureau. Eventually the bureau itself toppled. A few moments later, my mom stood in my doorway and said, with aplomb, "Looks like a tornado has been through here."

Five years later I stood on the lawn of my father's house, just home from summer camp. My oldest brother drove up the dead-end street in his gray Fiat and turned left into the short driveway. I ran over to see him. I recall, as I ran, feeling a false expansiveness. I wore a too-wide smile, like a clown scripted for a pratfall. As I began toward the car, my brother leaned over and rolled up the window on the Fiat's passenger side. Then he backed down the driveway and drove away.

When I was seventeen, I carried these and other fragments up the stairs of an old Victorian home in Cincinnati. As I sat in the waiting room of a psychiatry practice, I knew I was lonely, unhappy, even desperate. I did not know I was depressed. But that was the word that waited for me, a diagnosis that physicians since Hippocrates have been trying to elucidate and one that I would inherit.

The Hippocratic writers believed that gloom, abnegation, and misanthropy could be traced to excesses of black bile. Unlike the other three bodily humors (blood, phlegm, and yellow bile), black bile was never actually observed. Today, we know no such substance ever existed. Still, the Greek words for black (*melan*) and bile (*kholē*) dominated the language of inner states for more than two millennia.

In 1905, the influential American psychiatrist Adolf Meyer proposed that "melancholy" and "melancholia" be retired from the clinical vocabulary. He believed that the terms were used too broadly. They described "many dissimilar conditions" and also "implied a knowledge of something that we did not possess"—that is, the causal role of black bile. Meyer preferred the word "depression." Other physicians followed him, as did medical texts and the lay culture.

In the hands of modern writers, "melancholy" has recently experienced a renaissance. In *Darkness Visible,* William Styron charges that Meyer "had a tin ear for the finer rhythms of English and therefore was unaware of the semantic damage he had inflicted by offering 'depression' as a descriptive noun for such a dreadful and raging disease." The word "depression," Styron continues, has "slithered innocuously through the language like a slug, preventing, by its very insipidity, a general awareness of the horrible intensity of the disease when out of control."

It strikes me as telling that writers—for whom words are tools and imprecision deathly—knowingly use a term that is literally untrue; and that they use "melancholy," "depression," and other imperfect words interchangeably. These are two of many indications that the experience they describe has no true name. Styron, for instance, readily concedes the paradox that his memoir of melancholia is but a hazy shadow of something "indescribable." Most accounts of depression will have this sort of disclaimer. Others disclaim implicitly through dependence on metaphor and allusion.

Perhaps depression is simply hard to convey—even, as Styron

says, "indescribable." But I'd like to suggest another possibility: that what we call "depression," like the mythical black bile, is a chimera. That it is cobbled together of so many different parts, causes, experiences, and affects as to render the word ineffectual and perhaps even noxious to a full, true narrative.

It is ironic, given the criticism directed at him, that Adolf Meyer seemed to have in mind the limits of single-word diagnoses when he proposed that depression replace melancholy. Meyer believed the former word, obviously inadequate, would force doctors to tailor their descriptions to individual cases. "Nobody would doubt that for medical purposes the term would have to be amplified so as to denote the *kind* of depression," Meyer wrote (italics added). Perhaps Meyer even liked the insipid quality of "depression," believing it would announce (like a blank canvas or the blue screen on a film set) the absence of material to come.

If so, what transpired over the century can be counted among the great tragicomedies in the history of language: somehow, we have come to believe that "depression" *is* the art, *is* the phantasm of special effects, *is* the evocative detail or phrase or story—rather than a placeholder. The *DSM-IV* lists only a few qualifiers for "major depressive disorder." Psychiatrists and medical texts treat depression as a discrete entity, and assume it adheres to a particular course and treatment. Ads for drugs, herbal remedies, and nutritional supplements refer to depression as though it is a foreign invader, unrelated to the authentic self.

In lay culture, meanwhile, the word is often used with no context at all. A *New York Times* report on the rising suicide rate in Japan notes that the cause might be "depression," but does not offer even a single phrase to elaborate. In conversation, otherwise imaginative, articulate speakers toss around the words "depressive" and "depressed" as if they capture a person's essence. In his story "The Depressed Person," David Foster Wallace gives the eponymous character no other name, which I take as sardonic reflection on the way we drape over diverse sufferers a label that hides more than it reveals.

Perhaps, for many, staying hidden is part of the point. I think of Tipper Gore, who first spoke publicly of her depression in a front-page interview with *USA Today*. After her son recovered from a nearly fatal accident, Gore explained, she saw a social worker and was told she "had a clinical depression and one that I was going to have to have help to overcome."

She continued, "What I learned about it is your brain needs a certain amount of serotonin and when you run out of that, it's like running out of gas, it's like you're on empty. When you get to this point of being seriously depressed or what we call 'clinically depressed,' you just can't will your way out of that or pray your way out of that or pull yourself up by the boot straps out of that. You really have to go and get help, and I did. And I was treated for it successfully, I'm happy to report."

Gore did not describe in what way she felt depressed, nor how it affected her life—only that she had a clinical depression and was treated for it successfully. Her reticence might have been motivated by discretion, or a wish for privacy, and I do not begrudge her these. I appreciate her candor, insofar as many would choose to say nothing. Still, like so many public figures who have made similar confessions, she hinted at intimacy, then quickly withdrew behind a wall. The word "depression" was that wall.

It is inevitable that we abbreviate and simplify. (It is apparent even in this essay that I see no way around the words "depression" and "melancholy.") But it is one thing to use shorthand while straining against the limits of language. It is quite another to mistake such brevities for the face of suffering. Each year, seventeen million Americans and one hundred million people worldwide experience clinical depression. What does this mean, exactly? Perhaps they all have deficits of serotonin, feel hopeless, ruminate on suicide. But why? What wrinkles crease their minds? How are they impaired? For how long—two weeks? a month each year? an entire life? And from where does this depression come?

Rather than acknowledge these variations and uncertainties,

many react against them, taking comfort in language that raises the fewest questions, provokes the least fear of the unknown. Such is the case with the equation of emotional problems and mechanical fail- ure. Phrases like "running out of gas," "neurotransmitter deficits," "biochemical malfunctions," and "biological brain disease" are terri- bly common, and are favored by well-intentioned activists who seek parity between emotional and somatic illnesses. Pharmaceutical companies also like machine imagery, since they manufacture the oils, coolants, and fuels that are supposed to make us run without knocks or stalls.

This language not only reflects, but constructs, our reality. When we funnel a sea of human experience into the linguistic equivalent of a laboratory beaker, when we discuss suffering in simple terms of broken and fixed, mad and sane, depressed and "treated successfully," we choke the long streams of breath needed to tell of a life in whole.

Metaphor

Just as we hear music through intervals, experience is often easiest to understand in terms of contrast. And so despair is often best expressed in terms of what has changed. "I used to relish crowds on the street, but now people repulse me." Or, "I used to wake up with a feeling of expectancy. Now I can only wrap the pillow around my head and pray for more sleep."

When I began psychotherapy late in high school, I had a clear and persistent sense that something was wrong with me, but no vocabulary with which to describe it. I could not draw on contrast because I didn't remember a time when I felt differently or better. I did not have seasons of happiness followed by epochs of misery, or fall off cliffs and climb back up among the daisies. I felt as I felt for as long as I could remember. I did not go to therapy to understand, or to get through, an episode. I needed to understand and get through my life.

Since my "condition" is so deeply rooted, much of my personality has grown out of it and developed to cloak it. This made expressing myself even harder. I did well in school, stayed out of trouble, behaved like a son my parents could be proud of. I wrapped myself in a skin of normalcy and success but grew more hidden, from others and from myself. In high school, I wrote in a poem that I wished "to be a slug, to have an exterior that expressed what I felt." Like Gregor Samsa, I greatly desired to speak the whole truth. Instead, much of the time, I merely said, Thank you, thank you, I'm getting up now—going to school, going eventually to college and the bright future that everyone expected. But the present, which I tried so hard to dodge, could not be dodged.

In *Seeing Voices,* his book on the language of the deaf, Oliver Sachs notes that philosophers have long dreamed of "a primordial or original human language, in which everything has its true and natural name; a language so concrete, so particular, that it can catch the essence, the 'itness' of everything; so spontaneous that it expresses all emotion directly; and so transparent that it is incapable of any evasion or deception. Such a language would be without (and indeed would have no need for) logic, grammar, metaphor, or abstractions—it would be a language not mediated, a symbolic expression of thought and feeling, but, almost magically, an *im*mediate one."

I hoped for such fluid, full, direct communication in therapy. I tried to express the relentless stream of criticism that I directed at myself and others, the way I felt split in two, the dull and sharp aches that moved around my body as though taunting me. I wished to plug a probe from my brain to the doctor's so that he could see—without mediation—how I stood outside myself, watching and criticizing, and could never fully participate in a moment. How I felt bewildered, anguished, horrified.

Instead, I often found myself silent. When I spoke, it was with stumbles and stammers. Words—*unhappy, anxious, lonely*—seemed plainly inadequate, as did modifiers: *all the time, without relief.* Ordinary phrases such as *I feel bad* or *I am unhappy* seemed pallid. Evocative metaphors—*My soul is like burned skin, aching at any touch; I have the emotional equivalent of a dislocated limb*—were garish. Though this language hinted at how bad I felt, it could not express what it felt like to be me.

I suppose the combination of words, body language, and silence did, in some measure, convey the message, because my first therapist was able to offer me a helpful phrase. "Is it," he asked, "as though you have a soundtrack of negative thoughts in your head—the volume rising or falling, but never going silent?" I pictured an old reel-to-reel tape machine, sitting alone on a table in an empty room. I lingered over the image, comforted especially by the acknowledgment that it never stopped. And I felt a spark of recognition, a kind of introduction to the meaning of my own experience.

The soundtrack image was an imperfect one, as I do not "hear voices" in the sense of hallucination, nor are the bad feelings that echo inside me always in words, nor can I always discern the difference between self-criticism and observation, between a gratuitous self-slap and a guide to truth.

But of several hundred afternoons in that Cincinnati office, this moment stands out—the offer and acceptance of a liberating, idiosyncratic metaphor, one that would need many revisions, but at least got me on the page. By contrast, I have no memory of hearing the word "depressed," which was how I was described at that time to my parents and to insurance companies.

In his exhaustive survey, *Melancholia & Depression: From Hippocratic Times to Modern Times*, the historian Stanley W. Jackson concludes that "no literal statement" can convey the experience. But he found that, over 2,500 years, two images recur most often: "being in a state of darkness and being weighed down." If we consider "melancholy" and "depression" as condensations of these images—as more than diagnoses—they retain enormous power. One of my earliest attempts at essay writing dwelled at length on an image of a dark room lit only by the space beneath the closed door. I did not make a habit of spending time in such rooms. The image of darkness imposed itself upon me, as it has for so many, as a symbol of distress.

And my dislike for the word "depression" does not mean that it has no application to my life. I am often "bowed down greatly" (from Psalm 38), feel weighed upon, feel myself on lower than level ground. Compared with others, it seems, I get less pleasure from what's pleasurable and have a harder time with what's hard. My sex drive is often muted (even without antidepressant medication, which exacerbates this problem). Work and activity that require some suspension of self-consciousness—like playing team sports—are difficult, bordering on impossible. I've tended toward activities in which self-criticism can be an asset, like writing. A tightness, an anxiety, a desperation usually grips me when I wake, relaxes its hold only occasionally through the day, and accompanies me when I lie down.

But, even as metaphors, these words are too thin to contain a life. For example, the times when I do pass from withdrawn to talkative are often quite unpleasant. Darkness aches, but light blinds.

At this point I encounter in the margins a note from my editor asking for further explanation of what is written above. And I shudder from the memory of moments like this: I am trying to explain myself and I encounter "Why?" and "What do you mean?"—questions I fear can't be answered. I imagine the seams of this essay splitting, and the meaning and emotion I am struggling to convey here falling out like beans from a sack.

And so I remind myself: an imperfect word is sometimes better than silence, a pale metaphor better than suicide. Researchers and therapists want to understand problems in their broad dimensions; families and friends want to make sense of their afflicted loved ones; and, of course, those who suffer in isolation, starved for connection, mad with the sense that they will never be understood and never find relief, need to say *something*, even if it's wrong, or not wholly right.

Still, while we cannot be silent, or forsake the available word or metaphor for the perfect one that eludes us, we also cannot stop at those less-than-perfect words and metaphors. Insufficient or overused phrases—which resolve eventually into clichés—lose their power to evoke a fresh, startling image. They stop tapping into the field of primal meaning that precedes language and to which, through language, we are forever trying to return. Worse, poor language can cripple the capacity to imagine. "A man may take to drink because he feels himself to be a failure," George Orwell writes, "and then fail all the more completely because he drinks."

The failure begins when words intended to codify or categorize, what Maurice Merleau-Ponty calls "empirical speech," actually disrupts or preempts "creative speech," or "that which frees the meaning captive in a thing." Every breath and word is an effort at translation and, at times, that effort can seem impossible. But poems, lyrics, and stories can do an end run around the stubborn distance that separates us, helping us feel what it is to be alive. Words can create meaning, teach us our own thoughts, and perhaps even describe a life. But we have to plumb, with curiosity sustained over time, with toleration of uncertainty, the unsettling, elusive stories that make us who we are.

Story

Letters form meaning from lines and curves. Words form meaning from letters. Metaphors form meaning from words. None of these units is large enough to encompass, to identify, to "diagnose" a person. If pressed, one could call Ahab "mad," or Bartleby "depressed." But to *know* these characters, you must read the story. To tell a life, you must tell a story.

Which is not by any means a straightforward task. Freud's idea of "repression" suggests that unconscious experience is like water pressed against a dam, that we need only remove the blockage and allow our memories to pour out. This is a dominant image of emotional healing in our culture. I think of it as the Hawkeye Pierce model of psychotherapy, after the last episode in *M*A*S*H*, in which Alan Alda's character has been confined in an asylum and is coaxed into retelling a traumatic episode. One by one, the authentic details emerge until he remembers the repressed memory of a small child's death. He cries. He is healed.

My brothers fled the home as best they could. I, the adoring younger brother, tried to follow them. But they had no interest in me, except as an occasional object of humiliation. I suppose I reminded them of what they hated in themselves: the vulnerable, longing, suffering son of their parents.

When I tried to let out my own feelings—tearing apart that room, for instance—my family pretended they were invisible. I learned to not speak how I felt, soon stopped knowing, and slowly but certainly developed a way of being—a sense of being split, an aching numbness, a cascade of critical voices—that would keep things that way. Some psychiatrists have described this as "depersonalization." It is a diagnosis listed in the *DSM-IV* in the category of dissociative disorders, along with posttraumatic stress and what used to be called multiple-personality disorder. Depersonalization, the manual says, is characterized by persistent or recurring feelings of "detachment or estrangement from one's self, a sensation of being an outside observer of one's mental process, one's body, or parts of one's body.

"Often," the manual continues, "individuals with Depersonalization Disorder may have difficulty describing their symptoms."

No diagnosis can tell my story. Still, depersonalization has the advantage of nicely announcing what is missing. To treat this "disorder" requires nothing less than removing the "de" to find the person—whatever is real beneath.

There is no drug for depersonalization, which leaves me adrift in an era where pharmaceuticals offer identity: if Ritalin or lithium or Xanax ease your symptoms, you can fit into the narrative of the corresponding disorder (attention deficit, bipolar, anxiety). If an antidepressant helps, you can toss off the four letters preceding the hyphen and proudly affix to yourself the word that remains. I haven't been helped by medication. Many have. But I wonder if all of us are depleted by the way brand names, dosages, and combinations have eclipsed talk of agonies, fears, and dreams. Good stories must be reined in from chaos (the whole truth), which our imaginations are too feeble to comprehend. To shape and order our lives, without molding them into caricatures, is to hew a course between the poles of chaos and cliché—the course of authenticity.

The psychoanalyst Donnel Stern, in his book *Unformulated Experience,* suggests another way of thinking about "repression." He uses the metaphor of the rock at the bottom of a lake, which requires great and sustained effort to recover. Perhaps our lives are many such rocks. Perhaps we have to raise the ones we can, imagine the rest, and then, with these images and memories and emotions laid before us, find the patterns and shapes.

We are all natural storytellers. Even as we think we are just see-ing a concrete image or hearing a distinct sound, we are in fact filling in gaps, putting material in context, constructing a narrative. That muted howl from the apartment next door—is it a woman crying, or a child laughing, or the laugh track from a television set? We make such choices at every moment, usually without conscious thought. We compose stories about other people just as we construct one big story about ourselves.

But sometimes, for some people, the story is torn. The essential sense of who we are, of what the world means, becomes lost. All the bits of life's evidence that must be sifted, digested, or passed over, instead fly like shrapnel. This happened to me a long time ago. In high school, when I first saw my name over small stories and articles, those words "Josh Shenk"—in ink against newsprint—struck me with dumb shock. I was thrilled and horrified at a small glimpse of what it meant to be real. It may seem strange that someone haunted by the inadequacy of words would become a writer, but I've often felt no other choice but to struggle and claw for what should be a simple birthright: to tell myself and others who I am.

Like everyone, I start with a handicap, which is that I don't know my own beginnings. Births and early infancy precede memory. Many later memories, which we should in theory have access to, are still as elusive as mist. So we become historians of our own lives, dependent on unreliable, reluctant sources. I can describe with precision the home I grew up in, its brown paint and simple brick, the gnarled limbs on the trees outside. But what did it feel like to live there? How did it form me?

I need to find these feelings, because the facts communicate so little. For instance, I was the youngest of three children and my parents divorced when I was seven. This is a story too common to be distinctive, but too important to be ignored—the slow leakage of affection and kindness from my parents' marriage, the grim entrance of resentment, confusion, and anger. The unspoken rules of the house forbade expressing these emotions, and this remained true after the divorce.

This is a truncated memoir, an introduction to my own introduction to my story. I still need to imagine my life. I need to find my story by living it, following moments of emotional clarity through life's maze. I look for help in therapy, in relationships, and faith in its broadest sense—the faith of the gardener, the faith of the lover, the faith of the writer. The faith that I can experience what is real about the world, that I can hurt plainly, love ravenously, feel purely, and be strong enough to go on.

At the end of *As You Like It*, Shakespeare's famous "melancholy" character Jaques hears that a duke has "put on a religious life / And thrown into neglect the pompous court." Jaques instantly declares, "To him will I / Out of these convertites / There is much matter to be heard and learn'd." It is a striking contrast to his earlier cynicism that "All the world's a stage / And all the men and women merely players." It is the declaration of a character intent on finding some meaning.

But, in contrast to the smug assurance that passes for faith on the "700 Club," the truest faith reckons with uncertainty. It must account for the inevitable mystery, must survive the tension between the familiar and the shocking unknown (and the shocking unknowable). If one were forced to choose a single word to describe Jaques—who anguishes at the death of animals, wishes for love, longs for a fool's easy laughter—perhaps "melancholy" or "depressed" would be a good choice among poor options. Shakespeare chose "melancholy," but then had Jaques proclaim that he has neither the scholar's melancholy, nor the musician's, nor the courtier's, nor the soldier's, nor the lawyer's, nor the lady's, nor the lover's. Jaques has, he insists, "a melancholy of mine own, compounded of many simples, extracted from many objects." And off the stage he walks. Having hinted at his story, he goes to live it.

THE LEGACY

❧

Martha Manning

MY FAMILY IS HAUNTED BY depression. My mother can trace it back in her family at least six generations and it's in my father's family, too. When it hits, it hits hard. Some people find themselves or are found, others get lost forever. The melancholies, nerves, and breakdowns of my ancestors landed them in sanatoriums, rest homes, or upstairs bedrooms from which they never emerged. Treatment involved the state-of-the-art interventions of the time— cold packs, electric current, sedating drugs. Sometimes people got better. Sometimes they didn't.

Six months into my own treatment for an episode of depression that scared me in its speed, severity, and stubbornness, I had placed most of my emotional cards on the table, but was disappointed that my therapist still hadn't constructed some brilliant framework in which my difficulties could be finally uncovered and my dysfunction excised. Since he never volunteered his opinion on the subject, I finally just demanded, "Why are there so many problems in my family?" He shrugged and replied calmly, "Because there are so many people in it."

My first reaction was, "I'm paying a hundred dollars an hour for this?" And yet, eight years later, his comment still stands firm among my list of top-ten therapeutic interventions of all time. The poet Mary Karr, author of the celebrated *The Liar's Club*, a memoir of a colorful and tremendously chaotic family, recently echoed my therapist's comment when she wrote that her definition of a dysfunctional family is "a family with more than one person in it."

My therapist's comment looks naive compared with some of the more elaborate observations other therapists and clinical supervisors have made to me over the years. But in addition to comforting me with its commonsense approach to the variety of ways families suffer, his words have been an insistent caution whenever I am seduced too quickly into elaborate interpretations of psychopathology. There is, after all, a very thin line between theoretical elegance and bullshit.

For every connection we therapists find between our favorite theories and what we see in our consulting rooms, there are probably a hundred such families whose members defy our ideas about how dysfunctional their families are. Understanding the legacy of depression in a family requires more than genetic mapping, family diagrams, or symptom checklists. Each of us is the product of a complex weaving of genes and expectations, biochemistry and family myths, and the configuration of our family's strengths, as well as its vulnerabilities. To truly appreciate the complexity of the weave, we have to sort out the contributions of individual threads to the overall design.

My own memory of depression extends back to my great-grandmother, who lived into her nineties and died when I was about ten. As I began to put things together about the relationship between my grandmother and her mother, I started to wonder whether the dulling of self I sometimes experienced, and its power to contaminate energy and joy, played leapfrog with the generations—hopping over my great-grandmother and landing on my grandmother—leaping over my mother and crashing down on me.

My great-grandmother was either authoritative or controlling, depending on how negatively her behavior was affecting you at the time. When we visited my grandmother in Massachusetts, we knew our visit would include a pilgrimage to her mother, Grammy Hale. As young as six or seven, I knew that there was a whole lot more going on during those visits than I could grasp. My intuitions were confirmed whenever children were dismissed immediately following raised voices. I sensed something big happened during those dismissals. Something bad. Later I found out that these were the times my great-grandmother roundly castigated my grandmother—for my grandmother's break away from a middle-class Irish-Catholic neighborhood to reside on the WASPiest street in the town or for the tone of a brief comment my grandmother had made weeks before. The crime didn't matter. The punishment was always the same: my great-grandmother's total and complete disgust.

After each visit, I noticed the way my grandmother deflated and remained silent on the drive back to her house. She was almost impossible to distract from her brooding, even with our most entertaining attempts. When we arrived back at her wonderful beach house and celebrated our freedom from creaking musty houses and strange old women, my grandmother was elusive. She stayed in her room, shades drawn against the sun and the ocean, windows shut tight against the clean salt air. It frustrated me to think that she was making herself oblivious to the most obvious ways to feel better.

When we kids asked what was wrong with Grandmother, grown-ups always told us the same things. Grandmother was "tired," she "needed some rest," she "wasn't well." The only thing we could possibly do to make her feel better—"Be quiet"—was nearly impossible. Trays that were delivered to her room earlier in the day were retrieved untouched. She didn't even want to see me, her "golden girl," who could usually snap her out of anything. Sometimes I'd sneak into her room and lie next to her when she was sleeping, matching my breathing to hers and stroking her hair and face. She didn't have a fever, she wasn't throwing up, and I didn't see spots anywhere, so she wasn't sick in any way I knew about. I wondered if misery grew with age and actually made people sick. The reasons each siege of sadness finally ended were no clearer to me than the reasons it began. When I asked about these things, unlike other times when I knew information was intentionally withheld, I almost believed my mother when her smile flickered for a moment and she said she didn't know.

On her good days my grandmother was magic—extravagant, energetic, and interested. She allowed my cousins and me to tag along with her on her many errands and activities. She let us know that we were all perfectly wonderful children despite our parents' petty complaints about us. She was fun in a way my mother never was. But, on her bad days, my grandmother wilted before my eyes. There was nowhere to tag along, because she didn't go anywhere. She never got fully dressed. She didn't laugh. She didn't think I was perfect anymore. The air felt heavy around her, very still and hard to breathe. My grandfather, a CPA, seemed always to be working. My grandmother went to bed early (many times before dark). For a woman who spent this much time in bed, I was always puzzled by her daily complaint that she didn't get any sleep.

In early adolescence, my relationship with my grandmother changed. I felt some unspoken expectation that with my new maturity, I owed her something. Now she wanted me to listen to her complaints of how badly she slept or how my grandfather worked too much or how her children didn't understand her. Since I couldn't do anything about her complaints, I left each interaction frustrated and resentful. She scared me in a way I couldn't and didn't want to understand. I felt an uneasy resonance with her, a sonar that picked up on cues that predicted a shift in her mood.

My mother, on the other hand, was practical, rational, and smart. As a little kid I knew that and I loved her for it, because it meant that she would always take care of me, that no matter what happened, she was a constant. As I grew older, though, our personalities diverged and she seemed more formidable. My mother was in control of her feelings. Mine spilled out all over the place. To my mother, the fact that every day was a new day was a good thing. I was never so sure.

My mother had a no-nonsense approach to unhappiness. Stay busy, think of someone worse off than yourself, offer it up for the souls in Purgatory. At the pediatrician's office, when two or three of us lined up with our bare asses vulnerable to imminent medical intervention, one of us invariably burst into tears, protests, and screams. I remember more than once my mother leaning over and whispering, "If you *must* cry, cry quietly."

I recall her curiosity and impatience at my unremitting despair following being dumped by a boy when I was thirteen. She was sympathetic to the pain of such an experience and allowed that there was nothing like a good cleansing cry. It was the intensity and duration of it that proved problematic. My mother had about fifteen minutes in mind, whereas I was planning to make a weekend out of it.

Early on, I considered myself flawed in a way that she wasn't. Unlike my mother, I had difficulty with what she called "compartmentalizing." She could quickly extricate herself from awful feelings. I became mired in them. By my mid- to late teens, I began to struggle with the variability of my moods, something that my mother's steamroller approach to life could not control. I wondered which woman, my mother or my grandmother, was the preview of my future. My unspoken fear was that I was destined to become my grandmother.

I understood more about the nature of my mother's strength when I saw her in the context of my grandmother's vulnerability. As I grew old enough to realize that my mother and I could experience diametrically opposed feelings on the same subject, I realized she hated visits to my grandmother—the very same trips I loved. Once, I looked at the calendar and cried out, "Two more days till vacation." My mother's face got stormy. She clenched her teeth and spit out, "This is many things, but it is definitely not a *vacation.*"

When my grandmother's mood changed, my mother's did, too. Upon our annual arrival at my grandparents' beach house, my grandmother almost willfully fell backward into helplessness and depression. And, in response, my mother went into overdrive. After feeding her own six kids dinner in our adjoining cottage, she rushed up to the main house to feed my grandparents, who somehow made it through the other fifty weeks of the year just fine. And cooking was the least of my mother's duties. She was my grandmother's personal cheerleader, her therapist, the person who got her up and going, who tried to shift my grandmother's automatic negative outlook at least to neutral. One of my most common memories of those visits is the way my mother and grandmother sat around the kitchen table. My mother always looked like she was sitting on tacks and my grandmother always looked like she was sinking in mud. The sheer exhaustion she conveyed in the act of stirring her tea made it look like she was mixing cement.

My grandmother constantly sighed, something my mother never did. It was not an "Oh well" or a "That's life" kind of sigh. Hers was an exhalation that sounded like it could possibly end in her demise. It was a sigh of surrender. But as I got older, I understood that it wasn't pure fatigue or sorrow or hopelessness. It was, at its essence, an angry sigh. It was a challenge: "Just you try and make me feel better. I dare you."

As children, we believed all of my grandmother's promises that things would be better "If only . . ."—*If only you lived closer, I'd be happier; if only your aunt was easier to deal with; if only your grandfather didn't work so hard.* When I was ten, my mother (who rarely said bad things about people) insinuated that we shouldn't count on those extravagant promises our grandmother had made. When we leaped to our poor grandmother's defense, my mother responded, "This is the truth. It's what goes on. I'm giving you the truth. I never got that from my mother. But you will always have it from me."

My mother's and grandmother's conversations always stopped short when I walked in the room, but my mother didn't look at all like she looked in the many kitchen-table conversations she shared with her friends. When I became a therapist I realized that during those times my grandmother and mother were "in session."

In retrospect, I see how that pattern repeated itself with my therapist-husband when I was depressed, as we sat on the bed or at the table and he tried to get me to articulate what was wrong. Anyone who has ever been seriously depressed knows that that task is as daunting as asking a lame man to tap-dance. In addition, it leads to mutual frustration, anger, and ultimately helplessness. It was only when we both gave up the expectation that my husband could some-how "cure" me that we moved from pseudotherapy to true support. Instead of reaching out with well-intentioned "therapeutic" inter-ventions, he shifted to questions like, "What would help right now?"

My real therapist was always willing to include my husband in our sessions, and to recognize him and my daughter, Keara, as people who were suffering also. This freed them from the responsibility of those awful sessions at the kitchen table, where their feeling was that if they stayed for one minute longer, they would drown as well.

When I had my own child at the age of twenty-five, my mother became much more open in expressing her frustration—with my grandmother for not changing, and with herself for not being able to make her. In my late twenties and thirties, the depressive fog that had shadowed me for a long time grew more difficult to outrun.

I moved to Boston with my husband and daughter to do a post-doctoral fellowship at McLean Hospital. We found a house several miles away from my grandmother, to her great delight. I was thor-oughly unhappy with the fellowship, McLean, and the move, espe-cially as I realized why my mother had consciously put five hundred miles between her mother and herself. It was so sad to see my grandmother's magic consumed by something so insidious and powerful that neither my love nor my training could change it. I knew she was in her own hell, yet there were times I wanted to coax her or kick her out of it, dismiss her complaints and sighs, but I couldn't. And I feared I was looking at my future. I didn't want anyone to feel that way about me.

My first cousin—the firstborn in a family of seven children—was going through her own hell at the time from depression, a hell that culminated in suicide in her early twenties. My own deepening depression and my cousin's suicide catapulted me into psychotherapy with a psychiatrist referred by my health plan. I told him I was anxious. He told me I was depressed. Yeah, I admitted, I had my moods, but no way was I depressed like my cousin or my grandmother. As evidence against his diagnosis, I listed my accomplishments, the many responsibilities I fulfilled. But thirty minutes into my session with him I was convinced that I was indeed depressed. At the end of our first session he turned to me solemnly and said, "You really believe that life is something to be endured, to be overcome." I looked back at him suspiciously, wondering if it was a trick question. "It isn't?" I asked. We scheduled a session for the next week.

Our work in the five months that remained in my fellowship was fairly structured and involved learning ways to manage my anxiety and set limits in the many areas in which I felt overwhelmed. Perhaps the most significant result was that I decided to return to Washington to accept an academic position there.

Not long after we moved back, I began to hear my grandmother's sighs in my own labored breathing; I, too, felt the weight of the spoon as I stirred my tea. I knew that making a peanut-butter-and-jelly sandwich should be far less than a thirty-minute operation. I entered individual psychotherapy, found it extremely helpful, particularly in quieting the loud voice of perfection in my mind, and the panic that had begun to sneak up from behind and immobilize me.

But my depression continued—despite insight, despite a good marriage, despite a child I dearly loved. I finally agreed to try antidepressants and was horrified when my psychiatrist recommended Imipramine, the same medicine my grandmother had used in her late seventies, with moderate success, but difficult side effects. My psychiatrist must have registered the horror on my face. He reassured me that he always chooses a drug that has worked with other family members as the first antidepressant.

He was right. The medicine helped quickly and dramatically. It lifted a lifelong weight off my back and made me wonder, "Is this how regular people feel?" But like many people who take psychotropic medications for significant periods of time, I struggled with questions like, "Why can't I do this on my own?" or, looking at the tiny pills, "Is this all that stands between hell and me?"

Despite the benefits of the antidepressant, I still feared that I was destined to be my grandmother. No drug could erase this anxiety. I didn't want her resignation, her helplessness, her just-below-the-surface bubbling anger, or her genuine and horrible suffering. I also didn't want to have the impact that she had on her family, particularly on my mother. I did not want my daughter to take on the yoke of responsibility and resent me for it. I had already watched three generational scenarios: my great-grandmother's influence on my grandmother, both of their influences on my mother, and all three of their influences on me. The thing that scared me most was the the weight of all four of us on my eleven-year-old daughter.

My therapy focused on developing an understanding of the commonalities I shared with each woman, appreciating aspects of our shared legacies as some of the things I most valued in myself. I also had to articulate the differences between myself and each of them. I worked to understand that depression did not erase me, it just made my life different and difficult—hopefully for a limited amount of time, and that no one—genetically, biologically, or psychologically— is the blueprint for anyone else. Being haunted is not the same as being cursed.

The fact that in over a year's time, I descended into a very serious depression does not negate the impact of the psychotherapy or the medicine. For reasons that were never clear, I began to metabolize my medications so rapidly that to keep therapeutic levels in my blood, I required doses that became untenable.

My daughter tried to tease me, tempt me, annoy me, entertain me, and soothe me—all to no avail. Her constant question was, "Why are you so sad?" I had difficulty following the rambling conversations in the car that I usually loved. Her new friends' names were hard to remember. Our long-standing bedtime ritual with its whispers, soft songs, and backrubs dwindled down to a quick goodnight.

She and my husband hovered and worried. I tried to be straightforward with Keara, remembering what my mother had wished for in her adolescence—"Just some knowledge. What's going on and what's being done to help it."

Now, five years since my last serious depression, my daughter teases us that we went a bit overboard in providing the information my mother had wanted. She insists that the information we gave her about depression was a lot like the information we gave her about sex—a lot of big words with little context. Her concerns had less to do with having a technical command of depression than about the continuity of her care and protection. When she was sixteen she wrote:

> *The thing about having someone close to you suffer from depression is that your feelings go from worried to angrily impatient to guilty. One of the worst things was seeing my mom in so much pain and being constantly reminded that it wasn't my fault and there was nothing I could do to make her feel better.*

Despite pills, therapy, love, professional expertise, and faith, my symptoms worsened. I didn't sleep more than two hours a night. I stopped eating—it was too hard to swallow. I thought about the wisecrack about someone who is out of it—"The lights are on, but nobody's home." In depression, the lights are off, but somebody's definitely home. She just can't make it to the door to let you in.

My ruminations turned to comforting thoughts of death. I had always thought of myself as living in a series of concentric circles that connected me to life. My outermost circles included my interests and acquaintances, work and goals. Then came my friends. Then my parents and siblings. Then my husband and daughter. As the depression worsened, those connections dissolved. They were no longer reasons to stay in the game. Life could go on without me.

In the final days before my hospitalization, I was staying alive for my husband and my daughter. I never told them this. At the very end, I kept going only for my daughter. Every morning, Keara stumbles semiconscious into the bathroom and turns on the shower. Within the space of thirty seconds she starts to sing. She starts out humming so softly that her voice blends with the spray as it bounces off the wall. And then she chooses her song—sometimes sweet and lyrical, sometimes loud and rocking. Each morning, when I had to face another day on two hours of sleep and absolutely no hope, I leaned against the bathroom door waiting for her to sing and let her voice invite me to try for one more day.

One morning, finally convinced that suicide was an act of love not hate, I leaned for what I thought would be the last time against the door. I tried to memorize that voice, with all of its exuberance and innocence. With a sharp slap, her voice brought me to the realization that ending my life would be the surest way to silence that song. It was the best and worst of epiphanies. Best, because I committed myself to life. Worst, because that commitment meant undergoing electroconvulsive therapy (ECT).

Mine has always been the voice of the macho mother: I'd step in front of a speeding truck for my kid. The problem is that you never get to pick your truck. In my case, it was a psych unit and electricity. It was time to make good on my promise.

ECT was the tractor that pulled me out of the mud. Its power was hard to believe. Within several treatments, I was adding twenty, thirty minutes to my sleep per night. Having lost thirty pounds in three months, I began to look forward to meals. My face, which felt like a mask, regained its elasticity. It felt like several heavy backpacks had been taken from my shoulders. But it wasn't a magic cure. I still had to walk the whole way home—a journey that took over a year, assisted greatly by medicine, therapy, and the support of many people.

Finding my place again in my family took some time. When her bedtime approached on my first night home from the hospital, Keara announced, "I don't need you to tuck me into bed anymore. I do it myself now." For several weeks no one raised a voice or a broke a rule. I was being watched very carefully. At some point my daughter started challenging me again, testing the limits of my authority and my capacity for following through.

Over the course of that year, I had to struggle with self-recriminations about the ways I had failed the people I loved. I was ashamed that I'd been unavailable to Keara and embarrassed that she had seen me so vulnerable. As a psychologist whose profession has historically enjoyed mother-bashing as a blood sport, it was easy to apply it to myself. My daughter would be ruined for life and it would be all my fault.

For a long time after my hospitalization, my daughter dropped her middle name—Manning—and began making it clear that her name came only from my husband—Keara *Depenbrock*. I knew how important it was for her to see herself as separate from me currently—and, more importantly, in the future. My husband pointed out to me that while some of it was due to my depression, it was also a normal function of adolescence. When she wrote, "While I have a lot in common with my mother, I have inherited my father's mental health," I recognized it as a fact, as well as a wish.

Over the next several years I marveled at my child's blooming, despite the scarcity of light in our house at a critical point in her development. Keara later remembered:

> *My mom's depression was definitely an impediment to us being close at the time. Because she wasn't available to me, and because something so horrible was happening inside of her it was really*

hard for her to have this great relationship with other people. I
think that she spent all the time and energy she had with me and for
me—but it wasn't as much as I wanted. I don't blame her for that.
She didn't make a choice to be that way. But sometimes I'd get really
frustrated and impatient with her anyway.

I recalled the psychoanalyst D. W. Winnecott, one of the less
judgmental voices in the psychological wilderness, who disputed the
necessity of a "perfect mother" for a child's healthy development,
substituting the more attainable standard of "good enough mother."
My faith in Winnecott was confirmed the night my daughter invited
me back into her room for the nightly ritual that had taken so much
effort only months before. Now smoothing her rumpled sheets,
straightening her comforter to her exact specifications, and rubbing
her back with the precise level of finger pressure were gifts, not burdens.

Depression and I are not finished with each other. Four years ago,
two years after my first round of ECT, I started sliding in the same
dangerous direction. This time we all saw it coming. I had more ECT
treatments, this time on an outpatient basis. I left for the hospital in
the morning, after I'd seen Keara off to school, and I was back before
she returned home. Life was not business as usual, but we managed
the details with the help of our families and friends.

With the addition of a mood stabilizer (lithium), which I had
refused after my first ECT, I have since enjoyed the best years of my
life. They have also been the best years of my relationship with my
daughter. There was something in the combination of vulnerability
and stability that protected us. She saw me go to hell. But she was
there for the return trip as well. Her fears of depression invading our
family again were confirmed so quickly that, in some ironic way, she
found comfort in the evidence that our plans worked. We both
learned that lousy things can happen and that they can be so bad and
so powerful that they stand good solid relationships on their heads.

The differences between Keara and me are clear. Temperamentally she resembles my husband and my mother, not me. This knowledge frees her from having to deny the ways in which we are so alike. She can claim our similarities without the fear of turning into me. At the end of her senior year, she came home and leaned against the kitchen counter while I peeled carrots, and described having to fill out a form with her name exactly as she wanted it on her high-school diploma.

"I was afraid it wouldn't all fit," she told me.

"Yeah, Keara Depenbrock is a mouthful," I replied.

"No, Mom." She laughed. "It's worse than that. My *real* name— Keara Manning Depenbrock."

Our children inhale our imperfections and failings as easily as our love. Perhaps they are meant to. How else will they ever learn to tolerate themselves? My goal is no longer to make a perfect impression. Now I'm shooting for an imperfect impression and the ability to help my daughter deal with it. I pray that she is spared the torment of severe depression. I think she will be. But on the chance that she might get lost in it, or any of the other ways life tests our faith and our patience and our endurance, I wish for her exactly what she gave to me—a sweet voice in the distance that penetrates darkness and calls her gently toward home.

WISH YOU WERE HERE

❧

Nell Casey

M Y GREAT-GREAT-GRANDFATHER DIED in But-
lers, a hospital, as my mother was told, for the "alcoholically
insane." My great-uncle was institutionalized for importing a
château, stone by stone, from France to Long Island without any
money to pay for it. I have an aunt who, after the hormonal upheaval
of bearing three children in four years, began to see lion heads
instead of faces on the people she passed in the streets. A few years
ago my cousin explained to me, in the midst of a nervous breakdown,
that he'd been chosen to create a safer, more religious universe without technology (except for rotary phones).

My sister, Maud, was eighteen years old when she was hospitalized for the first time. Diagnosis: manic-depression. I was sixteen. When I visited her, we sat at a round table in a cafeterialike room filled with cigarette smoke and she asked me if she had a tampon in her spleen. I reassured her, *No, no, Maud, there is no tampon in your spleen. You do not have cancer. Dad is not dead.* I used to remember this experience as having a fairy-tale end—the doctors gave her medication, the strange behavior got a little less strange, and soon after, Maud got well again. I used to think of this as a neat little chapter in our exotic, fucked-up family life.

At twenty-nine, Maud was institutionalized again. This time— eerily aware that she was about to stop understanding reality—she decided to check herself in and asked a friend to accompany her to a hospital in Queens. She'd secretly quit taking the lithium that she'd been on for eleven years. She wanted to *feel* something from before, an unencumbered emotion, and didn't want to believe that she was a personality made up of medication. Slowly, unfairly, her mind unraveled.

"I'm happiest in the hospital," she told my mother and me in this hospital visitors' room. "This is the only place where I can really be myself. I think I'll have to stay here my whole life." We were sitting on orange plastic chairs, inches away from the other patients and their families, all of us in our tight little huddles of concern.

My own sanity, I realized later, must've seemed like magic to Maud in those moments. "You're so strong," she said then, eyeing me with suspicion and awe. The truth is, though, I am like Maud. We are both an erratic mix of fragility and strength. We are both worried. But I am a different breed—all wiry energy and rootless, dizzying panic attacks. I am a hypochondriac. I am obsessive. I fixate on one flimsy remark that yanks at the core of my personality and replay it in my mind for weeks. I tip the scales of anxiety often, wondering if someone has been in an accident, possibly killed, when they're twenty minutes late. Or maybe it's me who's dying—*what are these shooting pains in my arm, these dark undereyes, this odd feeling?* Once, at the height of my distress over Maud's second hospitalization, I couldn't read the menu at a restaurant. The letters did not cohere.

The words just stopped being reasonable. I wasn't convinced I'd officially learned the English language in the first place. I looked around the table to see if the others were noticing this rising hysteria bolting up through my body, threatening to levitate me altogether. *How do you live with a mind that can't hold on?*

In the beginning of Maud's second breakdown, however, I felt pure, heroic strength. I pictured those women you hear about who suddenly take on otherworldly powers in an emergency and lift trucks off their children. I even felt a brief and bizarre titillation around the crisis, a relief that someone else was taking up space, admitting to the monstrosities of life. In mobilizing around Maud's roiling emotion, I was able to give my own a purpose. I dealt with doctors and medical paperwork, waited patiently on the phone while Blue Cross had me on hold, held conference calls with Maud's employers, made the seventy-minute subway ride to the hospital in Queens almost every day after work and arranged for others to go when I couldn't make it. I informed friends and relatives about the situation—saying too much with a kind of dire rapture. (*Maud burned her arm with a cigarette! They put her in restraints last night! They've got her on constant surveillance—she can't even go to the bathroom alone anymore!*) Sometimes, I found myself consoling the person I'd just made cry with the grisly details. I admit a small part of me was spellbound, but mainly I hoped that telling friends everything would make it all more manageable, maybe even nudge the story along, encourage it to end.

And, through therapy, medication, and a month and a half in a hideous psychiatric hospital, Maud did become grounded again. That is, grounded in the sense that she no longer believed there was a bomb in the bed or a movie being made of her life, but not in the sense that she was, once again, Maud. After she reined it in and focused on life as we're asked to experience it on a daily level, she hurtled in another direction.

I want so much to explain the absence of my sister during her depression. The remove of personality. The hidden, shadowy terror of devouring misery. The hollow lifelessness of her pupils, cartoon-ishly exaggerated into large, black pools from medication. The listless physicality. I have watched Maud shuffle down hospital corridors—dirty sweatsocks, toes knocking into the backs of her ankles as she saunters up and down to nowhere. *Oh, for chrissakes, pick up your feet!* "It's like Maud is dead," my sister's best friend once said, beginning to weep, on the train ride back from the Queens hospital.

Maud went to stay with our mother in Illinois when she first got out of the hospital in July. We talked on the phone. She asked shy, brave questions about the parts of her hospital stay she only vaguely remembered. I tried to keep things light and not too scary while also filling in some of the gaps she so badly needed to recover. I joked with her about how the hospital was a dump and how confusing it was—*as if things weren't confusing enough!*—that there were two nurses named Jane and John (also the names of our parents).

"I really think some of the things I did had to do with how horri-ble the staff could be," she said in a far-off voice. "I just don't see how I could act so *angry* if they hadn't, you know, egged it on a little."

"You're right! You're definitely right! I thought that at the time, too," I agreed. "They were *awful*. It wasn't you, it just wasn't you." I wanted to smear forgiveness all over her now. An image of Maud in her hospital bed, ridiculously overmedicated and with greasy hair, surfaced in my mind. She could barely talk; her body was twitching uncontrollably. She reached out to give me a hug and then limply held on. "Maud, let your sister go," a plump nurse called from the hallway. "Geez, you can't be hangin' on her the whole visit!"

Sometimes Maud could only tread water when I talked to her in Illinois. She kept her answers brief. Waiting, I thought, for her own perspective to take shape. As long silences stretched out between us on the phone, I found myself missing the outgoingness of her mania. In the hospital, Maud had demanded to know how I could come see her wearing a sundress. *How can you come here dressed like nothing is wrong?* At least then I knew what she was thinking.

I threw myself again and again at the blank spaces—searching for an experience in my own life that would help me understand the full measure of Maud's pain. I thought about how I felt waking up after a night of drinking too much—the haggard half memories of my private self unleashed in public, the flashing images of once-guarded emotions ladled out so freely at the party the night before. Would anyone ever forgive or, better yet, forget? I tried to spin this out, breathe new life into it, method-act my way into Maud's rickety emotional state by thinking of it as a hangover.

Meanwhile, my mother took Maud to the hairdresser to highlight her hair. She got her professional massages at the Fox and Hounds Beauty Salon. She drove her to appointments with the interim psychiatrist and constantly produced maternal good cheer while quietly wondering if her daughter was permanently wounded.

The Illinois psychiatrist was more optimistic than my mother about Maud's progress (he wasn't the one talking her down from fierce bouts of self-loathing and guilt on the drive to and from his office). He was confident Maud was newly and successfully medicated—with an exhausting combination of antipsychotic, antianxiety, and antidepressant drugs—and on the road to recovery. My mother decided he must know best, that self-loathing and guilt were not uncommon among the sanest of people, and that Maud should be allowed—as she so eagerly wanted—to return to her life in New York. My mother thought it was the right decision, that she was drawing the line in the right place.

Maud came to see me—with those hungry, medicated pupils—right away when she came back to Manhattan in September. I cried in my bed all night afterward. It was impossible to decipher a real person in her. She seemed so tiny. She's not tall to begin with—maybe five-three—and she'd lost a lot of weight, but, most alarmingly, her spirit had vanished. She came over that night with all the trappings of a new lease on life, armed with a Gap bag full of clothes and an agitated, loopy smile. She tried on a pair of army-green pants she'd bought and slowly twirled in front of the full-length mirror. The too-tight pants pulled awkwardly against her little body as if everything now was conspiring to show how difficult it would be for her to reenter this world.

She was walking, talking, making sense, and somehow this was worse. There was enough of her there to imitate a functioning, viable person in the world (able to shop at the Gap), but the sum of these parts only added up to a ghostly version of the person she used to be. She stared into the mirror, moving in close to gaze blankly at her face and then backing up to get a good look at the whole person. She crawled into my bed. She was like a kind, strange infant of sadness in my arms. Her tenderness—able to reign over such intense misery— struck me hard. That and my own first flash of bottomless doubt. I'd caught up to my mother now. *Maybe this is it. Maybe this is as well as she gets.*

Maud's "recovery" in Illinois, as it turned out, was wishful thinking on all of our parts. It was supposed to be a time-out from her life—she got out of the hospital, she went to Illinois for a month, she got better and came back. But once in New York, Maud became more and more withdrawn, given over to an elusive, spooky mood. Some days, I thought she was hiding her torment, reluctant to show it to anyone. Other days, I decided she was too tormented to see beyond the murky swirl of her own mind. Either way, she was quiet in the scariest possible way, staring longingly at me, as if she would join us if she could.

When it did find a voice, Maud's depression opened up new worlds of insecurity: *Should I live in New York? Do I have a personality? Can I make it down the stairs? Do I know enough about history? Have I said the right thing? In the right language?* We had these conversations on the phone at night, sitting on the sidewalk (when she was too seized with anxiety to continue walking down the street), over brunch in homey restaurants, in our cramped New York apartments. I mostly gave practical, soothing answers (*I know what you mean, I worry I need to know more about politics, too... You've been through a lot, this is anxiety, it'll go away, we can make it back to your apartment and lie down*), but I was frighteningly close to asking myself the same questions Maud kept firing away. One moment I had total compassion, clear and vivid—*this, this* is what it's like to be Maud. The next, the feelings were eating me alive, threatening to hurl me downward as well. I had the taste of this thing on the tip of my tongue.

I wanted to be there for Maud, I knew that was what she needed (the one thing people always say about depression is that stubborn, consistent support helps even when it seems like it doesn't), but I didn't have the sturdiness of my own character to rely on. We were both young—with the amplified longings and alarms of people in their twenties. I had spent so much of my own life too heartily entertaining turbulent emotion, it seemed dangerous to peer into Maud's black hole of doubt. Sometimes it felt like a trade-off: I had to throw my life over in order to save hers.

In October, I made Maud promise that she would call me if she ever felt dangerously low. That's how I said it, *dangerously low*. And then, *You know, suicide.* I still don't know if she never felt that way or just didn't keep the promise.

There were several false starts with medications. While the interim psychiatrist in Illinois had effectively reduced many of the drugs Maud had been put on in the hospital, he had not predicted that the depression would subsequently deepen. When it did, Maud's doctor in New York began to play around with different antidepressants—starting with Zoloft, moving to Paxil, and then trying Wellbutrin. Each one brought its own personal, serious side effects. Not just of physical discomfort—dry mouth, weight fluctuation, sleepiness—but mind-altering chaos as well.

One weekend, during a visit to our father's home in Virginia, when Maud had just begun taking Zoloft, she rushed into my bedroom at six each morning to go through the same cycle of agitated thoughts. "I should leave New York. I think I need to move back here," she said, blanket wrapped around her face, a relentless campaigner for sadness. "I just need to start over. I think the problem is New York. I should leave New York."

"We should think about where you really want to live," I counseled. "Maybe New York *is* the problem." I knew this reassurance would be gobbled up and ignored along with all the others I'd spewed out over time, but a part of me always remained vulnerable to Maud's reasoning. I could never step back far enough to see that depression had made an impostor of my sister. *Maybe this is as well as she gets. Maybe the problem is New York.* It was a toss-up. *Maybe Maud is crazy. Maybe she knows what she's talking about.*

Once, a few months before she checked herself into the hospital, Maud and I stood on a busy, dirty New York street corner and she told me she felt bugs in her eyelashes. "I feel them everywhere," she said. "I don't see a thing," I offered, sifting carefully through her lashes. "They're all over though!" she yelled. I rubbed her arms, stroked her face. "I don't see anything. There's really nothing there," I pleaded. Frankly, I was concerned that if she did have, say, lice, I was getting them now too.

"I don't know who I am, what my personality is," Maud worried throughout her depression. I willed myself to remember something from the Maud before—she loved horses as a kid, she looked cutely chubby in her third-grade yearbook picture, her boyfriend in college played the accordian, she wrote a book of short stories called *Girls, Girls, Girls*—but I could only get at the facts. I knew she needed me to describe her essential nature, to remind her who she used to be so she could swim back to an old, stable shore. "You're filled with opinions. You have so many ideas," I explained. "You've written a novel. These things make up your very distinct personality." *I can't remember you from before.*

No one is a stranger to despair. It takes a resourceful mind to see, again and again, the purposeful good in broken-down ideals and renegotiated expectations. And, still, there are always private suspicions in the presence of the depressed: Is this person just spiritually weaker? Am I stronger? Couldn't it be worse? You have life! You have your health! I wondered if Maud was clinging to her sadness, stubbornly digging her heels in on a life that had become unwieldy and disappointing. In tearful conversations with friends, I thrashed about (*I think I might ... be ... having ... some kind of ... emotional collapse*) and, then, in the presence of Maud, I wondered if she just wasn't trying hard enough.

In November, a friend (and clinical psychologist) recommended a psychiatrist to go to for a second opinion. Maud and I went to see her together. Noelle. She was pretty, crisp, and smart. "It's not exactly reassuring, but if I had a nickel for every time I treated this kind of depression. . . ." She described Maud's mood with such blasé understanding, I was forced to see how common our own insular high drama must look to the rest of the world.

I watched Maud ask earnest questions about why the medications weren't working, why she still didn't want to get out of bed in the morning, why everything looked and felt so dull. I watched her plainly describe the immense, invisible pain she was in. Her practical tone ripped right through my ambivalence. I felt panicky and mean, as if I had perpetuated her problems with my own petty mistrusts.

Noelle said that Maud would start seeing the world in color again. The new medications should, in fact, start working by November 11, if not sooner. Outside, on the street, I conferred with Maud. "So November eleventh. That's not so far away!" I chirped, hoping my new enthusiasm might feel as contagious as her depression. Maud gave a faint smile.

At some indiscernible point (*after* November 11), things did start to get better. Maud's life started to take shape again. She made efforts that had once seemed too hearty for her feeble state. She cooked dinner for friends. She went on a few dates with a young psychiatrist she met at a party. (Even Maud had to raise an eyebrow at this.) She got an agent for her novel. She stopped telling me about the medications once they were settled.

As she pulled back—to regain composure, privacy—I lurched forward. I worried at the same fever pitch I had during the worst of her depression. I finished her sentences, laughed too hard at my own jokes when we talked, leaped forward at parties to help out with conversations when she was doing just fine on her own. I suffered from terrible headaches for months. "I have nothing left in me!" I sobbed to a puzzled acupuncturist. I whispered spitefully in my mother's face, "Do I need to check myself into a mental hospital to make you pay attention to my problems?"

For a while there was not enough of us all to go around, but, as I said, at some inscrutable moment things did right themselves. In December, at her thirtieth birthday party, Maud wryly commented to a group of friends that she hoped the coming year would be better than the last. It marked a new, hopeful phase. And yet, there was still a way her mood seemed dipped in honey—not *clinical depression* anymore, just sadness. She was a person who'd been places I am still trying to imagine.

In February, at the doorway of the East Village bar I was headed toward, I saw an impressive woman in a belted leather jacket. A spark of jealousy went off in me. *I need a leather jacket.* She was the kind of beautiful woman that throws me into a superficial tizzy, makes me reevaluate my life. *I shouldn't work such long hours at the office. I should really dress up more for these parties. I need to go shopping.* As I got closer, I saw that it was Maud.

She was talking to our friend Hank about her novel. Editors were interested. There was going to be a conference call with her agent to discuss it the next day. Hank was praising. Maud was gesticulating. Her eyes were lived in again, wise. Yes, I remember now, this is Maud.

I had a teetering, uncharitable moment: *That's it? You're better now?*

I wanted nothing more than to have Maud back, than to have Maud have Maud back, but now I didn't want to *forget.* Happiness was no longer an expectation, something big and looming to strive for, but actually right there in front of me, plain and simple, ready to be taken for granted again. Here was happiness: Maud standing before me in muscular exuberance. But Maud had also conjured the trembling subconscious of life (*I'm not real, I'm not here*). And watching it slink back to its hiding places, I needed to know that if we let it go, it wouldn't be roused again. It took me time not to want to needlessly slip the story into my conversations, yell it out all day long, to sternly remind Maud and myself how hard it had all been. I wanted to resuscitate the sadness if only to ward it off. Until slowly it dawned on me that Maud's sadness wasn't ever going away—it was right there in every swell and turn of my consciousness, smuggled always into our everyday lives. There it was in the curve of Maud's outstretched hand, rising up with her voice in conversation with Hank, settling down now in her hard-earned, knowing demeanor.

Yes, I remember now. *This* is Maud.

A BETTER PLACE TO LIVE

❧

Maud Casey

IT'S MARCH 1999, TWO MONTHS since I stopped wish-
ing I was dead. I read my mother's journal as I ride the F train to
the end of the line in Queens—179th and Hillside—to the psychiatric hospital where I spent most of last summer due to manic-
depression. Surprisingly—as I come from a family of relentlessly
nosy writers who believe anything not under lock and key is free
game—I have my mother's permission to read her journal that spans
my hospitalization and the five-month depression that consumed me
after my discharge. I am doing research, trying to find out what the
experience of my depression was like for other people. After my
release from the hospital—once I no longer believed that the hospital

staff was training a twenty-four-hour surveillance camera on me in order to eventually kill me—I was supposedly ready for the world. But was it ready for me? This is no saintly investigation, no purely altruistic walk in other people's shoes. The subject is still very much me, me, me.

Now that my depression has started to lift, I'm suffering from what I've come to think of as the hangover of the depressed: shame. I crawl out of bed some mornings like someone who has just woken up from a bender. I look in the mirror and think: Oh God, I did *that*? Who saw me? Maybe they won't remember; maybe they were really depressed, too?

This train ride is penance. My mother's journal is balanced on top of my own notebook, which teeters precariously on one knee. I—a former small-town girl who frequently falls *up* stairs and certainly no expert subway-riding-drinker-of-coffee—have a pen in one hand, a sloshing cup of coffee in the other, and the inevitable happens: I spill the coffee all over over my mother's journal and the crotch of my pants. The man next to me rolls his eyes and moves away, wanting no part of this, but the woman across the aisle digs Kleenex out of her purse and hands them to me, shaking her head at the chaos in my lap but smiling sympathetically like someone who frequently finds herself cleaning up other people's messes. Above her head is an ad for Maple Gardens, a private rental community with a twenty-four-hour manned gatehouse. There are festive pictures of people in bright clothing playing golf, chatting poolside, and jogging cheerfully on treadmills. "You can't find a better place to live," the caption reads. I wipe the coffee from my mother's words: *I feel Maud's misery and fear packed inside my senses. I wake in terror, always close to tears at dawn.*

I spent the fall of this year, and into winter, sleeping with my mother. In my Dial-A-Mattress bed in Brooklyn, I clung to her, often wrapping an arm, heavy and dead as my gone life, around her waist. I inhaled deeply her scent like smelling salts bringing me briefly back into the world. My mother worked full-time as a documentary filmmaker in New York, rushed to Prospect Heights to cook dinners I would otherwise skip, and traveled back and forth between New York and her home in Illinois. I tried to absorb that energy, her life force, like a plant absorbs the sun. But I wasn't that pure. There was desperation in my clinging—a kind of *Invasion of the Body Snatchers* life-draining suck and I had become pure suck, the alien pod.

SEPTEMBER 8, 1998: *Sleeping with Maud in her bed. The feeling both of laying my motherhood at her disposal and being a sponge to her deep fears and despair. The moon beams down on her through the window. I often think of her child body, child self, the joy she brought, how fascinated we were by everything she did; her stately, majestic, orderly procession through her skills and speech and school. These images return to me now as premonitions of pain to come. I look at her darling baby child self as wounded, as shrinking, shriveling in the shadows of her future suffering. Yet when I wake up at night, my child (a twenty-nine-year-old woman, but childlike in her pajamas, in her petiteness, in her funny little haircut and the simple sound of her breathing) is still there, my Maud bathed in the moonlight.*

During the weeks my mother spent in Illinois, my sister would sleep over on occasional nights. In her white nightgown with lace fringe around the neck, she was a radiant beauty—a successful writer and magazine editor who had recently fallen in love. She was my fairy-tale princess and my tentacles slithered out of their alien pod, wrapping themselves around her.

"I want to go back to the hospital," I would whisper to my mother trying to sleep next to me. "I want to die." "I want to go home," I would say to my sister as she rolled over to hold my shaking hands. The three—hospital, death, home—became interchangeable. "Tell me what's going on," my mother would whisper back, her warm body charged and ready like a nightlight, glowing with the possibility of emergency. "Maybe you could move to Virginia, live in

Dad's extra apartment," my sister would offer. And for a minute that would seem like the answer—if only it were possible for me to move and simultaneously leave myself behind in Brooklyn. Unfortunately, to be depressed is not to have words to describe it, is not to have words at all, but to live in the gray world of the inarticulate, where nothing takes shape, nothing has edges or clarity. A literal home was not what I meant.

Home was what my grandmother seemed to be talking about in the last months of her life. Here on the train, eighteen different combinations of antipsychotics, mood-stabilizers, and antidepressants later, I remember this. As my grandmother lay dying in the house she shared with her husband in South Hamilton, Massachusetts, she talked a lot about "going home." Would you like something to eat? Some water? More covers? Do you need to go to the bathroom? Her children and husband asked her these questions and she replied with stern practicality, "No, thank you, I'm going home." (In my version of the story, my grandmother wags her long, thin finger satirically at the asker, the way she always did to indicate that underneath her scolding, stern practicality was an appreciation for the naughtiness of the world.) For my grandmother, home was not in South Hamilton anymore. Home wasn't even in her body. She couldn't be bothered with the mundane details of the living—all of this eating, drinking, keeping warm, going to the bathroom, getting up, lying down, staying awake, going to sleep. Home was elsewhere, in death.

In the blackout drunk of depression, home was elsewhere for me, too. Not in my apartment in Brooklyn where I felt like a guest in someone else's falling-apart life—unanswered phone calls, unopened mail, rotting fruit on top of the refrigerator, and something unidentifiable and reeking inside, piles of dirty dishes, tumbleweeds of dust, books I didn't remember reading, furniture I couldn't remember buying, pictures of friends and family that seemed to belong to a stranger. Not in my father's extra apartment. Not in my mother's house in Illinois. Not under my psychiatrist's desk where I wanted to curl up and hide, resting my head on his sensible shoes. Not on my therapist's couch, waiting and waiting for, as Freud put it so succinctly, neurotic suffering to become everyday misery. Not in my body. Not in eating, drinking, keeping warm. Not going to the bathroom or lying down. Not in staying awake or going to sleep. Above the Kleenex woman's head, the glaring reds, nuclear yellows, and shocking blues of the Maple Gardens ad run together in a perky smear. Being depressed felt like living in a corpse, so being dead seemed like "a better place to live."

The depression that follows mania is rarely dealt with as aggressively as the mania itself. Once the hard throb of emergency is over, the presenting crisis passed, many people are left to deal with a depression that leaves them nostalgic for the wild, bucking panic of mania—in my case, all those revolutions to tend to, bombs to dismantle (in a moment of unintended irony, I called 911 from the hospital), all those actors playing my friends and family. This hospital is really a whorehouse fronting for a drug cartel, isn't it? No, come on, you can tell me. It is, right?

During my depression, I often thought of something a secretary once said to me as she explained my duties as a temp, leading me through a fluorescent-lit office with no windows where I was to spend the next few months. It's not hard, she said, but it makes you want to shoot yourself. The lifetime risk of suicide among manic-depressives is 10 to 15 percent. Every morning before I went to work as an administrator in a theater school (a job I managed to keep despite all of my efforts to quit—my incredibly patient and kind boss wisely told me I should hang on until my medication had been worked out), my mother and her girlfriend counseled me, in person or over the phone. I can't go, I would say. I can't leave my apartment. I can't get dressed. I can't take a shower. Take a shower, they would say. Put on your clothes—remember your favorite black pants? The green sweater you bought when you first moved to New York? Find your wallet. Your keys. Walk out the door and lock it behind you. Buy a seven-day Metrocard, they would say (*because you can last that long,* they meant). Get on the 2 train, switch to the 4 at Nevins, and ride it all the way to Union Square.

Once I'd made it to work, I made lists: pills, suffocation, subway, bus, cut my wrists. I was forever staring at the tender blue veins along the inside of my wrists, fragile twigs trapped under ice. "Whatever happens, promise me you won't kill yourself," my best friend pleaded. "If you commit suicide, I'll kill you," my mother told me.

SEPTEMBER 21, 1998: *Everything we worked for gone. She's slipped from being a high-functioning, promising, her-whole-life-ahead-of-her-young-woman to being someone beginning a downward grind. We'll have to take her home as a kind of second class citizen.*

When my father's twenty-seven-year-old godson shot himself, it had seemed to me like the mysterious act of a grown-up who had seen things that I, at the age of eleven, hadn't. But even then I knew those mysterious things might be waiting for me, and when I was two years older than he would ever be, I could understand the general impulse: Let me out of here! Let me out of this body! I want to go home! But then there was my father visiting me for the day, reduced to tears by my own self-hatred. "I have nothing to say because I don't have any thoughts in my head anymore," I told him over and over. And my mother busting into one of my therapy sessions, a maternal terrorist, demanding that my therapist convince me to stay at my job, that she force me to understand that I didn't actually want to go back to the hospital. "She'll go back to that hospital over my dead body!" And my sister's voice over the phone, stripped of its usual joyousness, smooth and basic as the bone it had become: "Do you know how horrible the hospital was for you? For all of us?" I limited myself to banging my head against the wall, pinching and scratching my twiggy veins for relief.

Trapped in the dead body of depression, I was able to find relief in touch—the touch of friends and family who wanted to keep me from hurting myself as well as from the pain I inflicted on myself. As I clung to my job at the theater school, an institution steeped in the Method, I found myself using the same sense memory—an exercise that allows an actor to create reality through the memory of touch, taste, sight, sound, and smell in the otherwise imaginary circumstances of an empty stage—that I described to potential students during interviews. A childhood friend—her mother lying in a hospital in Virginia after a near-fatal accident—came to *my* apartment and tickled *my* arm, stroked *my* hair as I stood mutely grateful. Her touch reminded me of the power of wordless physical connection, of what I would lose if I died.

One night, my best friend from college, disappointed that I had returned from the hospital (where she had visited almost every day) not closer to her but farther away, convinced me to have dinner with her at a loud, clattery restaurant rather than rush home to sleep. We sat opposite each other on long benches shared by other people, including a new, crooning couple next to us feeding each other noodles. My friend told me she wasn't sure what to do anymore, that she didn't know how to help me. Why wasn't I calling her? Why wasn't I sleeping on her couch, watching videos and letting her cook me dinner? I started to cry for the first time in months, relieved at the way her words shot through my medicine haze like a needle into my heart. As we held hands across the table, the anonymous buzz of people talking and laughing around us and our noodle-sharing neighbors oblivious, I remembered the specificity of friendship and was glad to be able to offer her my tears.

Sleeping next to the live bodies of my mother and my sister reminded me that I, too, had been alive once.

OCTOBER 3, 1998: *I am completely braced to do whatever necessary to bring Maud through. I have the clearest feeling of being supported by recent years of happiness (lest anyone mistake me for a selfless person). Packed with satisfaction and strength, I've lived out*

a lot of things I wanted to do so that it's possible for me to be at her
disposal. This feeling pours out for the most part (with occasional
moments of self-pity), I will lay my fat years at the service of her
lean one. I have a sense of the depth of the emergency. A visual
image of the hollow beneath her.

I put my mother's journal and my own notebook into my bag and
stand in my coffee-soaked pants to look at the subway map. The
Kleenex woman looks up from her book with a momentary flash of
concern but then returns to her reading. She's got her own destina-
tion. One hundred and seventy-ninth and Hillside is three stops away.
In my head, I say the names of the people who rode this train to visit
me: Jane B., Janet, Nell, Julia G., Jeremy, Lorraine, Alex, Annie,
Jacob, Dwight, Cree, Sofia, Lenore, Rick, Daniel, Rose, Matilda,
Molly, Caitlin, Linda T., Steve, Connie, Harold, Helen, Olivia, Virginia, Mike, Bliss, Jan. This list is like an incantation, a poem I have
memorized. I have filled entire pages with these names, afraid afterward that I've left someone out and afraid of the list itself, which still
has the capacity to split me wide open with humiliation. Like someone who tells her most secret of secrets as she dances naked and
drunk in front of everyone she knows, I can never be exactly sure
what I revealed. Then there are those who called, who wrote, who
saw: John, Ros, Clare, Julia C., Johnny, Lydia, Craig, Linda B., Van,
Bruce, Tim, Meredith, Jesse, Tracey, Darcey, Jane H., Tammy, Benjamin, Lily, Eve, Nava, Meg, Carolyn H., Nancy, Pat, Victoria, Anna,
Carolyn T., Thomas, Elizabeth. I can't remember them all. If I could
only name all of them I might gain some control over what otherwise
feels like a stadium full of people who witnessed this moment of
skinlessness. We are at the end of the line.

Hillside Avenue is a grim strip of discount electronic stores and
check-cashing places. Discarded fast-food wrappers and sheaves of
newspaper blow chaotically down the street. While my mother was in
New York taking care of me, she became obsessed with the everyday
trash that found its way into the streets.

NOVEMBER 11, 1998: *The streets are flooded with litter but most peo-*
ple have washed and dressed themselves in clean clothes. They pick
their way through garbage, as if they had nothing to do with it.
People make their way along the junky street, transcending the
plastic wrap, wax paper, underwear, intent on getting to the office, to
their apartment. This morning, when Maud opens her eyes, she is
restless and burning with self-hatred and fear. I can't, I'm stupid,
I'm not able, no memory. She looks at me and says: You look nice.
You're dressed as if there is nothing wrong.

I stand in front of Liquor World and an offtrack betting parlor
next to a group of teenagers—two boys and a girl. One of the boys is
describing how the girl he went out with last night was so mad tight
that it took him half an hour to get three fingers inside of her. I flag
a car and read from the tiny, coffee-splattered piece of paper on
which I've scrawled the directions: *Hillside to Palo Alto, 1 block to*
hospital. (I don't remember the trip here the first time—another
childhood friend, whose brother had also been hospitalized, bravely
and selflessly escorted me.) Hospital, home, death. I am finally going
back to this place I'd claimed I wanted to return. As we pull into the
circular drive of the hospital, a woman as thin as the sharp edge of a
road sign stands outside smoking a cigarette. She seems familiar—it's
as though we could be related. But the context comes back to me.
She's one of the mental-health workers who held me down while I
was being restrained.

"Hi," she says, stubbing her cigarette out on the hospital win-
dowsill. "How are you?"

"I'm fine," I say. "Well, pretty good. Okay, I guess. You know, all
right. So-so." What am I doing? I'm not wearing the right coat for
this windy day and I've lost yet another pair of gloves. I want something from this woman. I want her to take me back. Wrested from the
land of the living, I imagine myself sleeping the heavy sleep of sadness all day long—skipping groups, never changing out of my pajamas, and receiving only patients, like-minded people who understand

best the desire to disappear from the face of the earth, as I lie in my sterile, white, clean hospital bed running a salon for the insane. I want to go to a place where strangers take care of me, people whose pores are sealed, filled with their own rotten suffering. But I know better than that even before I walk back through the doors. Morning meds are at 8:00 A.M., if you aren't dressed you are put on constant supervision, patients aren't allowed in other patients' rooms, and there are no such things as sterile, white, clean beds in a psychiatric hospital. At this hospital, you're lucky to get a pillowcase. Saying I wanted to go back to the hospital was akin to holding a gun to my head.

> DECEMBER 3, 1998: *I am hanging on by a thread. I want Maud to hang on to her apartment and her job, to stay in the world as proof that she isn't going to be ground down, smashed by her depression or marginalized, one of those cousins who Aunt Dora used to include at family holidays out of kindness. Don't forget—often these terrifying, destabilized events occur and you are completely on your own with no idea how to proceed even with people around you. What are analogous stories? Having a baby?*

Saying I wanted to go back to the hospital was like waving a gun around at everyone I loved.

Still, I try again. "I want to speak with someone about attending outpatient groups," I tell the security guard sitting at the front desk. He is a huge and grouchy man who doesn't look up from the screens in front of him, screens filled with the threatening stillness of empty corridors.

"Take a seat," he says.

My former psychiatrist—a jumpy, handsome man with a ponytail that serves as a barometer for his nerves—bursts out of his office on the first floor. His ponytail swings wildly behind him. He scans the room, sees me, and, being a man trained to head directly for trouble, heads my way. "What are you doing here?" he asks. He thinks I'm back.

For a minute I consider turning myself over to him, telling him I want to hurt myself so that he will be forced to act on my behalf. But shame burns through me like acid, and instead I say something about outpatient groups. He looks me up and down. "For you?" he asks incredulously. "For you to *participate* in?" He asks me about my current psychiatrist, my latest drug cocktail, whether I'm employed, where I'm living. I answer him—smart and kind, Tegretol, Wellbutrin, Effexor, yes, Brooklyn—leaving out the rest, the parts that hover between the facts such as how I can't figure out how to live in the world after preparing to give up for so long, how I'd gone to the edge and thrown all of my tools over, how the choices involved with living overwhelm me, how I just need to lie down on the old unit and rest for a little while until I feel ready to move back into my body. But he is shaking my hand, congratulating me, and then he sails off, his ponytail a wiggly rudder steering him onto the next crisis.

The grouchy security guard, his eyes still glued to the screens offering a filtered reality easier to bear, buzzes me through doors onto a locked unit so that I can use the bathroom. I go into a stall, sit on the toilet, and weep because I am not welcome here. They won't take me back. I cry mostly because this wasn't the place I'd been wishing for all along. Because what I really wished for was to disappear, and for the first time I see the tragedy of this as clearly as if I was the person lying terrified in my bed next to me or desperately trying to reach me across the table in a crowded restaurant. I cry briefly, efficient as the cold white tiles of the bathroom floor, and then walk back into the lobby where my psychiatrist hovers over a woman and her panicked daughter gesturing wildly. I call a car and go out into the cold gray day to wait. As I stand there, another psychiatrist, the man who performed my intake, strolls up the semicircle of the driveway. He recognizes me vaguely with the wary smile of a man who has seen thousands of patients come and go. I might have been his patient ten years ago or two weeks ago.

"How are you?" he asks, still moving toward the door. He knows just how much he can afford to give.

"Okay," I say, definitively.

He's partly through the door when, without breaking stride, he says, "It's cold out here." Exactly. He feels it, too. It's cold out here for everybody.

The car doesn't come for another half an hour. I wait alone in my too-thin coat and think about calling my sister when I get back to Brooklyn. Recently, she sent me an essay by Lauren Slater on depression. At first, I was unable—unwilling?—to learn about my own disease. It was mine, all mine! The idea of sharing, the idea of hope, seemed cruel. I had read Kay Redfield Jamison's *An Unquiet Mind* twice, and took a stab at William Styron's *Darkness Visible,* but they left me feeling even more depressed. How was I, a not-yet-published writer who didn't have the energy to turn on her computer supposed to feel better by reading the stories of depressed, famous writers? But, when I finally came back to myself, remembering how often reading had saved my life, I sat down with the Slater essay.

In the margins of the copy my sister had sent me—the copy she had intended to keep for herself—there were notes scribbled in her familiar, spidery handwriting. My therapist would probably remind me that there are no accidents, but, frankly, this can be an exhausting concept. I *wanted* to see. *Maud's second breakdown and later depression broke my heart in a way I'd never known, a loss that even now, with her back and healthy, I can feel occasionally.* When I could breathe again, I began to see that the cruelty was not so much in the idea of sharing or the idea of hope as it was lodged in the layer of depression that is selfishness. My depression was not all mine, and as I read my sister's words again and again, relief loosened my relentless grip on my illness even as my heart broke, too.

When I call my sister, I won't tell her about this trip to the hospital. Not yet, I want to wait until the story is a gift and not a burden. Instead, I will tell her about a dream I had the other night in which we were the adults we are now wandering through my grandmother's Rhode Island house—a converted barn with beautiful high ceilings and an enormous window overlooking Narragansett Bay. The

Barn, as it was called by our family, no longer exists. My grandmother sold it, and in a perfect symbolic gesture of resistance to its new owners, it burned to the ground. In the dream, my sister and I wander in my grandmother's garden and we come upon myself as a child, pudgy and tan all over from never wearing clothes. We squeeze my squishy child legs and then my child self tells us she's happy. But my sister doesn't hear and my child self runs away, turns into one of the groundhogs that plagued my grandmother by biting the heads off her petunias, and scurries toward the bay. I decide to leave out the part about my child self and just tell my sister about visiting the Barn, how beautiful it was in the sepia tones of dream memory, how blissful it was to wander in the long-ago garden with her.

I check my wallet for carfare and pick the trash—gum wrappers, pens that don't write, paper clips—out of my bag. These mundane details of the living make up the sweet straitjacket of practicality that holds me to the earth. In my mind, I wander through my Brooklyn apartment, where the dishes are done and the floors swept, looking for my gloves—the fifth pair I've lost this winter. I'll find them when I get home.

CONTRIBUTORS

✍

A. ALVAREZ is a poet, novelist, literary critic, and author of many highly praised nonfiction books on topics ranging from suicide, divorce, sleep and dreams—*The Savage God, Life After Marriage, Night*—to poker, North Sea oil, and mountaineering—*The Biggest Game in Town, Offshore, Feeding the Rat.* His autobiography, *Where Did It All Go Right?*, was recently published by William Morrow. He lives in London and is a frequent contributor to *The New Yorker* and *The New York Review of Books.*

RUSSELL BANKS is the author, most recently, of the novels *The Sweet Hereafter, Affliction, Rule of the Bone,* and *Cloudsplitter.* His book of stories, *The Angel on the Roof,* was recently released by HarperCollins. He is the Howard G. B. Clark University Professor Emeritus at Princeton and lives in upstate New York.

ANN BEATTIE's last book, *Park City: New and Selected Stories* (Knopf), was her twelfth work of fiction. She divides her time between Maine and Key West, Florida.

MAUD CASEY's first novel, *The Shape of Things to Come* (William Morrow), will be out April 2001. Her short story collection, *Drastic* (William Morrow), will be released in Spring 2002.

NELL CASEY's work has appeared in such publications as *Elle, Mirabella, Salon,* and *The New York Times Book Review.* She is a 2000/2001

Carter Center fellow in mental health journalism. She is also on the board of *Stories at the Moth*, a nonprofit storytelling organization.

MERI NANA-AMA DANQUAH is the author of *Willow Weep for Me: A Black Woman's Journey Through Depression* (Norton/Ballantine) and the editor of *Becoming American: Personal Essays by First Generation Immigrant Women* (Hyperion).

LESLEY DORMEN's work has appeared in *Mirabella, Playboy, Mademoiselle, Glamour, Redbook*, and other magazines. She teaches fiction at The Writers Studio in New York City and is working on a short story collection.

DONALD HALL is a poet, fiction writer, and essayist. His work has been published in *The New Yorker, Harper's, The Nation, The New York Times, The American Scholar*, and *The Atlantic Monthly*, among other periodicals. He was nominated for the National Book Award in 1956, 1979, and 1993. His book *The One Day* (Houghton Mifflin) won the National Book Critics Circle Award in 1989. He is the author, most recently, of *Without* (Houghton Mifflin), which won the Pen-Winship Award for the best book of 1998, in any category, by a New England writer. He lives in New Hampshire.

VIRGINIA HEFFERNAN is a founding editor of *Talk* magazine and a Ph.D. candidate in English at Harvard, where her dissertation is on finance and fiction. Her work has appeared in *Lingua Franca, New York, Salon, Glamour, Metropolis*, and *Nerve*. In 1998, she wrote the Emmy-nominated documentary *Matthew's Murder* for MTV. A selection of her one-person plays, cowritten with the performer Mike Albo, appeared in *Extreme Exposure* (ed. Jo Bonney).

EDWARD HOAGLAND is the author of sixteen books. His work has appeared in numerous publications, including *Harper's, Outside, Civilization, Granta, National Geographic*, and the *New York Times*

Magazine. A member of the Academy of Arts and Letters, he teaches at Bennington College in Vermont.

KAY REDFIELD JAMISON, Ph.D., is a professor of psychiatry at the Johns Hopkins University School of Medicine. She is coauthor of the standard medical text on manic-depressive illness, which was chosen in 1990 as the most outstanding book in biomedical sciences by the American Association of Publishers, and author of *Touched with Fire: Manic-Depressive Illness and the Artistic Temperament.* Her memoir, *An Unquiet Mind,* which chronicles her own experience with manic-depressive illness, was cited by several major publications as one of the best books of 1995 and is currently under development as a feature film (Universal Studios). *An Unquiet Mind* was on the *The New York Times* best-seller list for five months. Dr. Jamison is the recipient of numerous national and international scientific awards, and in 1997 was appointed honorary professor of English at the University of St. Andrews in Scotland. Her most recent book is *Night Falls Fast: Understanding Suicide.*

DAVID KARP is a professor of sociology at Boston College. His books—*Sociology in Everyday Life, Experiencing the Life Cycle, Being Urban*—reflect an enduring interest in how we invest our daily worlds with meaning. He most recently published *The Burden of Sympathy: How Families Cope with Mental Illness* (Oxford University Press), a book on the experiences of family caregivers to mentally ill people. He lives in Chestnut Hill, Massachusetts, with his wife, Darleen. They have two grown children, Peter and Alyssa.

SUSANNA KAYSEN has written two novels, *Asa, As I Knew Him* and *Far Afield,* and a memoir, *Girl, Interrupted.*

NANCY MAIRS earned an M.F.A. in creative writing (poetry) in 1975 and a Ph.D. in English literature in 1984, both from the University of Arizona. A poet and an essayist, she was awarded the 1984 Western States Book Award in poetry for *In All the Rooms of the Yellow House* (Confluence Press, 1984) and a National Endowment for

UNITED INTL

DEVITO/DAVIDANGELO

Friday, May 03, 2013

FLIGHT

UA1642

Washington-Dulles
Raleigh/Durham
IAD to RDU

GATE

NOT YET
ASSIGNED

BOARD TIME

5:43 PM

Departs: 6:18 PM
Arrives: 7:28 PM

BOARDING
GROUP

5

SEAT

27B

Middle
Economy

Confirmation: **MX7CBX**
eTicket 0167211650925

Customer Notification Information

Effective Oct. 1,1998, All carriers are required to obtain the full name of U. S. citizens travelling to/from the United States on international flights.
To comply with the U. S. Department of Transportation ruling, please complete this form.

(Required)

Last or Surname   Middle Name or Initial   First Name

(Optional)

Emergency Contact:
Name/relationship
Area Code or City and   Country Code and Phone Number

er first work of nonfiction, *Plaintext:*
as published by the University of Ari-
, she has written a memoir, *Remember-*
al autobiography, *Ordinary Time: Cycles*
enewal, and three books of essays, *Carnal*
ecoming a (Woman) Writer, and *Waist-High*
ong the Nondisabled, all available from Bea-
project, entitled *Life's Worth: Rethinking How*
pported by a fellowship from the Soros Founda-
th in America.

ANNING, Ph.D., is a clinical psychologist and
currents: A Life Beneath the Surface, Chasing Grace:
Catholic Girl, Grown Up, All Seasons Pass: Grieving
nd coauthor of *Restoring Intimacy: A Patient's Guide to*
Relationships During Depression. She has written for
gton *Post, The New York Times Book Review, Glamour,*
Heu   *irabella,* and *New Woman.* She received the 1996 Presiden-
tial Award for Patient Advocacy from the American Psychiatric Association and the 1999 Stephen Lang Award from the National Alliance
for the Mentally Ill (NAMI) for her contribution to the understanding of brain disorders by a psychologist.

LARRY MCMURTRY received his B.A. from North Texas State College and his M.A. from Rice University, and he has done graduate
work at Stanford University as a Stegner fellow. He is the author of
two collections of essays and twenty-one novels, including the
Pulitzer Prize—winning *Lonesome Dove* and its sequel *Streets of
Laredo,* as well as *Comanche Moon, The Last Picture Show, Terms of
Endearment,* and *Horseman Pass By* (his first novel, and the basis for
the motion picture *Hud*). He operates antiquarian bookstores in
Washington, D.C., Texas, and Arizona. *Duane's Depressed,* the final
book in the trilogy comprising *The Last Picture Show* and *Texasville,*
was published in December 1998. *Walter Benjamin at the Dairy
Queen,* a memoir about his hometown of Archer City, Texas was pub-

lished in 1999. Most recently, McMurtry edited *Still Wild*, an anthology of western stories.

JOSHUA WOLF SHENK has contributed articles, essays, and reviews to *Harper's, The Nation, The Economist, The New York Times*, and other publications. He is a past fellow in mental health journalism at the Carter Center. He lives in New York City, where he teaches writing at the New School University. His first book, *The Melancholy of Abraham Lincoln*, will be published in 2002 by Viking Press. He can be reached at jwshenk@bigfoot.com.

LAUREN SLATER is the author of *Welcome to My Country, Prozac Diary*, and *Lying: A Metaphorical Memoir* (all published by Random House). Her e-mail address is lauren@channel1.com.

DARCEY STEINKE's first novel, *Up Through the Water*, was selected as a Notable Book of the Year in 1989 by *The New York Times*. *Suicide Blonde*, her second novel, has been translated into seven languages. She has also edited a collection of essays with Rick Moody entitled *Joyful Noise: The New Testament Revisited*. Her most recent novel, *Jesus Saves*, was published in 1997. She grew up in Virginia and lives in Brooklyn, New York.

LEE STRINGER is author of *Grand Central Winter: Stories from the Street*, a chronicle of his twelve-year odyssey living underground as a drug-fevered, homeless New Yorker. The book made the 1989 top-ten lists of *The New York Times* and *USA Today* and has been translated into ten languages and published in fourteen countries. Stringer's writing career began when he landed a column in *Street News*, New York's street paper for the homeless, where he eventually became editor in chief. His work has appeared in *The New York Times*, New York *Newsday, The Nation, In These Times, The Realist*, and *The Gauntlet*. *Like Shaking Hands with God: A Conversation on Writing* (Seven Stories Press), a collaborative effort between Stringer and Kurt Vonnegut, was published in 1999. Stringer lives in Mamaroneck, NY.

ROSE STYRON is a poet, journalist, and human-rights activist. She has published three volumes of poetry—*By Vineyard Light* (Rizzoli), *Thieves' Afternoon* (Viking), *From Summer to Summer* (Viking)—and collaborated on a book of biographies and translations entitled *Modern Russian Poetry* (Viking). Her poems and translations have appeared in quarterlies and anthologies, her essays in a variety of periodicals (*The New York Review of Books, The New Republic, The American Poetry Review*). Her monthly series of conversations with great novelists and poets, *Writers' World*, has been broadcast for Voice of America and syndicated by *Global Vision*. Ms. Styron has been chair of the National Advisory Council for Amnesty International U.S.A. and of PEN's Freedom to Write Committee and the Robert F. Kennedy Memorial Human Rights Award. She has traveled extensively for them and for the Lawyers' Committee for Human Rights. She is the wife of novelist William Styron and lives in Connecticut and Martha's Vineyard.

WILLIAM STYRON was born in Newport News, Virginia, in 1925. He attended Davidson College and Duke before wartime service in the marines. His first novel was *Lie Down in Darkness* (1951). After moving to Paris, he helped found *The Paris Review* with George Plimpton. Random House published his second novel, *Set This House On Fire*, in 1960, and *The Confessions of Nat Turner* (1968), which won the Pulitzer Prize. His other works include *The Quiet Dust and Other Writings* (1982), *Darkness Visible* (1985), his chronicle of depression, *Sophie's Choice* (1992), and *Tidewater Morning* (1993). He has received numerous awards and prizes, including the Commandeur de l'Ordre des Arts et des Lettres and the Commandeur Légion d'Honneur. Styron and his wife, Rose, were married in 1953.

CHASE TWICHELL is the author of five books of poetry, the most recent of which is *The Snow Watcher* (Ontario Review Press, 1998). She's the editor of Ausable Press, and teaches in the M.F.A Program at Warren Wilson College. She lives in the Adirondacks with her husband, Russell Banks.